A VOICE CALLED

Stories of Jewish Heroism

Yossi Katz

Typesetting by S. Kim Glassman
Cover Design by Zippy Thumim

Photo of Manya Shochat
courtesy of the Gershon Gera Collection, Beit Hashomer Archives.

Photo of Michael Halpern
courtesy of the Beit Hashomer Museum.

Photos of Barney Ross and Victor "Young" Perez
courtesy of the International Jewish Sports Hall of Fame,
Wingate Institute, Netanya.

Photo of Morris Katz's grave
courtesy of Yisrael Hartman, Kibbutz Lavi.

ISBN: 978-965-229-480-7

Gefen Publishing House, Ltd.   Gefen Books
6 Hatzvi Street   600 Broadway
Jerusalem 94386, Israel   Lynbrook, NY 11563, USA
972-2-538-0247   1-800-477-5257
orders@gefenpublishing.com   orders@gefenpublishing.com

www.gefenpublishing.com

Printed in Israel   *Send for our free catalogue*

Contents

Acknowledgments

A Voice Called: Stories of Jewish Heroism is the realization of a lifelong dream and I would like to acknowledge the many family, friends and colleagues who have helped me achieve the publication of this book.

Since 1980 I have worked as a Jewish educator at the Alexander Muss High School in Israel (AMHSI), located in Hod Hasharon. AMHSI is an award-winning academic experience in Israel for high school juniors and seniors from the United States. Students on the program study the four-thousand-year history of the Jewish people while visiting the sites of the actual historic events in Israel. The program's goal is to strengthen the Jewish identity of our students and to heighten their connection to their people, to their tradition and to Israel. As a teacher at AMHSI, I have sought to focus on the role of individual heroes in making Jewish history, with the hope that our students will not only learn about their past but will be inspired to help make the present and build a rich Jewish future. I believe with all my heart that our students are tomorrow's heroes.

I am grateful to the AMHSI chairman, Stephen Muss; to our headmaster Chaim Fischgrund; past principal Baruch Kraus; and to all the past and present teachers and staff and students of the Alexander Muss High School in Israel for their help and support and dedication over the years. I have learned so much from all of them and am eternally grateful for all they have given to me. A special chapter in this book is devoted to one of my colleagues from AMHSI, a dear friend and a great Jewish hero, David Sprung.

A VOICE CALLED

My late beloved parents, Miriam and Irving Katz, gave me a lifetime of love and inspiration and, though they both have passed away, they are still a presence in my life. I have never forgotten the lessons they taught me. They both were real heroes in every sense of the word and this book is dedicated to their memory. I am most grateful to my brother, Rabbi Michael Katz; to my sister, Ellen; and to my cousin, Bruce Lipton, for their love and support over the years. They have taught me much and, though the ocean separates us, they are always close in my heart. Throughout this project, I have had the constant love and support of my three wonderful children: Inbal, Meron and Yair. I dedicate this book to them.

I am most grateful to Murray and Ilan Greenfield, Smadar Belilty and all the wonderful staff at Gefen Publishing House for their help and support in helping to bring this project to fruition. Special thanks to Gefen's senior editor, Kezia Raffel Pride, for helping to refine my manuscript and bring it to print. I am especially grateful to Jonathan M. and Deborah J. Bruce of Milford, Massachusetts, and to all the dear friends who helped support this project financially. Your kindness and generosity are greatly appreciated. *Todah rabah!* Thank you so much!

Finally, I have devoted a chapter in this book to Michael Levin, the Israeli paratrooper from Philadelphia who fell in the Second Lebanon War on August 1, 2006. Michael was a former student of mine at AMHSI and was a dear friend. We both had grown up in Northeast Philadelphia, were active members of HaGesher Region USY and attended Camp Ramah in the Poconos. Though the records show that I was Michael's teacher in 2001, in life it was he who taught me the most important lessons and showed me what a real hero was. I will never forget him and hope that his story – and all the other chapters in this book that so inspired both of us – will touch our readers' hearts as well.

Yossi Katz
(September 2009)

Introduction

What is a hero? *Webster's New Collegiate Dictionary* defines "hero" as "an illustrious warrior; a man admired for his achievements and noble qualities; one that shows great courage." In one dictionary I even found the definition for "hero" as "a sandwich on a long roll in New York; a submarine." In the Talmud's *Pirkei Avot* (*Ethics of the Fathers*), Ben Zoma is quoted as saying, "Who is a hero?[1] He who controls his passion" (*Pirkei Avot* 4:1). But can't a hero be someone who uses his or her passion to fight for a noble cause?

So many questions arise from this four-letter word. Are only soldiers and warriors real heroes? Must they die in battle to be a hero? If a young soldier dies in battle, did he waste his life? Can women be heroes? What role does motivation play in heroism? Must a hero save a nation or can he be someone who exhibits an individual act of courage? Are heroes all selfless, kind, caring individuals or can a selfish egotist searching for glory also be a hero? What about outstanding athletes and famous movie and TV stars? Can they be considered heroes? Does hitting a clutch homerun or sinking a winning basket or scoring a decisive touchdown make a ball player a real hero, or are winning athletes just successful at playing their game?

Throughout the ages, philosophers and historians have debated whether it is great people who make history or history that makes

---

1. Literally, "Who is strong?"

xi

people great. Or perhaps it is a combination of both? While I believe the answers to the above questions can be found in the pages of this book, the reader will have to wrestle with these stories and find his or her own solutions. I do believe, however, that if you know a person's or a nation's heroes, you can know who that person or nation is and what their values are. A nation infatuated only with athletes, movie stars and "celebs" is condemned to mediocrity, selfish values and national decay. A people who looks up to true heroes will find the strength to face the world's challenges with dignity and courage.

This book, *A Voice Called: Stories of Jewish Heroism*, is a collage of my heroes and the people who have inspired me. I share them with you in the hope that not only will their stories touch you, but that in the end you will search for and find your own heroes to honor. They are out there.

I was born and raised in Philadelphia, a second-generation American Jew, and from the earliest days of my youth I remember how inspired I was by the stories of heroes. In sixth grade I did a report on Revolutionary War hero Nathan Hale, America's first spy, who was hanged by the British. I'll never forget the emotions I felt when I learned that facing the gallows, Hale courageously said, "My only regret is that I have but one life to give for my country." Then in junior high school, I read John F. Kennedy's *Profiles in Courage* and was inspired by the American leaders who stood up for their ideals and principles.

In Philadelphia, I also attended afternoon Hebrew school, which for most young Jews was a boring addition to an already exhausting day. My Hebrew teacher, however, was an amazing educator named Ruth Chinitz, the wife of the congregation's rabbi. In the months following the 1967 Six-Day War in Israel, she made the Jewish state's young heroes our curriculum. Prior to 1967, Jews were often seen as victims or weak patsies. For the first time in my life I learned about proud, courageous Jews who stood up and defeated the enemies that sought their annihilation. Mrs. Chinitz helped give me pride in my people and their history. The heroes she taught us about helped light my future path in life.

In 1968 I started attending a Jewish educational summer camp called Camp Ramah in the Poconos. Along with the regular camp counselors, swim instructors and sports staff, Camp Ramah brought a group of young Israelis to work at the camp. They were called the *Mishlahat* (Emissaries) and in 1968, most were in their early twenties and had fought in the 1967 Six-Day War. Now, for the first time in my life, I met strong, proud, courageous Jews who were fighters and heroes – the very people Mrs. Chinitz had taught us about.

On the first morning of the 1968 summer at camp, I went with my bunkmates to the morning prayer service in our camp social hall, called the *Merkaz*. Sitting next to me was a tall, handsome, muscular man from the *Mishlahat*. His name was Yitzhak Hochman but everyone called him "Hochla." Hochla, a national sports star in Israel, was the first religious Israeli to make the Israeli national basketball team and was in camp as a sports instructor. Before services I was mesmerized as he spun a basketball on his finger like a Harlem Globetrotter, but what really amazed me was when he sat down next to me in prayer services and helped me put on my tefillin (two leather boxes with straps, containing sacred parchments with words from the Torah, worn on the head and left arm by Jews during morning prayers). He wore his on his muscular arm and prayed with *kavanah* (true intent) and passion.

For the first time in my life I saw a Jew who was not only an accomplished athlete, but also a proud, strong Jew. Later in the summer, Hochla and his fellow *Mishlahat* members came to my bunk one evening and told us about fighting in the Six-Day War. I was so excited to learn about and meet real Jewish heroes. Camp Ramah taught me that a Jew could play sports and have muscles and also put on tefillin every morning and pray. I have not missed a day of putting on tefillin or *davening Shaharit* (saying my morning prayers) in the past forty years and much of that, like my decision to eventually make Aliyah (move to Israel), is due to Hochla and Camp Ramah.

In the 1973 Yom Kippur War, Hochla served in an elite commando unit of the Israel Defense Forces (IDF) and fell heroically in battle in the Sinai Desert. A brigade intelligence officer, Hochla was rushing to the aid of besieged comrades in Suez City when his half-track was hit by enemy fire, killing him instantly. He died trying to save others. It was shocking for me to learn of Hochla's death and I will never forget him; most of all, I will always remember how he lived his life – caring for his fellow human beings.

My high school years coincided with the early 1970s and the struggle of Soviet Jews for their freedom from the USSR. I remember hanging pictures of Soviet Refusniks (brave Soviet Jews who were refused permission to immigrate to Israel and were often arrested by the KGB and imprisoned in Soviet gulags) on my wall and thinking that if my grandparents hadn't had the courage to flee czarist Russia in the early 1900s for the USA, this heroic but tragic story could be mine. I attended rallies and protests to free Soviet Jews though I was doubtful they could actually be freed. When the Soviet Union collapsed and the "Iron Curtain" was opened in the early 1990s I learned a lesson of the power of the just. Just as tiny Israel defeated all its Arab neighbors in wars for its survival, so too did the tiny Jewish people bring the Soviet bear to its knees.

Jewish history has had heroes like Mordechai Anielewicz – who died in the fires of the Warsaw ghetto, preserving Jewish honor – but also heroes like Avigdor Kahalani and Zvika Greengold, who saved Israel in the 1973 Yom Kippur War and brought their people victory. In December 1973, at the end of the Yom Kippur War, I traveled to Israel for the first time on a two-week trip. I saw the battlefields where Kahalani, Greengold and thousands of unsung Israeli heroes had fought just weeks earlier to save the Jewish state. I remember contrasting the heroic young Israelis who fought to preserve their freedom with my Jewish classmates back in the USA, some of whom only cared about what college they got into.

One day during my visit to Israel, I bought a falafel in Jerusalem and was intrigued by the falafel salesman, who looked like he was my age. He was handsome, strong and proud – very different from the Jews

I knew back at home. A day later, I met the same young man in the National Military Cemetery in Jerusalem, mourning his older brother who had fallen in battle at the Suez Canal on the first days of the Yom Kippur War. I came to understand that in every Israeli home there were heroes who were willing to give their lives for their people and their country – now, my people and my country.

In June 1976, during my college years, an Air France airbus with 250 people aboard was hijacked out of Athens on a flight from Tel Aviv to Paris. The hostages were taken to Idi Amin's Uganda, where a selection was conducted and the non-Jewish passengers were released; the 105 Jewish hostages faced execution by Arab terrorists. Yitzhak Rabin, Israel's prime minister, courageously gave orders to the Israel Defense Forces to fly thousands of miles over enemy territory and to rescue the hostages and bring them home. Despite Israeli military estimates of 70 percent casualties in the daring operation, only one Israeli soldier was killed in battle during the successful rescue mission – the ground commander Yonatan "Yoni" Netanyahu.

After Netanyahu's death, his family published a book of his personal letters called *Self Portrait of a Hero: The Letters of Jonathan Netanyahu*. I received the book as a gift, shortly after its printing, and read Yoni's letters and words. I was touched to the core of my soul by the ideals and values of this great Jewish hero. In one letter Yoni writes about lying as a soldier in ambush on a hilltop all night long protecting civilians celebrating the Rosh Hashanah, the Jewish New Year, down below in the valley. He described the scene to his family in these words:

> This year, too, I won't spend the holidays at home. Again we are lying in ambush on the borders at a time when the entire House of Israel is happily celebrating at home.
>
> It's extraordinary, the distance between soldier and civilian. In town people are having parties. In brightly lit rooms there is music, and people stay up until the morning. I, too, was up until morning, the only difference being that I was

lying on the ground on a dark cold night without a single ray of light to brighten my surroundings, alert to every suspicious sound and movement around me....

Despite all this, there is a magic in everything we are doing now. I have lain like this in ambush more than once and shall do so many more times. I just wanted to share with you some of my impressions on the eve of the New Year.[2]

Israelis and free people everywhere are safe because heroes like Yoni are standing on guard. We must make sure that they are not alone.

With the book in hand, I made Aliyah (immigrated) to Israel, where I have lived since 1978. Shortly after arrival in my new country, I was drafted into the Israel Defense Forces; I will never forget the feeling of pride in wearing the IDF uniform. I felt like I was carrying on the same struggle that Joshua, Samson, David, Judah the Maccabee and Bar Kokhba had fought, thousands of years ago. Throughout my life I had learned about and been inspired by Jewish heroes; now I had the opportunity to play my small part in my heroic people's history. In one of Yoni's last letters he wrote about feeling like a link in the chain of Israel's existence and independence. I felt the same way about living in Israel and serving in the IDF: it was my responsibility to continue and strengthen the chain built by my ancestors over a period of four thousand years. I served in the army and later in the combat reserves as a reconnaissance soldier in the Israeli Armor Corps.

Upon completion of my military service, I began working as a teacher of Jewish history and a tour guide to Eretz Yisrael (the Land of Israel) at the Alexander Muss High School in Israel (AMHSI), where I have been for over thirty years. At AMHSI we teach about many of the heroes in our nation's four-thousand-year history. This book seeks to share with the reader the stories of some of my favorite heroes from modern times. Most of the chapters are written in third person, but

2. Jonathan Netanyahu, *The Letters of Jonathan Netanyahu: The Commander of the Entebbe Rescue Force* (Jerusalem: Gefen Publishing House, 2001), 79–80.

where I have added personal connections and anecdotes, the writing is in first person.

The first chapter is about Theodor Herzl, father of modern Zionism. As I learned more about the "real" Herzl, I gained new admiration for this great thinker and writer who often is treated more as a symbol than the real man he was. That real man, in my humble opinion, is an even greater hero than the symbol.

Many Jewish heroes are women. That is not a point added for "political correctness" – it is simply a fact. When I was a young boy in Hebrew school we learned a silly song for Chanukah that spoke about "Mrs. Maccabee, who made the latkes for the Jewish fighters." As a ten-year-old I thought the song was funny; today I find it offensive! Jewish women can do so much more than make dinner for their husbands. In this book you will read about great Jewish heroines such as Manya Shochat, Sarah Aaronsohn, Rahel the Poetess, Hannah Senesh, Zivia Lubetkin, Roni Zuckerman and Naomi Shemer. Some fought with a rifle while others inspired with pens; all were great heroines who left us an everlasting legacy.

My father, of blessed memory, bucked the stream of popular culture in America and taught me not to idolize professional athletes simply because they played a children's game well and often were not kind, outstanding human beings. He was right and Americans and Israelis would do well to find different role models than their sports stars or movie actors. Yet in this book of heroes you will also find athletes. Victor "Young" Perez and Barney Ross were great world boxing champions, but it was their behavior out of the ring that made them heroic. Tal Brody is arguably Israel's greatest sportsman, yet it is the lessons he taught his people off the court that made him truly great.

While I want to stress that a hero need not be a soldier with a gun, it is a fact that reality has demanded of the Jewish people the ability to defend themselves. In this book you will read about Jewish military heroes like Michael Halpern, Dov Gruner, Moshe Barazani and Meir Feinstein, David Marcus, Avigdor Kahalani, Zvika Greengold, Morris

Katz, Yoni Netanyahu, Rafael Eitan, Alex Singer, Yonatan Ben Meir and my former student and dear friend, Michael Levin. You will also read about men of letters like Eliezer Ben Yehuda and Haim Bialik and men of conscience and courage like Murray Greenfield, Jacob Birnbaum and Natan Sharansky.

This book will tell stories of great leaders like Menachem Begin, the brave astronaut Ilan Ramon and courageous espionage agents like Eli Cohen. You will even find here the story of a religious Christian, Orde Wingate, who became a great hero of Jewish history, as well as the stories of a colleague and some of my former students who went on to make Jewish history. Finally, you will read here about my parents, Irving and Miriam Katz, of blessed memory, who taught me about Jewish heroes through stories and most importantly, through their own personal examples. It is to their memory that I dedicate this book with the hope that I can pass on to the reader through these stories at least a fraction of the inspiration that they gave me in their lives.

Hannah Senesh, the great Hebrew poetess and fighter who sacrificed her life in the Holocaust, once wrote in a poem: "A voice called and I went." The true test of a hero is not only in hearing the voice of inner conscience or a people's cry for help, but in answering the call. May the stories in these pages help us all to hear the voices calling out to us and find the courage to answer and act because we are the heroes of today and tomorrow.

THEODOR HERZL
"IF YOU WILL IT, IT IS NO DREAM!"

> **Theodor Herzl (1860–1904)**
> - Father of modern Zionism
> - 1896 Wrote *Der Judenstaat* (*The Jewish State*)
> - 1897 Convened First Zionist Congress in Basel, Switzerland
>   *"In Basel I founded the Jewish State."*

In September 1894 a French counterespionage agent searching in the wastebasket of the German military attaché found the "Bordereau," a promise in French to deliver French military manuals to the Germans. It was clear to the aide to the chief of French intelligence, Colonel Henry, that a German spy was working in the midst of the French army. Colonel Henry announced in October that the spy had been discovered and was a French artillery officer named Captain Alfred Dreyfuss. The handwriting on the "Bordereau" did not match Dreyfuss's nor was their any reason to suspect him. He became the scapegoat for this terrible affair simply because he was Jewish.

Dreyfuss was arrested, jailed, accused of treason and court-martialed by the French military court. Colonel Henry told the tribunal judges that he had "secret proof" of Dreyfuss's guilt but could not divulge it in the courtroom; otherwise his sources would be compromised. The judges accepted Colonel Henry's statement and found Captain Alfred Dreyfuss guilty of treason and sentenced him to life

1

in prison on Devil's Island, off the coast of French Guiana. In January 1895 Dreyfuss's degradation ceremony took place in France. His ranks were ripped from his shoulders and his sword was broken in two as thousands of anti-Semitic Frenchmen shouted, "Death to the Jews!" Dreyfuss was driven to the port and shipped off to the world's most infamous prison on Devil's Island.

Covering this dramatic affair for Europe's leading newspaper, the Viennese *Neue Freie Presse*, was the paper's Paris correspondent, Theodor Herzl. Herzl, like Dreyfuss, was an assimilated Jew who loved his adopted homeland (for Dreyfuss, that homeland was France; for Herzl, it was Germany). Herzl first believed Dreyfuss was guilty but then, as the case unfolded in court, Herzl realized that Dreyfuss was completely innocent. Alfred Dreyfuss loved France with all his heart; Herzl knew that an assimilated Jew like himself would never be a traitor to his new country. Dreyfuss was rich and had no need for money and there was no reason to suspect him other than pure anti-Semitism.

As thousands of Frenchmen screamed, "Death to the Jews" at the French captain's degradation, Dreyfuss naively hollered back, "Vive la France!" Theodor Herzl witnessed this heart-wrenching scene and wrote in his diary: "Death to the Jews! howled the mob, as the decorations were being ripped from the captain's coat… Where? In France. In republican, modern, civilized France, a hundred years after the Declaration of the Rights of Man."[3] What, he lamented, was to be expected of less civilized countries?

Herzl was in effect saying that if it could happen in France, it could and would happen everywhere else. In 1895 Theodor Herzl was already predicting the outbreak of virulent anti-Semitism in Europe that would ultimately reach its horrific climax in the Holocaust. In the next nine years he would dedicate himself to founding the political movement called Zionism and planting the seeds that would ultimately see fruition in a Jewish state on May 14, 1948. It was the Dreyfuss Affair that

---

3. "Theodor Herzl: A Biography, Based on the Work of Alex Bein," in Theodor Herzl, *The Jewish State* (Mineola, NY: Dover Publications, 1988), 34.

helped mold this great Jewish leader and hero.

Theodor Herzl was born on May 2, 1860, in Budapest, Hungary, to Jacob and Jeanette Herzl, wealthy and assimilated Hungarian Jews. Herzl's father was a successful businessman and directed a small bank. The family had little connection to its Jewish roots and young Theodor did not have a bar mitzvah ceremony in a synagogue but rather a "confirmation" ceremony at home. His real passion was for all things German – literature, language, culture and history. In his free time Theodor wrote short stories and poems in German and dreamed of being a German writer. In 1878 the Herzl family moved to Vienna to be closer to the cultural world they longed for. Theodor loved the city and frequented its theaters, operas and literary cafes. He enrolled in the University of Vienna Law School and joined a German nationalistic fraternity called Albia.

In 1883 the famous German composer and anti-Semite Richard Wagner passed away and Herzl's fraternity held a service in his memory. At the memorial for Wagner, Herzl's frat brothers made vicious anti-Semitic speeches; Herzl was later expelled from the fraternity for raising his voice in protest to their expression of hatred for the Jews. It was one of the first times that he began to seriously contemplate his Jewish identity. In 1884 he received his doctorate in law and two years later he met his future wife, Julie Naschauer. She was pretty, blonde and the daughter of a millionaire. Herzl wrote in his diary, "A sweet kiss from Julie. I am in love!! Unbelievable!!"

The couple were married in 1889 and only then did Herzl discover that his beautiful bride had been psychotic from birth. His marriage was a painful affair and Herzl contemplated divorce several times but remained in the relationship for the sake of the couple's three children, Pauline, Hans and Trude. Sadly, all three children suffered from mental instability themselves. Pauline died of a heroine overdose after suffering from mental disorders. Hans, who at one stage converted to Christianity – though he later recanted this step – committed suicide, distraught with guilt over not having taken better care of his sister. Finally, Trude, who frequented mental clinics, was sent to a concentration camp by the Nazis where she died of starvation.

Trude's only son and Herzl's grandson, Stephen Theodor, was schooled in England and became a British officer in World War II. In 1946 he visited Israel, showed interest in Zionism and promised to return. After World War II, he worked in the British Embassy in Washington, DC, and tragically committed suicide after hearing of the death of his parents at the hands of the Nazis. He jumped off a bridge into the Potomac River. Herzl's wife, Julie, had died in 1907 at the age of thirty-nine; she was cremated. Her final resting place is unknown. One story has it that her son Hans lost the urn of her ashes.

In October 1891 Herzl was appointed as the Paris correspondent of *Neue Freie Presse*, and quickly enhanced his stature as an already prominent journalist. In 1893 he covered the collapse of the French attempt at building the Panama Canal. There were a number of Jews on the board of the French company attempting to build the canal and the French used the Jews as a scapegoat in the company's failure. Anti-Semitism rose in France as Edouard Drumont's 1886 anti-Jewish diatribe *La France juive* (Jewish France) sold over a million copies and made the best-seller list.

In 1893 Herzl proposed asking the pope to fight anti-Semitism and in return he would bring millions of Jews to St. Stephen's Cathedral and all would proudly baptize and convert to Christianity. However in 1895 the Dreyfuss Affair broke and Herzl saw how assimilated Jews were still hated for their Jewish identity, despite giving up all vestiges of Judaism. Herzl realized that even if the Jews converted, they still would be hated for being Jewish! Theodor Herzl began to work on a new, radical solution to the Jewish problem. He shared his new ideas with the famous European Jewish physician and writer Dr. Max Nordau, who answered, "If you are insane, we are insane together. Count on me!"[4]

Nordau encouraged Herzl, who published an eighty-six-page

---

4. Quoted by Nordau's wife and daughter in their biography of him: Anna and Maxa Nordau, *Max Nordau: A Biography* (New York, 1943), 120.

pamphlet in February 1896 entitled *Der Judenstaat* (The Jewish state).
The booklet would change the history of the world. Herzl wrote in it:

> The idea which I have developed in this pamphlet is an an-
> cient one: it is the restoration of the Jewish state.... The world
> needs the Jewish state; therefore it will arise.... The Jews who
> will try it shall achieve their State; and they will deserve it....
> We are a people – one people. We have honestly endeavored,
> everywhere, to submerge ourselves in the surrounding com-
> munity and to preserve only the faith of our fathers. We are
> not permitted to do so.[5]

Herzl then outlined his proposal to create a state for the Jewish people
and concluded *Der Judenstaat* with the following words:

> Therefore I believe that a wondrous breed of Jews will spring
> up from the earth. The Maccabees will rise again. Let me
> repeat once more my opening words: The Jews who will it
> shall achieve their state. We shall live at last as free men on
> our own soil, and in our homes peacefully die. The world
> will be liberated by our freedom, enriched by our wealth,
> magnified by our greatness. And whatever we attempt there
> for our own benefit will redound mightily and beneficially
> to the good of all mankind.[6]

Theodor Herzl's radical proposal was mocked by Western assimilated Jews.
They called him the "Jewish Jules Verne," but in Russia where four million
Jews lived, Herzl was cheered as the new Messiah. In May 1897, Herzl
began publishing his ideas in the Zionist newspaper he had founded, *Die
Welt* (The world). Herzl was not just a man of words; he was a true leader
and man of action. In August 1897, Theodor Herzl convened the First

---

5. Theodor Herzl, preface to *Der Judenstaat*, translated from German by I.M.
    Lask (Tel Aviv: M. Newman Publishing, 1958), 29, 33, 38.

6. Arthur Hertzberg, *The Zionist Idea: A Historical Analysis and Reader* (New
    York: Atheneum, 1969), 225–26.

Zionist Congress in Basel, Switzerland. He brought together 208 delegates from sixteen countries and created the modern Zionist movement.

From A to Z, Herzl organized every aspect of this history-making conference. He chose the hall and even addressed the congress's invitations on his own! Herzl asked his assistant, David Wolfson, to prepare a flag for the congress and after much thought, Wolfson decided to use the Jewish prayer shawl, the *tallit*, as the basis for the Jewish flag, adding a Star of David to the white background with the two blue stripes. Naphtali Herz Imber's song "Hatikva (The hope)" was chosen as the movement's anthem, declaring that "Our hope is not yet lost/The hope of two thousand years/To be a free people in our land/The land of Zion and Jerusalem." At the congress, the World Zionist Organization (wzo) was created with Herzl as its first president. The First Zionist Congress stated the goals of the new Zionist movement in the Basel Program:

> Zionism seeks to establish a home for the Jewish people in Eretz Israel secured under public law. The Congress contemplates the following means to the attainment of this end:
>
> 1. The promotion by appropriate means of the settlement in Eretz Israel of Jewish farmers, artisans, and manufacturers.
>
> 2. Organizing and uniting all Jewry by means of appropriate institutions, both local and international, in accordance with the laws of each country.
>
> 3. Strengthening and fostering Jewish national sentiment and national consciousness.
>
> 4. Preparatory steps toward obtaining the consent of governments, where necessary, in order to reach the goals of Zionism.[7]

---

7. Theodor Herzl, Reuben R. Hecht, Ohad Zemorah, *When the Shofar Sounds: Herzl – Image, Deeds and Selected Writings* (Haifa: Moledeth, 2006).

Meanwhile, covering the First Zionist Congress were twenty-six world correspondents including the famous American humorist and writer Mark Twain, who wrote tongue in cheek, "I am not the sultan and I am not objecting but if that concentration of the cunningest brains in the world was going to be made into a free country, I think it would be politic to stop it! It would not be well to let that race find its strength. If horses knew theirs, we should not ride anymore."[8] Theodor Herzl summarized the congress on a more serious note when he wrote in his diary, "In Basel I have founded the Jewish state.... Perhaps in five years, certainly in fifty years, everyone will admit it." Herzl would prove to be prophetic when the Jewish state would arise exactly fifty-one years later.

Theodor Herzl was a political Zionist and sought to achieve Zionism's goal of founding a Jewish state through political negotiation. Herzl sought to obtain a charter from the Ottoman Turkish Empire (which ruled the Land of Israel at the end of the nineteenth century) to permit Jewish settlement in Israel. In search of this charter, Herzl met with Kaiser Wilhelm of Germany (Turkey's ally) three times and with the Ottoman Turkish Sultan Abdul Hamid. Herzl even offered to repay the Ottoman Empire's enormous public debt but in the end, his offer was refused. Herzl also had unsuccessful meetings with Austrian, Portuguese, Belgian and Russian diplomats. In 1902 Herzl met British colonial secretary Joseph Chamberlain and proposed Jewish settlement on Cyprus or in El Arish but the plans were rejected.

Then in 1903, just five days after the terrible Kishinev pogrom, Joseph Chamberlain proposed to Herzl that he consider building his Jewish homeland in Uganda. Herzl, worried about the survival of Russian Jewry in the face of pogroms and persecution, decided to accept the offer and made the proposal to the Sixth Zionist Congress. Herzl called Uganda "Little Palestine" and saw it as a *Nachtasyl* (night haven) on the path to an eventual home in Israel. Herzl was anxious not to

---

8. Mark Twain, "Concerning the Jews," *Harper's New Monthly Magazine*, March 1898.

insult the English by rejecting their magnanimous offer. Russian Jews at the Sixth Congress, however, responded in anger and stormed out of the congress. There was only one Jewish home for these Jews raised on Jewish tradition and history: the Land of Israel! A young Jewish woman at the congress ran up to the dais and ripped off the map of Uganda hanging there. Herzl remarked in astonishment, "These people have a rope around their necks, but still they refuse!"

In order to preserve the unity of the Zionist movement, Herzl forged a compromise with the establishment of two committees, one that would continue exploring the possibility of Uganda, the other El Arish. He continued to stress that a Jewish homeland in Eretz Yisrael was his ultimate goal, and closed the convention with the words in Hebrew, "If I forget thee oh Jerusalem, may my right hand lose its cunning!"[9]

The bitter disappointment at the Sixth Zionist Congress sapped Herzl of his last strength. He literally exhausted his body of its vitality in the name of Zionism. Theodor Herzl took no compensation for his work and spent his entire family fortune on Zionist affairs. In June 1904 he was taken to a resort in Vienna to rest after suffering a mild heart attack; but on July 3, 1904, he died of heart failure…some say of a "broken heart." Herzl died feeling he was a failure but he had great accomplishments in his short life of forty-four years. He helped create the World Zionist Organization, the Jewish National Fund, and the Jewish Colonial Trust (later to become Bank Leumi) and helped put Zionism on the world map. Though his negotiations with world leaders were unsuccessful, their very existence proved that Zionism was a new force to be reckoned with.

Two years before his death, Herzl wrote a short novel depicting his utopian vision of a future Jewish state. It was called *Altneuland* (Old-new land). Nachum Sokolov translated it into Hebrew using the title *Tel Aviv*. In 1909 a city was founded on the Mediterranean sand

---

9. Psalm 137:5.

dunes and given that name to honor Herzl. Theodor Herzl's legacy was summarized in *Altneuland* with the words, *"Im tirtzu, ein zo aggadah* (If you will it, it is no dream)!"* Herzl's dream became a vision and forty-four years after his death, the vision became a reality.

Few are the heroes who have had such an impact on their people's history in so few years. When David Ben-Gurion declared Israel's independence on May 14, 1948, it was Herzl's picture that looked down on the assembled at Independence Hall in Tel Aviv. Herzl, like Moses, would not live to see that moment, but more than any other, he would be the one who laid its foundation. After the creation of the Jewish state, his remains were reinterred in Jerusalem on the mountain that now bears his name. Today Theodor Herzl lays at rest on Mount Herzl in Jerusalem, eternal capital of the Jewish nation. His vision, work and sacrifice were not in vain.

HAIM NAHMAN BIALIK
A POEM THAT AWAKENED A NATION

Haim Nahman Bialik (1873–1934)
- Greatest modern Hebrew poet
- 1903 Wrote "In the City of Slaughter"
- Created "Oneg Shabbat" custom in Tel Aviv
  "Satan has not yet created the vengeance worthy of the murderer of a little child."

Haim Nahman Bialik, the greatest Hebrew poet of modern times, was born in 1873 in the Russian village of Radi, near Zhitomir. Bialik would not only have a great effect on the development of Hebrew culture in Eretz Yisrael (the Land of Israel) but he would also have a profound influence on the course of modern Jewish history. It is rare for a poet to have such an influence on the path of his people but Bialik did with his pen what scores of generals could only dream of doing with their swords. In many ways, this Russian-Jewish poet could be called one of the spiritual fathers of modern Jewish self-defense and, in effect, the mighty Israel Defense Forces (IDF or Tzahal, *Tzeva Haganah l'Yisrael*, in Hebrew).

Haim Bialik grew up in a traditional Jewish home in Russia. His father, Isaac Joseph, a Talmudic scholar, and his mother, Dinah Priva, gave their children a warm, loving home but when Haim was seven, his father passed away and the family became destitute. The Bialiks moved to Zhitomir and Haim was raised by his well-to-do but stern Orthodox grandfather, Jacob Moses. At the age of fifteen, Haim convinced his grandfather to send him to the famous Volozhin Yeshiva, perhaps the greatest Talmudic academy in the world. Bialik immersed himself in the erudite teachings of Talmud but soon doubts developed in his mind about that path. He had great respect for the yeshiva students' devotion and perseverance but disliked their narrow view of the world.

At the age of eighteen, Bialik left the Volozhin Yeshiva for Odessa, the center of the "Haskalah" – the modern Jewish "enlightenment" – in southern Russia. It was there that he joined a literary circle led by the famous Zionist writer Ahad HaAm, who had a great influence on him. Bialik was penniless and made a living teaching Hebrew. In 1892 he published his first Hebrew poem, "El hatzipor" (To the bird), a song of longing for Zion, which received critical acclaim. In 1901 his first volume of poetry was published and Bialik was hailed as the "poet of the national renaissance." In 1904 the young poet moved to Warsaw and became the literary editor of Ahad HaAm's weekly magazine *HaShiloach*.

Meanwhile revolutionary winds blew in Russia, home to four million Jews, the world's largest Jewish community. On March 13, 1881, Czar Alexander II was assassinated by Russian revolutionaries from the "Narodnya Volva" (Will of the people) group. His son and successor, Czar Alexander III, blamed liberal elements and Jews for the assassination. Fearing for his throne, Alexander III organized attacks on Russia's Jews as an attempt to divert the Russian people's anger from the ruling Romanov family. These attacks, known as *pogroms* (the Russian word for "devastation") began in 1881 at the instigation of the czar. His chief advisor, Pobedonostev, developed the "Thirds Plan for Russian Jewry": one-third of Russian Jews would be murdered in the pogroms, one-third would be expelled from Russia and the final third would be forcibly converted to Russian Orthodox Christianity.

Alexander III and Pobedonostev's plan was a slow death sentence for Russian Jewry. As these pogroms spread across Russia, the country's Jews were forced to find solutions to their deadly predicament. Some traditional Jews said this suffering was part of being Jewish and patiently prayed and waited for the Messiah. Some, like Leon Trotsky, became Bolshevik Communists and sought to change Russia from the inside. These Jews believed that Jewish blood would be "the oil that greases the spokes of world revolution." Over two and a half million Russian Jews would flee the pogroms for safety in the West – most going to the United States. A small but significant minority of Russian Jews responded to the pogroms, not by fleeing to a new exile or becoming communists, but by becoming Zionists and moving to Eretz Yisrael where they hoped to build a Jewish state in our ancestral homeland. Bialik was one of the latter. His response to the infamous Kishinev pogrom in 1903 would greatly affect the course of modern Jewish history.

In 1894 Nicholas II took over from his father who died of a kidney illness. Facing increasing revolutionary activities, Czar Nicholas II and his minister of the interior, Vyacheslav von Plehve, both rabid anti-Semites, began to plan the biggest of all the pogroms, the April 6, 1903, Kishinev pogrom. They hoped to divert the Russian masses' attention from the Romanovs' corruption by instigating against the Jews. Kishinev was the capital of the Russian province of Bessarabia. It had 140,000 inhabitants, one-third of whom were Jewish. Von Plehve paid the editor of the local newspaper, the *Bessarabetz*, to publish articles against the Jews and in early 1903 the newspaper published headlines like "Death to the Jews!" and "Crusade against Hated Race."

In February 1903 the mutilated body of a Russian peasant boy was discovered near Kishinev. Though his uncle confessed to the crime, the *Bessarabetz* accused the Jews of murdering the boy as part of a ritual killing to use his blood to make matzah for Passover. Though the charges against the Jews were unfounded and ridiculous, they spread like wildfire. Handbills were handed out in Kishinev calling on Christians to inflict bloody punishment on the Jews. Even the head of the local police published anti-Semitic articles in the local newspaper. The pogrom exploded on Easter Sunday, April 6, 1903, a date that coincided with the last day of the Jewish holiday of Passover. As thousands of Russian churchgoers left their houses of worship, they were met by twenty-four gangs of armed Russian hoodlums who urged them to join in taking revenge on the Jews.

The pogrom would last for over two days, and the Russian police refused to intervene to protect Kishinev's Jews. In fact, both the Kishinev bishop and police chief rode around in a car blessing the rioters. When the pogrom finally ended 49 Jews were dead, 495 Jews were severely injured and 123 Jewish children had become orphans. Though the destruction seemed minor compared to what the Nazis would do to the Jews forty years later, the Kishinev pogrom was one of the worst and most traumatic attacks on the Jewish people in history. American president Teddy Roosevelt condemned the attack along with both houses of the u.s. Congress and even Germany's Kaiser Wilhelm, an anti-Semite himself, protested the pogrom to the czar.

The barbarism and atrocities inflicted on Kishinev's Jews were devastating. Jewish men were castrated and hanged from latrines. Jewish women were gang raped while alive and while dead – sometimes a daughter in front of her mother! Jewish babies were found with their heads split open and their brains splattered. Some women had their bellies cut open and filled with feathers from ripped quilts. Jewish victims were found with nails driven through their skulls. In response to the Kishinev pogrom a great Yiddish poet named Shimon Frug wrote a poem called "Hot rachmones" (Have pity). Part of it read:

> Streams of blood and tears in rivers
> Seethe and flow and spread.
> Our ancient terrible trouble
> Has laid its hand on our head....
>
> Brothers and sisters have pity!
> The need is terrible, dread!
> Give the dead their winding sheets,
> Give the living bread....

Too weak is our arm for fighting,
Terrible is our smart,
Come with love and consolation,
Good Jewish heart!

Frug's poem was meaningful and well intentioned but it smacked of two thousand years of Jewish passivity and weakness. Frug was afraid to curse the Russian attackers and begged for pity for his injured people. He openly declared that "too weak is our arm for fighting" and his poem was indicative of Jewish weakness in the Diaspora.

At the same time Haim Bialik was sent to Kishinev on behalf of the Jewish Historical Commission in Odessa to report on the atrocity. After touring the town and interviewing survivors, he wrote a short poem called "Al hashehitah" (On the slaughter) calling on heaven to execute immediate justice. The poem's most famous line read, "Cursed be he who says 'Revenge,' As Satan has not yet created the vengeance worthy of the murderer of a little child."

Over the next three months Bialik wrestled with what he saw in Kishinev, and in the summer of 1903 he published a second poem on the Kishinev pogrom. This epic was a fourteen-page attack on the Russian murderers, and on God Who allowed the pogrom to occur, but mostly it was Bialik pouring out his wrath on the Jewish men of Kishinev who cowered in their hiding places while their wives and daughters were raped and murdered. Bialik was angry with Jews like Yisrael Steinberg who ransacked his own house to fool the Russian attackers into thinking they had already been there, and later watched in hiding as his father was murdered. The poem is called "B'ir haharegah" (In the city of slaughter) and it sent shock waves through the entire Jewish world.

Arise and go forth to the city of slaughter
    and come into the courtyards,
And with your own eyes you will see....
The congealed blood and the hardened brains
    of the corpses....

Do not stand on the ruins. Pass from there to the road –
Acacia trees are blossoming there before you,
Sprinkling into your nostrils their spices.
Their buds are half covered with feathers,
     and their fragrance is like the odor of blood.…
     For God called forth the spring and the slaughter
     together:
The sun shone, the acacia blossomed
     and the slaughterer slaughtered.
You flee, and come to the courtyard;
     in the courtyard is a heap.
On this heap, two were beheaded: a Jew and his dog.
One axe beheaded them,
     and onto one garbage heap they were thrown.
In the evening, pigs will pick and wallow
     in the blood of these two.
Tomorrow, rain will fall and wash it away
     to one of the desolate streams.…
And all will be as if nothing happened.…

So ask the spiders – they are living witnesses,
     eyewitnesses; they will tell you all:
The story of a stomach torn apart
     that they stuffed with feathers.
The story of nostrils and nails, of skulls and hammers.
The story of a slaughtered people hung on rafters.
And the story of an infant found
     by the side of his impaled mother –
As he sleeps, and in his mouth
     is the nipple of her cold breast.
And the story of a child torn apart.
     He died crying "Mommy!".…

Go down from there and come to the dark cellars,
The place where the pure daughters
    of your people were defiled.…
One woman after another
    under seven of the uncircumcised.
The daughter in front of her mother,
    the mother in front of her daughter,
Before the slaughter, during the slaughter
    and after the slaughter.…

See in the dark of that same corner,
Under the mortar used for this Passover's matzah,
    behind the same barrel.
Lay husbands, grooms, brothers – peering through holes
At the twisting of the holy bodies
    beneath the flesh of donkeys,
Choking in their defilement,
    swallowing the blood of their throats.
Like a man passing around treats,
    the abominable goy passed around their bodies.

They (the Jewish men of Kishinev) lay in their shame
    and they saw, they didn't move or budge;
    Perhaps each man prayed to himself, in his heart –
"Master of the Universe! Perform a miracle!
    May this evil not come upon me!".…
See with your own eyes, where they were hiding,
Your brothers, the sons of your people,
    descendants of the Maccabees!.…[10]

---

10. This translation of "B'ir haharegah" (In the city of slaughter) is by Rabbi
    Michael Katz, of Westbury, Long Island, who has researched the pogrom ex-
    tensively. His translation appears in *Sourcebook #4 : Emancipation, Haskalah,
    Zionism* (Hod Hasharon: Alexander Muss High School in Israel, 2006).

Bialik described how Kishinev's Jewish men, descendants of the courageous Maccabee warriors, hid in fear as their wives and sisters and
daughters were raped and murdered. He castigated his people for their
passivity in the face of murderous attacks and mocked their preoccupa-
tion with Jewish ritual matters instead of fighting back and defending
themselves. The Jewish elders of Kishinev banned the condemning
poem but young Jews across Russia read it in forests and in outhouses,
far from the sight of their weak communal leaders. Bialik's poem, like
the pogrom itself, was a wake-up call to young Jews to take their destiny in their own hands and stand up and defend their people. Jewish
historian Yisrael Berman wrote of Bialik's effect on young Russian Jews
in an article on Kishinev:

> The slogan "self-defense" which was sounded by someone in
> a small group of young people during the reading of Bialik's
> poem became like a pebble thrown in still water. From that
> pebble came a small circle, and after it a larger circle, and after
> the second, a third, and then a fourth – one circle larger than
> the previous one. Thus did this slogan encircle all of the young
> Zionists and Jewish self-defense became a reality. In secret
> meetings of defense groups we read the poem, explained it
> and argued about it and after every meeting new members
> would come forth to enlist.
>
> Two and a half years later, during the pogroms of 1905,
> the rioters in Kishinev and Odessa and other towns felt they
> were dealing with a different kind of Jew. Hundreds of rioters
> paid with their lives for trying to plunder and kill Jews.
>
> And if during the terrible pogroms in Israel in 1920, 1921,
> 1929 and 1936–39 dozens of young Jews successfully stood up
> to gangs of hundreds and thousands of armed Arab murder-
> ers and drove them off, and if Jews no longer hid but were
> prepared to defend their honor and their nation's honor then
> one of the main reasons is without a doubt the poem "In the

City of Slaughter." Thus, Kishinev, the birthplace of the poems
of wrath, was also the birthplace of Jewish self-defense![11]

Bialik lived in Odessa till 1921 and then moved to Berlin. In 1924 he
made Aliyah to Israel and settled in Tel Aviv where he spent the rest of
his life. Bialik taught at the Herzliya Gymnasium, the first Hebrew high
school in modern Israel, and helped found the Hebrew University in
Jerusalem. Along with Yehoshua Rawnitzki, he helped compile the great
Rabbinic stories from the Talmud in the classic work *Sefer HaAggadah*
and instituted the popular concept of "Oneg Shabbat," a now worldwide
custom of study on Shabbat.

Haim Bialik was the greatest Hebrew poet since Yehuda HaLevi
and his genius has left an indelible mark on the modern State of Israel
and Hebrew culture. His poetry not only played a vital role in the revival of the Hebrew language but his responses to the Kishinev pogrom
helped spur the rise of Jewish self-defense and a new spirit in the Jewish people that would lead them to freedom and independence. Haim
Bialik died on July 3, 1934, and he is buried in Tel Aviv. His house in
Tel Aviv is now a museum and the street it's on bears his name in his
honor and memory.

POSTSCRIPT: Bialik wrote his epic poem of wrath "In the City of Slaughter" in Hebrew. Most Russian Jews read the translation of the poem
into Russian that was done by another Jewish poet and writer, Zeev
Jabotinsky. Jabotinsky was born in 1880 in Russia and visited Kishinev
immediately after the pogrom. As Jabotinsky toured the ruins of
Kishinev's Jewish quarter he came upon a synagogue that had been
desecrated and burned. Jabotinsky began to cry as he saw a destroyed
holy ark with burnt Torah scrolls in front of it – the work of Kishinev's
Russian murderers. Suddenly in the midst of the ash and destruction,

---

11. Yisrael Berman, "Im H.N. Bialik b'Kishinev [With C.N. Bialik in Kishinev],"
in *HaPogrom b'Kishinev b'Mil'ot Shishim Shana, 1903-1963*, edited by Chaim
Shorer (Tel Aviv: HaIgud HaOlami shel Yehudei Bessarabia [World Federation
of Bessarabian Jews], 1963), 75–80.

Jabotinsky noticed a small piece of parchment with two words from the Torah clearly visible. The words were *b'eretz nochriyah* (in a strange land). Jabotinsky immediately recognized the words from Exodus 2:22, where Moses explains the origin of his son Gershom's name, by saying, "I was a stranger in a strange land."

Jabotinsky was a cosmopolitan assimilated Russian Jew at the time but the parchment he found that day in Kishinev changed his life. He believed that these two words carried the secret to the redemption of his people. As long as Jews lived in strange lands, they would face persecution and pogroms. Only in Eretz Yisrael would Jews be able to build a secure future for their people. Jabotinsky understood that no one would hand the Jews a state in Israel on a silver platter. He knew they would have to stand up and fight for their rights. Jabotinsky would later move to Israel and create the Jewish Legion in 1917, the first Jewish armed force in two thousand years. He and his followers would create the underground defense group called the Haganah in Jerusalem in 1920, and its splinter group the Etzel (*Irgun Tzva'i Leumi*, National Military Organization), founded in the 1930s. His legacy would give birth to a new Jew: proud, fierce and strong. That legacy was born in Kishinev in 1903.

MICHAEL HALPERN, MANYA SHOCHAT
AND THE HEROES OF HASHOMER

Michael Halpern (1860–1919)
- Inspired Jewish self-defense in Russia and Israel
- Dreamed about forming a Jewish army in Israel
- 1911 Courageously sang "Hatikva" in lions' cage
  "Join the Jewish army!"

Manya Shochat (1880–1961)
- Russian revolutionary and Zionist
- 1904 Made Aliyah to Israel
- 1909 Helped found HaShomer defense organization
  "In blood and fire Judea fell;
  in blood and fire Judea shall rise again!"

HALPERN   SHOCHAT

In 1880 there were twenty-five thousand Jews in Israel, mostly ultra-orthodox living in the Holy Land's four holy cities: Jerusalem, Hebron, Tiberias and Safed. These Jews of the "Old Yishuv" (the Land of Israel's old Jewish community) studied in yeshivas (Talmudic academies) and lived off of the "*Chalukah*" – donations from overseas Jewish communities. Their only goal was to study, pray, die and be buried in the Holy Land. In 1882 a new wave of Jewish immigration began to come to Eretz Yisrael (the Land of Israel). Jews, mostly from Russia but also from

Yemen and elsewhere, began to immigrate to Israel with the goal of building a new life for the Jewish people in our ancient homeland. They were the first Zionist pioneers (*halutzim*) and about twenty-five thousand arrived in the years 1882–1903. They built twenty-eight moshavot (farm-villages) including Rishon LeZion, Petah Tikvah and Zikhron Yaakov.

Conditions in Israel were very rough in those days and the land had not been farmed in over two thousand years. Many of the first pioneers broke down and left their old-new land. Financial help from the world's richest Jew, Baron Edmond de Rothschild of Paris, helped save the day but brought with it new challenges. He donated over six million dollars to buy lands in Eretz Yisrael and help set up new settlements and factories. Due to his generosity and help he became known as the "Father of the Yishuv" ("Yishuv" referring to the new Zionist community growing in Israel).

While the First Aliyah laid the seeds for Zionist achievements, much of the "harvesting" was done by the "Second Aliyah," the new wave of Zionist immigrants that came to Eretz Yisrael between 1904 and 1914. About forty thousand Jews, mostly from Russia, came during the "Second Aliyah," fleeing pogroms and persecution but also looking to build a new Jewish homeland in Eretz Yisrael. Their motto was "*Anu banu artza livnot u'lehibanot bah* (We came to Israel to build a new homeland and to be rebuilt ourselves)."

These *halutzim* were angry at the old Orthodox Jews who sat around and prayed and waited for the Messiah. They sought to create a new Jew who would take control of his own destiny and bring redemption with his own hands. Their three goals were to work the soil of Eretz Yisrael, to speak Hebrew and finally, to defend their land and people with their own hands. The *halutzim* of the Second Aliyah achieved three great accomplishments in the year 1909.That year they founded the first kibbutz (communal farm settlement), Degania, on the shores of Lake Kinneret (the Sea of Galilee); founded the first modern Hebrew city, Tel Aviv (which celebrated its hundredth birthday in

2009); and created the first modern Jewish self-defense organization, HaShomer ("the guard").

The precursor to HaShomer was an amazing Jewish personality named Michael Halpern. Halpern was born in 1860 in Vilna to a wealthy family. He was a big, strong, muscular man and learned horseback riding and saber fighting from the Cossacks. Michael had a heart as big as his muscles and was very idealistic. Once he saw a pimp mistreating prostitutes in the town of Smolensk. He used family money to "buy" them from their pimp, rented a train and freed the young women. When he received a big inheritance he used much of the money to buy land in Eretz Yisrael and helped found the settlements of Yesod HaMaalah and Nes Ziona. In 1881 he joined the Zionist youth movement Chovevei Zion ("lovers of Zion") and visited Israel in 1885, traveling the length and breadth of the country by foot.

In 1886, in the midst of violent pogroms in Russia, Michael Halpern made Aliyah to Israel. His dream was to create a Jewish army in Israel and liberate the Jewish homeland. In those days he was seen riding on horseback, jumping over campfires with an Israeli flag in hand, screaming, "Join the Jewish army!" Halpern labored in the fields of Israel and struggled against Baron de Rothschild's bureaucrats. In 1903 he returned to Russia and after the Kishinev pogrom (April 6–7, 1903) he helped organize Jewish self-defense in the land of the czars. Many of the young men and women he inspired in Russia made Aliyah to Israel and helped found HaShomer, the first modern Jewish self-defense organization.

Halpern returned to Israel in 1905. The story for which he is best known occurred in 1911 when the circus came to Jaffa. The main attraction was a lion tamer, who seeking big ratings challenged the ethnic groups in the audience to enter the lion's cage. He called upon the Muslims, who sent forward their bravest soul. The Muslim hero approached the lion's cage and put his foot through the bars. The lion leaped forward and the Muslim ran away screaming, "*Allahu Akbar* (God is great)!" The Muslims in the audience roared their approval for their hero. The lion tamer then called for a Christian hero to come forward. The Christians laughed and declined the offer by saying that they had bad experiences with lions during the Roman period!

Finally, the lion tamer called for a Jewish hero to come forward. The audience broke out in raucous laughter. A "Jewish hero" – that is an oxymoron! The Arabs in the audience began to mockingly chant in Arabic, "*Walid al maut* (children of death)," a derisive label used for Jews, who were thought to be weak patsies. As the audience laughed, Michael Halpern stepped forward holding an Israeli flag and volunteered to be the Jewish contestant. He approached the lion's cage and suddenly pushed the lion tamer away, entered the lion's cage and locked himself inside. The crowd watched in shocked silence, expecting to see the fool mauled to death. The lion rushed at Halpern, who stared down the beast and roared back at it. The lion halted, as if in shock itself. Michael Halpern lifted the Israeli flag high in the air, eyed down the frightened beast, and sang with all his might the Jewish national anthem, "Hatikvah." The Arabs were amazed, having seen a brave, courageous Jew for the first time, and legends about the modern-day Samson spread far and wide.

Halpern passed on the legacy of Jewish heroism to many, including his own son, Jeremy. Jeremy Halpern was born in 1913 and joined Zeev Jabotinsky's Zionist youth group Betar. In 1929 he helped lead the defense of Tel Aviv during Arab riots and in 1934 he set up the first modern Jewish naval academy in Civitavecchia, Italy. One of the graduates of that academy was Shlomo Erel, who was commander of the Israeli navy during the 1967 Six-Day War.

Meanwhile, in 1907, ten young Jews gathered in the Jaffa apartment of Yitzhak Ben Zvi and founded a secret society to defend the Jewish people and their land in Israel. The organization was called "Bar Giora" after the commander of the great revolt against Rome in Jerusalem. Shimon Bar Giora was the last defender of Jerusalem in 70 CE and was executed in Rome. The group adopted their motto from Yaakov Cahan's poem "Zealots." It was, "In blood and fire Judea fell, and in blood and fire Judea shall rise again!"

The driving force in the creation of Bar Giora was Israel Shochat, who was born in Grodno in 1886. Shochat helped organize Jewish self-defense in Russia after the 1903 Kishinev pogrom. He, like many of his comrades, was dually inspired by Haim Bialik's poem "In the City of Slaughter" and by the personal example and teachings of Michael Halpern. Israel Shochat made Aliyah in 1904 and in 1907 helped organize Bar Giora. He pulled together a unique group of tough, brave Jewish heroes including Yitzhak Ben Zvi, Yehezkel Chenkin, Yehezkel Nisanov, Mendel Portugali, Alexander Zaid and Israel Giladi.

Ben Zvi helped lead the defense of Poltava, Russia, during pogroms there in 1905. He later helped found the Israeli Labor Party and became Israel's second president.

Chenkin led the defense of Homel, Russia, during pogroms there in 1903. At one point he leaped on a horse and with saber in hand charged at the attacking Cossacks who fled in shock. He made Aliyah in 1903 and later founded the Maccabi Jaffa Sports Club and became the first modern Jewish hunter.

Nisanov organized Jewish self-defense in Sevastapol, Russia, and made Aliyah in 1906. He was killed in Israel defending a farm from Arab robbers. At his funeral, his mother said, "Boys, don't cry! Go kill the Arab murderers and let their mothers cry! I don't cry because my son fell for the holiness of Eretz Yisrael!"

Mendel Portugali's family was descended from the Spanish exile. He too led the defense of his shtetl in Russia during the pogroms. He came to Israel on the Second Aliyah and worked the fields by day and guarded them by night. When he came home late at night he would dance with his wife, happy that there were now Jewish guards.

Alexander Zaid was born in Siberia in 1886. Inspired by Halpern, he trained thirty Jews to fight the pogromchiks in the forests. He came to Israel in 1904 and helped found Bar Giora. He also learned stone masonry and worked in the ancient Jewish profession. While guarding lands near Beit Shearim, he discovered an ancient Jewish burial site including Rabbi Judah HaNasi's grave and synagogue. On July 11, 1938, he was ambushed and murdered by Arabs while guarding his post. His sons later discovered and assassinated the murderers. Today a statue of Zaid on horseback stands over the Jezreel Valley.

Finally, there was Israel Giladi, who was born in Russia and led the defense of his town during the 1905 pogroms. He made Aliyah to Israel and walked barefoot because he felt, "Our feet must feel the soil of Eretz Yisrael." The ten members of Bar Giora settled in 1907 at Sejera (Ilaniya), a training farm where they met a remarkable woman named Manya Wilbuschevitch.

Manya was born in Russia and had been active in Communist revolutionary groups. She became disillusioned with her Communist comrades after the 1903 Kishinev pogrom and even tried to assassinate the Russian minister of the interior responsible for the pogrom, Vyacheslav von Plehve. She made Aliyah to Israel in 1904 and in 1907 came to Sejera where she helped organize a collective that became the prototype for kibbutzim. In 1908 she joined Bar Giora but began to convince her fellow guards that they needed to cease being a small, secret society and take over the public guarding of all Jewish settlements in Eretz Yisrael. When the Jewish manager of Sejera refused to let the Bar Giora members guard the training farm, Manya stole the settlement's mule, being watched by Circassians, proving the ineffectiveness of the non-Jewish guards. Sejera's manager turned the guard duty of the settlement over to Bar Giora and Zvi Becker became the first Shomer.

In April 1909 Manya and the members of Bar Giora met at Mesha (Kfar Tavor), at the foot of Mount Tabor where once Deborah and Barak fought, and founded HaShomer ("the guard"). It was the first Jewish self-defense organization in two thousand years. They adopted the Bar Giora motto and wore exotic garb including Arab keffiyas, Circassian kulpaks (hats) and Russian rubashkas (shirts). The Jewish guards rode on horses and carried an *Abu Hamsa* (five-bullet rifle), a *shabariya* (dagger), a *nabut* (club) and a pistol. Yehezkel Chenkin could stand up on his horse and hit a bull's-eye with his rifle while riding! HaShomer became the toughest group of young Jews in two thousand years and soon its members were guarding Jewish settlements all over Israel.

In 1908 Manya married fellow guard Israel Shochat and became Manya Shochat. In 1920 she and her husband moved to Kibbutz Kfar Giladi, the first kibbutz founded by HaShomer. During the 1921 Arab riots in Jaffa, Manya Shochat dressed up as a nurse and bravely rescued many of the Jewish wounded. When a massacre of Jews took place at the Ajami House in Jaffa, Manya learned the name of the Arab murderer from a twelve-year-old orphan survivor. She found the Arab policeman who led the massacre and executed him in the name of Jewish justice. In 1948 she joined the Mapam political party and settled in Tel Aviv. Manya Shochat died in 1961 at the age of 81.

In 1920 HaShomer disbanded and its members helped found the Haganah, the Jewish underground army. Then on May 28, 1948, during the War of Independence, the Haganah was disbanded along with the Etzel and Lehi undergrounds, and Tzahal, the Israel Defense Forces, was created. David Ben-Gurion once said that the Israel Defense Forces had many fathers but only one "grandfather" – HaShomer.

ELIEZER BEN-YEHUDA
"IVRI, DABER IVRIT!"

Eliezer Ben-Yehuda (1858–1922)
- Father of modern Hebrew
- Wrote seventeen-volume dictionary of modern Hebrew
"Ivri, daber Ivrit!" (Jew, speak Hebrew!)

The Ben-Yehuda pedestrian mall in Jerusalem is one of Israel's most vibrant and exciting tourist attractions, yet few of the people visiting and shopping there know the story behind the man for whom the famous street is named. Eliezer Ben-Yehuda, ardent Zionist and father of the modern Hebrew language, was born as Eliezer Yitzhak Perelman in Luzhky, Lithuania, in 1858. His parents were Orthodox Jews and Eliezer had a traditional Jewish education. Ben-Yehuda's father, a Habad hasid, died when Eliezer was five years old and when the boy reached his bar mitzvah (age thirteen), he was sent to his uncle in Polotsk, where he attended yeshiva. The head of the yeshiva was a Maskil ("enlightened" Jew) in secret and introduced the young boy to secular literature. Ben-Yehuda also learned Russian and eventually transferred to and graduated from the secular Dvinsk Gymnasium in 1877.

The Russo-Turkish War of 1877–78 and the struggle of the Balkan nations for their freedom planted in Ben-Yehuda the idea for the renaissance of Jewish independence in their ancient homeland of Israel. Ben-Yehuda came to believe that the Jewish people had a historic land and language and that a new movement was needed to bring both back to life. He would later write, "In those days it was as if the heavens had suddenly opened, and a clear, incandescent light flashed before my eyes, and a mighty inner voice sounded in my ears: the renascence of Israel on its ancestral soil."

Eliezer became determined to make Aliyah to Israel and settle in his people's homeland but first he needed a profession to provide for his livelihood. In 1878 he traveled to Paris and began to study medicine at the Sorbonne. While in France, he was greatly influenced by the importance of the French language in French nationalism. In 1880 he wrote his fiancée, Deborah Jonas, "I have decided that in order to have our own land and political life it is also necessary that we have a language to hold us together. That language is Hebrew, but not the Hebrew of the rabbis and scholars. We must have a Hebrew language in which we can conduct the business of life."[12]

In Paris, Ben-Yehuda met the Jerusalem scholar Abraham Moses Luncz who spoke to him in Hebrew and convinced him to make the Sephardic pronunciation the format for modern Hebrew. In 1881, the twenty-three-year-old Ben-Yehuda married his fiancée and the two boarded a boat to Eretz Yisrael (the Land of Israel). On board, the two vowed to speak no other language but Hebrew – a vow they never broke.

In Israel, Eliezer and Deborah set up the first modern Hebrew-speaking home and Eliezer officially adopted the pseudonym Ben-Yehuda. The couple's first son, Itamar Ben-Avi, was only allowed to hear Hebrew and since no nanny could speak the ancient tongue, he was only allowed to hear his parents speak. Itamar did not utter a word for the first four years of his life and at first was thought to be mentally handicapped; however, at the age of four the tot opened his mouth and began speaking full sentences in Hebrew, making him the first modern Hebrew-speaking child in history.

Though the Ben-Yehudas had five children, not even a non-Hebrew-speaking maid was allowed in the home. The Ben-Yehuda

---

12. Quoted in Yosef Eisen, *Miraculous Journey: A Complete History of the Jewish People from Creation to the Present* (Jerusalem: Targum Press, 2004), 319.

children were not allowed to play with other kids lest they be influenced by languages other than Hebrew. They practiced their Hebrew with cats and dogs, using male and female genders, and the animals became the first "Hebrew-speaking" pets in the world!

The family suffered from poverty and from attacks from Jerusalem's ultra-Orthodox Jews who saw Hebrew as only a holy tongue and feared Ben-Yehuda's attempts to revive the language as a living one. Ben-Yehuda was also opposed to and spoke out against the old Orthodox tradition of "*chalukah*" where men studied Talmud and lived off of donations – in effect welfare. Ben-Yehuda's office was stoned by ultra-Orthodox Jews and he was later excommunicated by them. Young religious children called him *HaMeshuga* (the crazy man) and when his wife Deborah died, she was refused burial in the Ashkenazi cemetery.

In 1884 Ben Yehuda began to publish a Hebrew newspaper called *HaZevi* which had about two hundred subscribers. In the paper he promoted Zionist settlement and agricultural labor in Israel as well as opposing *chalukah*. In *HaZevi* he championed, of course, the revival of the Hebrew language and spared no effort to coin new words and phrases in the reborn language.

In 1891 his wife, Deborah, died and six months later he married her younger sister, who adopted the Hebrew name "Hemdah." In 1894 Hemdah published an article in *HaZevi* in which she wrote to her fellow Zionists, "Let us gather strength and go forward!" Ben-Yehuda's ultra-Orthodox enemies used the opportunity to inform on him to the Ottoman Turkish authorities, then ruling Palestine, and said the phrase really meant "Let us gather an army and proceed against the Turks." Ben-Yehuda was sentenced to a year in prison but after a worldwide appeal he was released. The affair shows the great animosity felt towards him by the ultra-Orthodox, who felt Hebrew was only a language for prayer. His house is located near the religious neighborhood of Meah Shearim in Jerusalem and each time a memorial plaque is placed on the building, it is immediately ripped off.

Ben-Yehuda's greatest accomplishment, perhaps, was his compilation of a seventeen-volume dictionary of modern Hebrew. Already upon his arrival in Israel he began to gather notes with words and phrases he had created in Hebrew. Ben-Yehuda used the Tanakh (Hebrew Bible) to adapt new words in Hebrew to modern life. He created the word *chashmal* for "electricity" from the biblical word for sparks coming off of Ezekiel's chariot. Eliezer Ben-Yehuda, with the support of the Zionist movement and Baron Edmond de Rothschild, published five volumes of his *Complete Dictionary of Ancient and Modern Hebrew*. Three volumes were published after his death and nine more were completed from Ben-Yehuda's manuscripts – a total of seventeen volumes. Ben-Yehuda also founded the Vaad HaLashon HaIvri (Academy of the Hebrew Language) which then, as today, supervised the modernization and spread of Hebrew as a spoken language for the Jewish people in Israel. Wherever Ben-Yehuda traveled to in Israel, he always spread his motto, "*Ivri, daber Ivrit* (Jew, speak Hebrew)."

In 1913 the Haifa Technical Institute (later to be called the Technion) announced that its board of directors, mostly German Jews from the Hilfsverein der Deutschen Juden, a German-Jewish aid association, had decided to introduce German as the official language of instruction in its fifty schools and in the college in Israel. Ben-Yehuda led a vigorous campaign against that decision and his struggle soon became known as the "war of the languages." He even threatened that "blood [would] flow in the streets" for this sacred cause.

The first strike in modern Israel was not for increased wages but was carried out by Ben-Yehuda and the Hebrew Teachers Association in order to have all subjects at the Hilfsverein schools in Israel taught in Hebrew. Four months later the board of directors of the Haifa Technical Institute reversed their decision and announced that all subjects would be taught in Hebrew. Ben-Yehuda won the war and already by 1916 40 percent of the Yishuv in Israel spoke Hebrew as their first language. When Eliezer Ben-Yehuda died in December 1922, thirty thousand people escorted his body to the grave and the Yishuv declared three days of official mourning.

While Ben-Yehuda's enemies considered him crazy, he certainly was eccentric. The story is told that Ben-Yehuda attended the first performance of *Zerubabel*, the first Hebrew opera in Israel. At the end of the performance the crowd rose to its feet and gave the singers a standing ovation. They chanted "Bravo, Bravo!" in Italian as per the European custom. Incensed at the sacrilegious use of a foreign tongue, Ben-Yehuda leapt from his seat and beat his fellow opera-goers with his program, screaming the correct Hebrew phrase for approval, "*Hedad, Hedad!*"

Visionaries are often thought to be crazy. Many thought Herzl was insane when he wrote *Der Judenstaat* in 1896 and proposed a Jewish state. Just over fifty years later that state was a reality. Ben-Yehuda dreamed of a day when modern Hebrew would be the spoken language in an independent Jewish state. Today over six million Jews speak Hebrew in the State of Israel and the rebirth of the ancient tongue is perhaps the most underrated miracle of the twentieth century. Hebrew newspapers, Hebrew novels, Hebrew rock songs and Hebrew movies and television shows are accepted norms today, yet just over a hundred years ago, Hebrew was almost a dead language. Today Hebrew has come back to life and with it the Jewish nation, which owes an eternal debt of gratitude to Eliezer Ben-Yehuda.

SARAH AARONSOHN
AND THE NILI SPIES

Sarah Aaronsohn (1890–1917)
- Sabra (native-born Israeli)
- Together with her brother, led Nili spy organization
- 1917 Committed suicide after being arrested and tortured by Turks
  "Netzach Yisrael lo yishaker."
  (The Eternity of Israel will not deceive)

In 1915 a group of young Jews in Eretz Yisrael (the Land of Israel) had a dream. They envisioned a day when Israel would be free from the oppressive rule of the Ottoman Turks and when the Jewish people would have their own independent homeland. Knowing that dreams are realized only through action, they founded the Nili spy organization and set out on a road of danger and sacrifice.

Israel, at the turn of the century, was part of the Ottoman Turkish Empire. The Turks were vehemently opposed to Zionism and treated the Jewish Yishuv (community) in Israel with brutality. Many Jews, having witnessed the Turkish genocide of the Armenian people, feared a similar fate. In 1914 World War I broke out with the Turks and Germans aligned against England and the Western powers. It was within this atmosphere that Nili was created.

Nili was a secret spy organization founded by young Jews in Eretz Yisrael in 1915. It numbered about sixty members, most of whom were native-born Israelis ("sabras") from the First Aliyah moshavot (Jewish

agricultural settlements in Eretz Yisrael built by Zionist pioneers between 1882 and 1904) of Zikhron Yaakov, Hadera and Rishon LeZion.
Their primary aim was to supply British intelligence with information
about the Turkish military presence in Palestine with hopes that the
British would oust the Turks from Eretz Yisrael and grant the Jews an
independent homeland.

The original founders of Nili were Dr. Aaron Aaronsohn, a world-
famous agronomist from Zikhron Yaakov, and Avshalom Feinberg, who
from the age of twelve dreamed of liberating Eretz Yisrael for the Jewish
people. Aaronsohn ran an experimental agricultural station on the Mediterranean coast at Atlit (near Haifa) where he carried out his renowned
research on strains of wheat and other crops. Feinberg served as the
assistant at the agricultural station and later became engaged to Aaron's
sister, Rivka. (Feinberg would later write Rivka a beautiful love letter with
the phrase "*elef neshikot* (a thousand kisses)" made famous years later by
Israeli songwriter and singers Zvika Pik and Yehoram Gaon.)

At first Avshalom suggested a Jewish military operation against
the Turks but Aaron's view, that espionage would be more effective and
practical, prevailed. Aaronsohn and Feinberg recruited members and
their spy organization began to grow. Meanwhile a plague of locusts
struck the Middle East and the Turks appointed Dr. Aaron Aaronsohn
as inspector general of the war on the locusts. This gave Aaronsohn and
his "assistants" free entry into Ottoman government offices and Turkish
military camps throughout Palestine. In this manner Nili was able to
easily acquire great amounts of valuable intelligence information.

Convincing the British of Nili's value, though, was not to be as
easy. Aaronsohn sent his brother Alex and later Feinberg to speak with
British officials in Cairo about Nili but both emissaries met with failure.
Only in the summer of 1916 did the Nili spy organization receive official
approval when Aaronson met with British officials in London. They
became impressed with Nili's work and sent Aaron to British headquarters in Cairo where he was to advise the British officers planning
the invasion of Ottoman-held Palestine.

Feinberg, unaware of Aaron's success in London, tried to reach British lines in Egypt with Nili member Yosef Lishansky. The two tried to cross the Sinai Desert on foot but were attacked by Bedouins near Rafiach. Avshalom Feinberg was killed but Lishansky, who was wounded in the attack, made his way to Cairo where he found Aaronsohn. Avshalom Feinberg's body was discovered after the 1967 Six-Day War when Sinai Bedouins showed Israeli troops his grave. A palm tree had grown out of dates that Feinberg had in his pocket when he was murdered. The Bedouins called the spot "the Grave of the Jew" and considered it holy because of the palm tree. Avshalom Feinberg's remains were brought to Jerusalem in November 7, 1967, and were reburied in the National Military Cemetery on Mount Herzl.

Lishansky returned to Israel in February 1917 and along with Aaronsohn's sister, Sarah, ran the espionage ring at Atlit. Several times over the next nine months the British Royal Navy yacht *Menagem* anchored off the coast at Atlit and received intelligence reports from the Nili spies. On one occasion Aaron sailed on the *Menagem* and secretly met one of his spies, Liova Schneerson, a relative of the Lubavitcher Rebbe. Aaronsohn asked Liova if he could think of a good name for their clandestine undertaking. Schneerson took out of his pocket the Tanakh (Bible) he had been given as a gift by Avshalom Feinberg and randomly opened the holy book to I Samuel 15:29. The biblical verse "*Netzach Yisrael lo yishaker* (the Eternity of Israel will not deceive)" caught his eye and the acronym for it, Nili, became the group's name and secret password.

In the spring of 1917 the Turks expelled the Jews from Jaffa and Tel Aviv. Nili sent this information to Aaron Aaronsohn in Cairo who publicized the deportation around the world. Aaronsohn was able to organize worldwide protests against the Turks and raised two thousand English pounds in gold coins for the Jewish Yishuv in Israel. Nili's efforts brought much relief to the Yishuv at this troubled time.

When the *Menagem* was no longer able to approach the coast at Atlit, Nili began sending intelligence reports to Cairo by carrier pigeon.

In September of 1917, the Turks caught one of these pigeons and this provided clear proof of a Jewish espionage network in Palestine. A week later they captured Nili spy Naaman Belkind, who after being tortured gave his interrogators information about Nili and its operations.

The leaders of the Jewish Yishuv in Israel denounced Nili before the Turks. Though they may have agreed with Nili's goals, they were fearful that Nili would bring Turkish retribution on the entire Yishuv. On October 1, 1917, the Turks surrounded Zikhron Yaakov and although Yosef Lishansky succeeded in escaping, Sarah Aaronsohn was arrested.

Sarah Aaronsohn was a sabra, born in Zikhron Yaakov in 1890. In 1914 she married a Bulgarian Jew and moved to Constantinople. Her marriage was unhappy and a year later, she returned home to Israel. In April 1917 she visited her brother Aaron in Cairo and he tried to convince her to stay there for her own safety. Sarah would hear nothing of this. She returned to Atlit and from there directed Nili's operations while Aaron remained in Cairo.

When the carrier pigeon was discovered she ordered all Nili spies to disperse but she remained in Zikhron Yaakov to facilitate their escape. After her arrest the Turks demanded that she divulge the whereabouts of Lishansky and the other Nili spies. Sarah refused. First the Turkish police tortured her father and brother Zvi before her eyes. Their screams were heard all throughout the terrified village. Then for the next four days Sarah Aaronsohn was put through the most terrible tortures the Turks could invent. They burned her all over her body and beat the soles of her feet with a whip called a *falaka*. Sarah still refused to talk. Her heroic stand saved many lives in Zikhron Yaakov and throughout the Yishuv.

On October 4 Sarah was transferred to a Turkish prison in Nazereth for more intensive interrogation. Sarah requested to change her bloodied clothes before departing. All of Zikhron Yaakov's Jewish inhabitants watched through their window shutters as Sarah was marched up the main street of the village to the Aaronsohn home by Turkish soldiers. Though her feet were swollen from the *falaka* beatings and caused her excruciating pain, she walked erect and proud. She knew the townspeople were watching and she didn't want to show any weakness. Sarah entered the house and went into the bathroom alone where she jotted down the following letter:

[...] I was beaten murderously, and they bound me with ropes. Do remember, to describe all our suffering to those who shall come after we have passed away. I do not believe that we shall survive after having been betrayed, and the whole truth about us probably exposed. The news of victory must eventually come, and, as you will be seeing my brothers, tell them about our martyrdom, and let them know that Sarah has asked that each drop of her blood be avenged measure for measure...that no mercy shall be shown, just as they have shown no mercy to us. Believe me, I have no more strength left to endure, and I prefer to kill myself than to be tortured any more at their bloodstained hands. They say they will send us away to Damascus; there they will surely hang me. I shall try to get hold of some small firearm or poison. I do not want them to maul my body. My sorrow is the greater for seeing my father suffering in innocence. But there will come a day of reckoning; we have died as warriors, and have not given way.... They have come, and I can write no longer.[13]

Then Sarah Aaronsohn pulled out a pistol she had hidden earlier in the house, put the barrel in her mouth and pulled the trigger. When the Turks heard the shot they burst open the bathroom door and found her mortally wounded on the floor. Sarah lay suffering for two days while the Turks tried to save her for "further investigation." Her last wish was for the villagers to look after her elderly and beaten father. She died on October 9, 1917, and was buried in the Zikhron Yaakov Cemetery.

Yosef Lishansky tried to make his way on foot to Egypt but was caught, and along with Naaman Belkind, was transferred to a Turkish prison in Damascus. The two were sentenced to death by hanging and were executed on December 5, 1917. Aaron Aaronsohn survived the war

---

13. Quoted in Shmuel Katz, *The Aaronsohn Saga* (Jerusalem: Gefen Publishing House, 2007), 333–34.

but died in a mysterious plane crash over the English Channel in 1919. Many believe he was killed by the very British he had helped, for their fear that one day he might demand fulfillment of the English wartime promises to Nili and the Jews.

With Aaron's death, Nili finally disbanded but by then the British had liberated Eretz Yisrael and signed the Balfour Declaration, calling for an independent Jewish homeland in Palestine.

Until this day the Nili saga is surrounded by debate and controversy. There are those who claim Nili was irresponsible in acting on its own and could have brought tragedy to the Yishuv. Nili's accomplishments, however, are impressive. Nili reported to the world about the Turks' deportation of Tel Aviv and Jaffa's Jews and the protests that followed helped put an end to the Turkish brutality. Nili raised thousands of dollars for the Jewish Yishuv in Eretz Yisrael at a time when poverty and starvation were rampant. Finally, Nili played a major role in the British conquest of Palestine and was an important consideration in the giving of the Balfour Declaration. Sarah Aaronsohn and the Nili spies were the precursors and inspiration for a new generation that grasped Jewish destiny in its hands and helped to bring about the liberation of the Jewish homeland and Israel's independence. Their sacrifice was not in vain.

RAHEL AND SHELLY
MY HERO AND MY FRIEND

> **Rahel the Poetess (1890–1931)**
> - 1909 Moved to Israel on "Second Aliyah"
> - Became *halutzah* (pioneer) and Hebrew poetess
> - 1931 Died of tuberculosis, buried at Kinneret
> *"Only a tree have my hands planted..."*

Rachel (Rahel) Bluwstein was born in czarist Russia on September 20, 1890. She grew up in a traditional Jewish home, the granddaughter of an Orthodox rabbi. Rachel, or "Rahel," as she was known in Hebrew, studied first at a traditional Jewish elementary school and later at a Russian high school and developed a deep love of poetry and painting. At the age of seventeen she moved to Kiev and began studying painting but those were the days of murderous pogroms (organized attacks on the Jewish community) in Russia. While over two and a half million Russian Jews fled the pogroms to America in the early 1900s, Rahel was one of the few ardent Zionists who chose a different path. In 1909 she made Aliyah to Eretz Yisrael (the Land of Israel) as part of the wave of Zionist immigration called the "Second Aliyah."

Some forty thousand Russian Jews came to Eretz Yisrael between 1904 and 1914 as part of the "Second Aliyah." These highly motivated immigrants sought to build a new life for their people, not in a new Diaspora like America, but in the Jewish people's ancient homeland, Eretz Yisrael. These immigrants were known as *halutzim* (Zionist pioneers) and were dually motivated by the ideals of Zionism and socialism. Many of the *halutzim* were disillusioned with traditional Judaism and its attitude of waiting for a Messiah to save our people. The *halutzim* sought to create a new Jew who would take control of his destiny and bring about redemption through labor and deeds.

Rahel could have been the poster child for this special generation. On arrival in Israel in 1909 she pledged with her sister to speak only Hebrew, a language that had been dead for over two thousand years. In those days a great Zionist thinker named Eliezer Ben-Yehuda was writing a seventeen-volume dictionary of modern Hebrew. He believed that there could be no Zionist revival of Israel as a nation without the Hebrew language to be the cement to hold the Jewish people together. He felt that Zionism and Hebrew were symbiotic, and Rahel believed wholeheartedly in his ideas.

When she arrived in Israel, Rahel settled in Rehovot and began working in the orchards there. She found that the only place in the small settlement to learn the new language was in a nursery school. Rahel swallowed her pride and sat amongst the little children and learned her new tongue with determination and perseverance. In 1910 Rahel enrolled in the Girls' Agricultural School at Kinneret by the Sea of Galilee. She was taught by Hana Meisel, the renowned agronomist who would later teach another Jewish heroine named Hannah Senesh.

At Kinneret Rahel found a mentor in Aaron David Gordon, the white-bearded Zionist philosopher and pioneer who taught the idea that the Land of Israel and the Jewish people were both sick after two thousand years of neglect and exile. A.D. Gordon taught that the Jews could heal both the barren land and their persecuted people by working the soil of Eretz Yisrael. Gordon became the father of Labor Zionism and Rahel was to be the movement's heart and soul.

In 1911 a Russian Jew named Zalman Rubashov made Aliyah to Israel but like many of the naive idealists, he was quickly disillusioned on his arrival in the Holy Land. After just days in Israel, Rubashov decided to return to Russia, as did 80 percent of the immigrants on the

Second Aliyah. Zalman first traveled to Kinneret to say goodbye to a friend but on his dawn arrival at the Agricultural School he saw Rahel in a white dress coming out the front gate with a flock of geese that she was shepherding. He described the picture in these words:

> I heard...a commanding voice in fluent Hebrew. I was capti-vated. I stood completely still. And here, from out of the gate, there spilled forth a bustling multitude of cackling geese all over the hill, and behind them a shepherdess with a white dress and striking blue eyes, graceful as a doe and beautiful as the Kinneret itself. In her hand she held a palm branch aloft and, with this as a staff, and her young warm voice, she kept order over the spilling throng, and took her flock of geese out from the yard to pasture. Holding my breath, I hid in the shadow of the wall until this white procession had passed me by. The shepherdess was the poetess Rahel.[14]

Zalman Rubashov fell in love with Rahel, though they were never to marry. Many of her love poems, however, were dedicated to him and she did inspire him to remain in Israel. He stayed and eventually be-came Israel's third president from 1963 to 1973 under the name Zalman Shazar.

Meanwhile Rahel settled on Degania, the first kibbutz, and was asked by A.D. Gordon to travel to the University of Toulouse in France to study agronomy in order to help the struggling Zionist farmers. Rahel readily agreed and traveled to France but World War I broke out and studies at the university were cancelled. Rahel was unable to return home to Israel as it was in the territory of the Ottoman Empire, enemies to the French. Then, Rahel was suddenly offered a wonderful opportunity to study art in Rome. It seemed to be a dream come true but she also learned that a Jewish orphanage in Russia was looking for help to take care of needy Jewish children. It was not an easy decision

---

14. *Sourcebook #4 : Emancipation, Haskalah, Zionism* (Hod Hasharon: Alexander Muss High School in Israel, 2006).

for Rahel but in the end she traveled back to Russia and began working at the orphanage. She gave the little Jewish orphans love and affection but unknowingly contracted tuberculosis from the sickly children.

In 1919, with the war over, Rahel returned home to Israel and settled on Kibbutz Degania. One day while working in the fields, she fainted and was soon diagnosed with the deadly and contagious disease of TB, tuberculosis. Rahel could no longer work in the fields she so loved or even teach the children she adored. She was taken by horse cart to Tel Aviv and quarantined in a tiny apartment on the second floor of a building on Bograshav Street. There, alone and dying, she spent the last years of her life. She died on April 16, 1931, at the age of forty. In those last years of her life she poured out her heart on paper and wrote some of the most beautiful poems ever written in Hebrew. If she could not give Israel her deeds, then she would give the land her words.

Rahel became Israel's most beloved poetess and today, some eighty years later, her poetry continues to inspire generation after generation. Israeli rock stars like Arik Einstein, Rita and Achinoam Nini (Noa) include her poems in their albums and even the late Israeli astronaut, Ilan Ramon, was pleasantly awakened in the Columbia space shuttle by his wife Rona, when she broadcast the first Hebrew song ever in outer space. The song "Zemer nugeh" (A sorrowful song) by Rahel spoke of love and parting, themes that would prove most prophetic and tragic when the Columbia exploded on reentry to the Earth's atmosphere on February 1, 2003.

Rahel is buried in the beautiful Kinneret Cemetery on the shore of the Sea of Galilee. Her unique grave lists her name simply as "RAHEL" and has a bench connected to it with a book of her poetry tied to the memorial by a chain. Israelis, young and old, make pilgrimages to her resting site and sit under the palm trees around her grave reading her beautiful Hebrew poems. Her poetry is simple and passionate and has inspired myriads of Zionist pioneers to follow in her footsteps.

One of the many touched by her words was a dear friend of mine, Shelly Greenspun from Haddon Heights, New Jersey. I met Shelly in

1974 when I was in college and was leading youth services (*knesset noar*) on Shabbat mornings at Shelly's synagogue. Her two youngest kids, Larry and Jeannie, were regulars at my service where I was known as "Reb Yossi with the Time Machine." Larry and Jeannie were so sweet and well behaved and quickly became some of my favorite "congregants."

One Shabbat morning Shelly came and sat down on one of the little chairs in our small auditorium. I told her that the adult services were in the main chapel down the hall but she told me that she didn't feel comfortable there and wanted to pray with the children. I didn't think of it at the time but it was just like Rahel when she studied Hebrew at the nursery school in Rehovot. Shelly and I became dear friends and at the end of the year she gave me as a gift a wonderful book on Jewish history signed "in love and gratitude from Larry and Jeannie Greenspun"...her little children who could barely write!

In 1978 I made Aliyah to Israel where I have lived since. While in Israel I learned that cute little Jeannie had developed cancer. Luckily our prayers were answered and Jeannie went into remission but sadly, about the same time, her mom, Shelly, developed cancer of the larynx that proved to be terminal. It was then that many people learned Shelly's amazing story.

She came from an assimilated Jewish family and Judaism and Israel were far from her soul. One day she was at the local JCC, where her son attended nursery school, and noticed a sign advertising an upcoming lecture about poetry which she decided to attend. It turned out to be a lecture by an Israeli professor about Rahel and her poetry. The tragic story about Israel's beautiful poetess and her love for Israel touched Shelly deeply. She began to read and learn everything she could about Rahel the Poetess, the *halutzim*, Zionism and Judaism. She studied Hebrew so she could read Rahel in the original and visited Israel and dreamed of moving there one day. She got in touch with her own Jewish identity and became more religious and even applied to the Conservative movement's rabbinical school at the Jewish Theological Seminary, but they did not ordain women as rabbis in those days.

Shelly got involved in her local Jewish Federation and became a leader in the Jewish community. She also longed to have a bat mitzvah and have an Aliyah to the Torah. She reached that day the same time that the cancer had taken away her voice and when she rose to the bima (the main stage in the synagogue) to read from the Torah, her voice could not be heard. Everyone in the audience shed tears as they followed Shelly's lips reading the sacred blessings. Though the circumstances were tragic, it was one of the happiest moments in Shelly's life – holding the Torah's handles and becoming fully part of her people.

In her last days, Shelly wrote the Kinneret community and told them how Rahel's story and poetry had brought her back to her people and to Israel. She told them that she had adopted the Hebrew name "Rahel" and, like her mentor, was destined to die in the prime of her life. Shelly's last request was to be buried in the land she loved near the grave of her light and inspiration, Rahel the Poetess. The members of Kvutzat Kinneret (a kvutza is a small kibbutz) were touched by Shelly's letter and made room just to the left of Rahel's grave in the Kinneret Cemetery. Shelly died on February 26, 1985, and was buried next to Rahel by the Sea of Galilee. Thanks to Rahel, she was finally home.

A true *halutzah*, Rahel the Poetess felt guilty that she was unable to work the land while she was sick. She wrote an apology to the Land of Israel in a beautiful poem from 1926 entitled "El artzi" (To my land). It began:

I have not sung to you, my land
Nor have I glorified your name
With deeds of heroism,
Or with the spoils of war.
Only a tree have my hands planted
Along the quiet shores of the Jordan.
Only a path have my feet conquered
Across the surface of the fields....[15]

15. *Rahel* [in Hebrew], edited by Uri Milstein (Tel Aviv: Zmora-Bitan, 1985), 156. Translation mine.

Rahel died feeling she had not done enough for Israel and Zionism, yet if we look at her life we can see how much she accomplished. She made Aliyah to Israel and learned Hebrew. She worked the land and planted trees and helped found the first kibbutz. She helped bring life back to Eretz Yisrael and the Jewish people. Rahel gave up personal desires to help Jewish orphans in Russia and when she became sick she shared her heart and ideals with others through her poetry and words.

Rahel Bluwstein, or as we remember her, "Rahel the Poetess," was a true hero of Israel. Though she never carried a rifle or fought in a battle she did heroic deeds that remain an inspiration to us all. She inspired Shelly Greenspun and millions of other Jews throughout the last generations to love their land and their people. She is someone we all can admire and aspire to be like. My hero, Rahel Bluwstein, and my friend, Shelly Greenspun, will never be forgotten.

ORDE WINGATE
"HAYEDID"
FRIEND AND HERO

Orde Wingate (1903–1944)
- British Christian military officer
- 1938 Founded Special Night Squads (SNS)
- Zionists called him *HaYedid* (the Friend)

"Go in this strength of yours and deliver Israel."

In 1977 I was a student of Jewish history at the Hebrew University in Jerusalem. It was during that same year that I won the Israeli National Boxing Championship at Israel's National Sports College – Wingate Institute, south of Netanya. When I first stepped through the gates of the Wingate Institute, I knew little of the great Christian hero for whom the school is named. However, in many ways, it would be a most fitting place for a student of Jewish history and a boxer to win his pugilistic title, as Orde Charles Wingate was both a fighter and one of the great heroes of Jewish history.

Orde Charles Wingate was born on February 26, 1903, in Naini Tal, India. His father, George, came from an old Scottish family which traced its roots back to the days of William the Conqueror. Apparently their original family name was the French "Winguet." George entered the British army in 1871 and eventually was transferred to service in India, where the Scot had a religious experience that led him to join the Plymouth Brethren, a conservative Christian fundamentalist sect. George married late in life, at the age of forty-six, to Ethel Orde-Browne, whose family were also members of the Plymouth Brethren. The couple worked as dedicated missionaries and passed on their love of the Tanakh (the Hebrew Bible) and its heroes to their children, especially to Orde Charles. When Orde reached age two his father, who was a colonel in the British army, received his pension and moved back to England where Orde was schooled.

The Wingate family had a Sunday afternoon custom of calling upon their children to memorize and recite whole chapters of the Tanakh, which Orde eventually mastered. Orde's favorite biblical hero was the judge (tribal chieftain) Gideon who, with an elite commando force of three hundred men, defeated the Midianites and won the ancient Israelites their freedom three thousand years ago. Wingate was especially impressed with Gideon's use of night fighting and guerrilla tactics which would one day become his hallmark as a British soldier. In the Book of Judges, God commanded Gideon, "Go in this strength of yours and deliver Israel from the Midianites. I herewith make you my messenger" (Judges 6:14). Orde Wingate felt as if God was speaking to him personally in this command to Gideon and the desire to serve God's Chosen People as a messenger began to nurture in the young Scot's heart.

In 1921 Orde Wingate took his first steps towards an illustrious military career when he entered the Royal Military Academy at Woolwich, England. The young cadet was small in frame – only five foot six inches tall – but he was strong and stubborn. Once, after committing a minor offense against the rules at Woolwich, Wingate was subjected to a ragging ritual named "running" in which he was stripped naked and forced to run a gauntlet of senior students who were to beat him as he ran the set path. On reaching the end of the gauntlet the first-year cadet would then be thrown into an icy cold cistern of water. When it came time for Wingate to run the punishment line, he walked straight up to the senior student at the head of the gauntlet, stared him straight in the eye and dared him to strike. The senior declined. Wingate moved to the next senior and did the same; he too refused. In turn each senior refused to strike and coming to the end of the line Wingate walked to the cistern and dived straight into the icy cold water. The episode gained new respect and several lifelong friends for Wingate, who graduated in 1923 with his gunnery officer's commission.

In the army Wingate became an accomplished equestrian and also became interested in the Middle East. He studied Arabic at the London School of Oriental Studies and was eventually posted in the East Arab Corps of the Sudan Defense Force on the border of Ethiopia. There, using ambushes and guerilla tactics, Wingate fought against slave-traders and poachers. In 1933 Wingate returned home to the United Kingdom via boat from Egypt. On that voyage he met his future wife Lorna Moncrieff Patterson, whom he married two years later. The couple had one son, Jonathan, who later rose to be a colonel in the British army. In 1936, Orde Charles Wingate was assigned to the British Mandate in Palestine where he was to serve as a staff intelligence officer. It was that posting that would change his life.

In Palestine, Wingate spent three months in Haifa at the Savoy Hotel. Originally he came to Palestine with false information that the Jewish Zionists had stolen lands from the Arabs, but in the country he learned on his own how Jews had bought back their promised land for exorbitant prices demanded by Arab landowners. As he studied the Holy Land's history and met the peoples in the land, Wingate became an ardent Zionist. Once, when asked how he, a non-Jew, could become such a passionate proponent of Zionism, he replied, "When I was at school I was looked down upon, and made to feel that I was a failure and not wanted in this world. When I came to Palestine I found a whole people who had been treated like that through scores of generations, and yet in the end of it they were undefeated, were a great power in the world, building their country anew. I felt I belonged to such people!"[16]

In Haifa Wingate met one of the most prominent Jews in the country, David HaCohen, head of a large contracting company. The two would become lifelong friends. HaCohen recalled that Wingate

---

16. Quoted in Christopher Sykes, *Orde Wingate* (London: Collins, 1959), 110.

"had the looks of an ascetic, dressed in a simple worn uniform which strangely became his emaciated and serious face."[17] In their first meeting Wingate told HaCohen that he had met few Jews in his life but that his sympathies were with Zionism. HaCohen asked Wingate if he had read any books on Zionism and the British officer replied, "There is only one important book on the subject: the Tanakh, and I've read it thoroughly!" Then the religious Christian made a confession of faith to the Jewish stranger:

> This is the cause of your survival. I count it as my privilege to help you fight your battle. To that purpose I want to devote my life. I believe that the very existence of mankind is justified when it is based on the moral foundation of the Bible. Whoever lifts a hand against you and your enterprise here should be fought against. Whether it is jealousy, ignorance, or perverted doctrine such as have made your neighbors rise against you, or "politics" which make some of my countrymen support them, I shall fight with you against any of these influences. But remember that is your battle. My part, which I say I feel to be a privilege, is only to help you.[18]

Wingate would spend much of the coming years in doing just that – helping the Jewish people and the Zionist movement.

In 1936 the Arabs in Palestine began a three-year assault on the Jews in Israel, known as the Arab Revolt. In addition to their murderous attacks on the Jews, the Arabs also hit British installations and sabotaged the TAP oil pipeline. Led by the mufti of Jerusalem, Haj Amin el-Husseini, the Palestinian Arabs massacred over five hundred Jews and left two thousand Jewish casualties. The mufti's men also annihilated over thirty-seven hundred Arab moderates willing to coexist with the Zionists. The Haganah, the Jewish Yishuv's underground army,

---

17. Ibid., 111.
18. Ibid., 112.

had an ineffective policy of *havlagah* or restraint in dealing with the Arab terrorists.

Wingate taught the Yishuv how to fight back against Arab terrorism and in 1938 formed an elite commando unit called the Special Night Squads (SNS). Many of its first members, like Yigal Alon and Moshe Dayan, would later found the Palmach, the elite strike force of the Haganah that would help Israel win its War of Independence in 1948. Wingate and his Special Night Squads brought the war into the enemy camp. His methods were aggressive and effective. During the Arab Revolt, a northern kibbutz was complaining of attacks from terrorists based in Lebanon. Wingate took a squad of SNS men and infiltrated the terrorist village at night and killed the terrorist leaders in their beds. The attacks on the kibbutz ceased.

Wingate's tactics were seen by some as harsh but they helped bring an end to the Arab Revolt. He used night fighting and guerilla tactics learned from the heroes of the Tanakh – like Joshua, David and Gideon. Wingate and his SNS crushed the Arab Revolt in six months and he was awarded the Distinguished Service Order (DSO) in 1938.

On one occasion Wingate, David HaCohen and some fighters from the SNS were atop Mount Gilboa overlooking the Jezreel Valley. Suddenly Wingate remarked, "Why was he defeated? The man is a fool! He should have won this battle!" David HaCohen looked at his fellow SNS commandos and wondered out loud who Wingate was talking about. The religious Scot answered, "I am talking about King Saul! He could have won this battle and defeated the Philistines. He should have attacked in a flanking movement at night instead of going to the witch of Ein Dor. He could have won. King Saul could have won!" Some considered Wingate eccentric and almost insane but for this great hero the Tanakh was a living manual and its heroes were his.

On another occasion Wingate attended a Jewish party with David HaCohen, who entertained the crowd with a Yiddish story called "The Goat." David explained how a Jewish man once complained to his rabbi about his life of poverty and problems. The rabbi told the man to bring a cow into his house and on the following days chickens and finally a goat. Life became unbearable and the man complained to his rabbi, who immediately told him to take away the animals. The story ended with the man expressing his newfound happiness to the rabbi. The audience at the party roared in laughter as HaCohen shared the humorous yarn from the shtetls of Europe, but Wingate was angry. He told his Jewish friend, "Squalid stories like this give Jews a bad name and make them despised. Why don't you do away with this embarrassing folklore? The whole purpose of the 'Return to Israel' is to stop the Jews from being associated with that kind of story."[19]

Wingate wanted the Jews to be like their biblical ancestors – proud, dignified and strong. He did everything he could to turn the Zionist dream into reality and dreamed of one day becoming the chief of staff of the Jewish army and leading Israel to victory in their war for independence. In the Jewish Yishuv, Wingate was called *HaYedid* (the Friend) but he was hated and feared by the British Colonial officials and officers in Palestine who sided with the Arabs. In 1939 Wingate was returned to England and his service record was amended with the comment, "...a good soldier but, so far as Palestine is concerned, he is a security risk. He puts the interests of the Jews before those of his own country. He should not be allowed in Palestine again." His British passport was stamped "The bearer of this passport should not be allowed to enter Palestine."

Wingate soon went on to other glories. In 1941 he organized the "Gideon Force" and with a band of seventeen hundred defeated over twenty thousand Italian soldiers and won Ethiopia its freedom. Between 1942 and 1944 Wingate, now a major general, fought the Japanese in Burma with a band of local guerilla fighters called Chindits. They disrupted Japanese plans and made an important contribution to the Allied war effort. On March 24, 1944, Orde Wingate was on a reconnaissance flight over Burma when his plane crashed into the Burmese

---

19. Ibid., 116.

countryside, killing him and the eight others on board. British prime minister Winston Churchill remarked, "With him a bright flame was extinguished." As the majority of those killed in the crash were American, the mass grave was placed at Arlington National Cemetery in the USA, where Major General Orde Charles Wingate now rests.

On May 14, 1948, Israel declared its independence and the Jewish army Wingate helped train won the war that ensued. During one of the battles in Israel's War of Independence, the Arabs besieged the Mount Carmel Jewish settlement of Ramat Naphtali (also called Yemin Orde in Wingate's honor). Lorna Wingate, Orde's widow, flew overhead in a light plane and parachuted a small package to the defenders. When they opened it, they found it was Orde Wingate's personal Bible in Hebrew, a language he had learned to master. In it she wrote,

> *To the Defenders of Ramat Naphtali – Since Orde Wingate is with you in spirit, though he cannot lead you in flesh, I send you the Bible he carried in all his campaigns, from which he drew the inspiration of his victories. Pray it be a covenant between you and him, in triumph or defeat, now and forever.*[20]

Orde Wingate's teachings and legacy helped bring the Jewish people their independence after two thousand years of exile. In addition to the Wingate Institute near Netanya, and Yemin Orde, a Wingate Forest on Mount Gilboa and streets throughout Israel honor Orde Wingate's memory. Most importantly, he is remembered by a grateful Jewish nation. *HaYedid*, our friend Major General Orde Charles Wingate, will never be forgotten.

---

20. Robert St. John, *They Came from Everywhere: Twelve Who Helped Mold Modern Israel* (New York: Coward-McCann, 1962), 206.

HEROINES AND HEROES
OF THE WARSAW GHETTO

Zivia Lubetkin (1914–1976)

- Asst. Commander of Eyal,
  Jewish fighting organization in Warsaw ghetto
- 1943 Escaped burning Warsaw ghetto through sewers
- 1949 Among founders of Ghetto Fighters Kibbutz in Israel
- Grandmother to Israel's first female fighter pilot,
  Roni Zuckerman

"Jewish education is the real secret
of our movement's strength."

Warsaw, the capital of Poland, was home to over 400,000 Jews at the outbreak of World War II. The Jews made up over one-third of Warsaw's population and the city was home to Europe's largest Jewish community. World War II began on September 1, 1939, with the Nazi Blitzkrieg into Poland, and Warsaw fell to the Germans on September 28. Immediately, the Nazis began large-scale persecution and mistreatment of Poland's Jews.

Already in December 1939, the first Jewish resistance group was founded by members of the Zionist youth group Betar. They were called the zzw (Jewish Military Organization) in Polish, or the Etzey in Hebrew, and were led by Pavel Frankel. On November 15, 1940, the Germans ordered Warsaw's Jews to move into a newly created ghetto making up only 2 percent of the city's area. The ghetto had two separate sections joined by a wooden walking bridge which was surrounded by an eight-foot-high wall.

In 1941 another 100,000 Jewish refugees were flooded into the Warsaw ghetto and its population grew to over half a million. The Nazis deliberately created conditions in the ghetto to cause disease and starvation, hoping most Jews would die. The Jews received only 184 calories per day, basically a piece of bread, made of sawdust and potato peels. Typhoid and other diseases ran rampant. Young children became the heroes of the ghetto as they courageously climbed through holes in the ghetto wall in order to smuggle food from Warsaw's Christian sector to their starving families. When caught, these young children were shot on the spot by the Nazis.

The dramatic story of life in the Warsaw ghetto was recorded by a unique individual named Dr. Emanuel Ringelblum, who was born in a small Ukrainian shtetl in 1900. Ringelblum moved to Warsaw to study at the local university and completed his doctorate in the history of Warsaw Jewry. He had a strong social conscience and set up evening courses in Jewish history for poor workers. In August 1939 Ringelblum was a delegate to the twenty-first Zionist Congress in Geneva and could have moved to Israel but felt he had an obligation to his brothers in Warsaw and remained in the Polish capital.

When the Nazis forced half a million Jews into the Warsaw ghetto, Dr Emanuel Ringelblum founded a clandestine organization made of educators, writers, historians and others to record every aspect of life in the ghetto so the memory of Warsaw's Jews would not be obliterated from the earth. The secret organization was called "Oneg Shabbat" (Sabbath pleasure) because they met on Saturday afternoons to carry out their sacred work. Ringelblum knew that the Nazi persecutions were unprecedented and he was determined to record the history unfolding in Warsaw. He and his colleagues collected historical data and wrote articles about life in the ghetto and the Jewish resistance movements. They also documented the deportation and extermination of Polish Jewry and sent the information to the Polish underground, which smuggled it out of the country. In this manner, Emanuel Ringelblum helped expose the Nazis' atrocities.

The Oneg Shabbat materials were stored in three milk cans and buried in Warsaw at separate locations. One of the sites was uncovered in 1946 and a second in 1950; the other has yet to be located. Ringelblum and his wife and thirteen-year-old son succeeded in escaping to the Aryan side of Warsaw in 1943 and hid with thirty-five other Jews in the cellar of a Polish worker's home. A Polish informer led the Gestapo to the home and all thirty-eight Jews and their Polish protector, Mieczyslaw Wolski, were executed. The Oneg Shabbat archives remain the most in-depth record of life and events in Warsaw during the Holocaust, and Ringelblum's heroic efforts will never be forgotten.

By July 1942, eighty thousand Jews had died in the Warsaw ghetto from hunger and disease but the Nazis were not pleased and decided to accelerate the process with deportations to the Treblinka death camp. On July 22, 1942, the Nazis began sending over 300,000 Warsaw Jews to the gas chambers of Treblinka from the Umschlagplatz (railway loading station) in the ghetto. The date chosen for the mass deportations was no coincidence. July 22, 1942, fell on Tisha b'Av in the Jewish calendar, the anniversary of the destruction of the First and Second Temples in Jerusalem. The Nazis learned the Jewish calendar and often used it for their sadistic and murderous plans.

The Jewish Council of Warsaw, called the Judenrat, was led by Adam Czerniakow. The Nazis wanted them to do their dirty work and commanded: "To you, the Judenrat, we entrust the carrying out of this task. Should you neglect to acquit yourselves satisfactorily, you will all hang from the same rope!" Realizing that the Judenrat was being tricked into helping the Nazis carry out their murders, Adam Czerniakow took poison and committed suicide. Though he could not save his people, he would not be a tool in their murder by the Germans. During July and August 1942, over 300,000 Jews were sent from the Umschlagplatz in Warsaw to the gas chambers of Treblinka. It was during those days that one of the most moving and heroic stories of the Holocaust took place – the saga of Janusz Korczak.

Janusz Korczak was born as Henryk Goldszmidt in 1879 in Warsaw to a wealthy, assimilated Jewish family. Goldschmidt studied medicine at the University of Warsaw and became a renowned pediatrician. During the summers, Henryk worked at a summer camp for under-privileged children and became deeply concerned with their plight. As a result of his experiences, he published two controversial books under the pen name Janusz Korczak. The first was called *Children of the Street* and described how homeless orphans learned to steal food to survive in the streets but still kept their sense of right and wrong. The second book was called *A Child of the Salon* and painted a contrasting picture of a pampered, wealthy child whose life revolved around money.

Korczak became a world famous educator and writer. In 1911, he gave up his successful private practice to take over the Jewish orphan-age in Warsaw. Janusz Korczak had a revolutionary approach to educa-tion. He brought up the orphans in his institution in an atmosphere of self-respect and affection and allowed the children to run their own government and court and publish their own newspaper. As a result of his experience at the orphanage, Janusz Korchak published several internationally acclaimed books including *How to Love a Child* and *A Child's Right to Self-Respect.*

With the rise of Nazism in Germany, Korczak's Jewish conscious-ness deepened. He even visited Israel twice, in 1934 and again in 1936. Korczak fell in love with the Jewish homeland, especially the kibbutzim, and wanted to make Aliyah but felt he couldn't abandon his orphans; he returned to Poland. In 1939, the Nazis took the Polish capital and Janusz Korczak was locked in Warsaw's ghetto. On August 5, 1942, the Jewish orphanage in Warsaw was ordered to be deported to Treblinka but Korczak, as a renowned physician, was given a reprieve. Though he was safe, he felt he could not abandon the little orphans. Janusz Korczak dressed up two hundred children in their best Shabbat clothes and led them singing to the Umschlagplatz.

Although he knew the final destination, he told the children they were going on a picnic to sunshine and green fields. In his arms, Korczak carried a sick child. An eyewitness remembered:

And so a long line is formed in front of the orphanage on Slisks Street. A long procession, children, small, tiny, rather precocious, emaciated, weak, shriveled and shrunk. They carry shabby packages, some have schoolbooks, notebooks under their arms. No one is crying. Slowly they go down the steps, line up in rows, in perfect order and discipline as usual. Their little eyes are turned toward the doctor. They are strangely calm – they feel almost well. The doctor is going with them, so what do they have to be afraid of? They are not alone, they are not abandoned.[21]

From the Umschlagplatz in Warsaw, Dr. Janusz Korczak and his two hundred children were sent to the gas chambers of Treblinka. Korczak sacrificed his life so the children would not die alone. His heroism was no less than that of those who would soon fight in the ghetto's ruins with pistols and grenades.

There now remained seventy thousand Jews in the Warsaw ghetto. On July 28, 1942, young Jews from Warsaw's leftist Zionist youth movement founded the Jewish Fighting Organization, known by its Polish initials ZOB or its Hebrew acronym Eyal (for Irgun Yehudi Lohem). The leaders of Eyal were Mordechai Anielewicz, Itzhak ("Antek") Zuckerman and Zivia Lubetkin – all in their early twenties. One of the bravest fighters in the ghetto was a woman named Nita Teitelbaum, known and feared by the Nazis as "little Wanda with the braids." Nita was born in 1918 to a Hasidic family but did not follow in their religious path. In 1939, she began studying psychology in a Polish university but when the Nazi invasion came, she was herded into Warsaw's ghetto.

Nita was one of the first to join the Jewish underground and

---

21. Nora Levin, *The Holocaust: The Destruction of European Jewry, 1933–1945* (New York: Crowell, 1968), 326.

quickly became one of the most active Jewish fighters. She explained her actions thus: "I am a Jew! My place is among the most active fighters against Nazism, in the struggle for the honor of my people!"[22] Nita, with her blue eyes and blond hair, was able to sneak out of the ghetto and carry out acts of sabotage against the Nazis. She blew up railway lines and killed German soldiers in Warsaw's cafés. The Nazis began to speak of "little Wanda with the braids" who fearlessly attacked their troops and installations.

One sunny day, Nita ("Wanda") walked into Warsaw's Gestapo headquarters wearing her hair in childish braids. She batted her pretty eyes and requested to see the Gestapo commander on a "personal matter." The guards winked and let her in. When the Gestapo commander saw her, he remarked, "Why if it isn't Heidi of the mountains!" "Wanda," without replying, opened her pocketbook, pulled out a pistol and shot the Nazi officer dead in his chair. Then she calmly left through the main exit smiling at the guards. "Wanda" was immediately placed on the Gestapo's most wanted list and eventually was captured by the Nazis. The Gestapo tortured her for weeks, seeking information about the Jewish underground, but she never betrayed her comrades. In July 1943 she was murdered in the Gestapo torture chambers.

Meanwhile on January 18, 1943, the Nazis began a second wave of deportations to the Treblinka death camp. Hastily, the Jewish underground called the remaining Jews in the ghetto to rebellion. Their leaflets urged, "Jews – the enemy has moved onto the second phase of your extermination! Do not resign yourselves to death! Defend yourselves! Grab an axe, an iron bar, a knife! Let them take you this way, if they can!"

That same day, a group of Jewish fighters led by Mordechai Anielewicz made a frontal assault on the Nazi forces, inflicting heavy casualties on the Germans. In one of the ghetto buildings a group of forty young Jews from the Zionist youth movements waited for the

---

22. Quoted in Yuri Suhl, *They Fought Back: The Story of the Jewish Resistance in Nazi Germany* (New York: Schocken, 1967), 52.

Nazis with pistols, grenades and cups of acid. Their leader was the famous Jewish poet and teacher Yitzhak Katzenelson, who inspired them with these words: "We must be happy for we are about to meet the enemy with ammunition, though it be to die; we will fight with arms, not for ourselves but for future generations! Let us have courage! The Germans can kill millions of us but they will never overpower us. The Jewish nation lives and it will live forever!"[23] As Katzenelson finished speaking, the Nazis broke into the room, and the youths opened fire killing several soldiers and capturing their weapons. The other Nazis ran in fear. Over a four-day period in January 1943 over twenty Nazis were killed and the myth of German invincibility was crushed. Fearful of further violence, the Nazis halted the deportations.

In February, 1943, Heinrich Himmler, commander of the Nazi ss, ordered the complete annihilation of the Warsaw ghetto to take place on April 19, 1943. He figured the action would take one day and on the morrow, April 20, he could hand Adolf Hitler a birthday present of a *Judenrein* (free of Jews) Warsaw. Waffen ss General Jurgen Stroop was appointed overall commander of the operation. Meanwhile the Jewish underground made preparations for the battle, digging bunkers and a maze of interconnecting hideouts. On Monday, April 19, 1943, two thousand heavily armed ss troops marched into the ghetto singing Nazi marching songs, followed by thousands of German reserves and Ukrainian Fascists. As the Nazis passed Zamenhof and Mila Streets, they were met with a hail of bullets and Molotov cocktails. ss troops began to panic and flee. Two German tanks were hit by Molotovs and went up in flames. Nazis were seen fleeing, crying hysterically, "*Juden Waffen, Juden Waffen* (Jews – guns, Jews – guns)!"

The Nazis retreated and Jews poured into the streets celebrating and calling out to each other, "*Mazal tov!*" One fighter remembered: "We were happy and laughing. When we threw our grenades and saw German blood on the streets of Warsaw, which had been flooded in the

---

23. Quoted in Nora Levin, *The Holocaust: The Destruction of European Jewry, 1939–1945* (New York: Crowell, 1968), 344.

past with so much Jewish blood and tears, a great joy possessed us!"[24] On one of the rooftops, underground fighters from the Etzey unfurled the Zionist flag, as the Jewish fighters rejoiced. The Nazis issued an ultimatum to the Jews to lay down their arms but the Jews answered with their guns. Zivia Lubetkin, a female commander in Eyal, laid an electric mine and recounted, "We allowed the Germans to pass our hidden positions until they reached the mine spot. Then we pushed the electric button and soon saw the torn limbs of scores of Germans flying in the air!"[25]

General Stroop was resting at home in bed figuring his police chief, Von Sammern, could handle the operation. Van Sammern came running into Stroop's bedroom screaming, "All is lost in the ghetto! We have dead and wounded. We must fly in bombers and blow up the ghetto." General Stroop said that flying in the German air force to wipe our a few *Untermentschen* (subhumans) would be an embarrassment to the Third Reich. General Stroop personally took over command of the operation in the Warsaw ghetto and began to clear out ghetto houses one at a time. He used incendiary squads and set the entire ghetto on fire. Back in Germany, Himmler wrote, "The combing of the Warsaw ghetto must be carried out thoroughly, with a hard heart, without mercy. It is best to proceed rigorously. The incidents in Warsaw prove how dangerous these Jews are."[26]

The Nazis began to pump poison gas into the sewer canals where many of the Jewish fighters were hiding. On May 8, 1943, the Nazis surrounded the Eyal Bunker at 18 Mila Street. Inside were about twenty fighters including Eyal commander Mordechai Anielewicz. A ferocious

---

24. David Altschuler, *Hitler's War against the Jews* (New York: Behrmann House, 1978), 166.

25. Zivia Lubetkin, *Biyemei kilayon vamered* [In the days of destruction and revolt] (Tel Aviv: HaKibbutz HaMeuchad, 1953), 127.

26 Quoted in Lawrence N. Powell, *Troubled Memory: Anne Levy, the Holocaust, and David Duke's Louisiana* (Chapel Hill: University of North Carolina Press, 2000), 239.

battle broke out during which sixty Jewish fighters were taken prisoner. Then the Nazis began pumping poison gas into the bunker and many of the Jewish fighters, including Anielewicz, chose to die as free men and committed suicide. A few days earlier, on April 23, 1943, Mordechai Anielewicz penned the following last letter:

> It is impossible to put into words what we have been through. One thing is clear, what happened exceeded our boldest dreams. The Germans ran twice from the ghetto.... I feel that great things are happening and what we dared do is of great, enormous importance.... It is impossible to describe the conditions under which the Jews of the ghetto are now living. Only a few will be able to hold out. The remainder will die sooner or later. Their fate is decided. In almost all the hiding places in which thousands are concealing themselves it is not possible to light a candle for lack of air.... The fact that we are remembered beyond the ghetto walls encourages us in our struggle. Peace go with you, my friend! Perhaps we may still meet again! The dream of my life has risen to become fact. Self-defense in the ghetto will have been a reality. Jewish armed resistance and revenge are facts. I have been a witness to the magnificent, heroic fighting of Jewish men in battle.
>
> −Mordechai Anielewicz[27]

When the bunker at Mila 18 fell, a small group of Jewish men and women succeeded in fleeing into the sewers led by Eyal's assistant commander Zivia Lubetkin. Zivia led the survivors on a perilous thirty-hour journey under the city of Warsaw in the rat-infested sewers. Eventually they came out in the Aryan side of Warsaw and hid in a furniture factory. Zivia called a Polish trucking company and asked them to send a truck to pick up a shipment of furniture from the factory at Prosta Street.

---

27. Yitzhak Arad, Israel Gutman, *et al.*, *Documents on the Holocaust: Selected Sources on the Destruction of the Jews of Germany and Austria, Poland, and the Soviet Union*, 8th ed. (Lincoln, NE: University of Nebraska Press, 1999), 315.

When the truck arrived, the fighters pulled out guns and demanded to be driven to the Lominaka Forest where they joined the partisans and continued their struggle for Jewish freedom.

When asked where she found her strength, Zivia Lubetkin answered that she owed it all to the Zionist pioneering youth movements:

> This is the real secret of the Movement's strength. The Movement always knew how to demand everything from its members. The Movement's goal has always been to educate a new kind of man, capable of enduring the most adverse conditions and difficult times while standing up for the emancipation of our people, of the Jew, of mankind. It was our Movement education which gave us the strength to endure.[28]

On May 16, 1943, General Stroop blew up the last remaining building in the Warsaw ghetto, the Great Synagogue on Tlomackie Street. The same day Stroop reported, "The former Jewish residential district in Warsaw is no longer in existence." Over fifty-six thousand Jews were killed in the month-long revolt in the Warsaw ghetto. Only a handful of the brave Jewish fighters survived – among them, Anielewicz's assistant commanders: Antek Zuckerman and Zivia Lubetkin. The two continued to fight the Nazis as partisans in the forests of Poland and eventually married. At the end of World War II, they made Aliyah to Israel and founded Kibbutz Lohamei HaGhettaot in the northern Galilee. The kibbutz's English name is "Ghetto Fighters' Kibbutz" and it sent a message around the world that Jews in the Holocaust did not all go like sheep to the slaughter but that many fought back in impossible conditions.

The kibbutz opened a Holocaust museum dedicated to Jewish resistance in the Shoah and the legacy of the Warsaw ghetto's courageous underground fighters has been passed down from generation

---

28. Zivia Lubetkin, *In the Days of Destruction and Revolt* (Tel Aviv: Hakibbutz Hameuchad, 1981), 276.

to generation. Antek and Zivia became the grandparents to a brilliant, sharp-witted granddaughter named Roni Zuckerman. On June 29, 2001, Roni made history of her own when she became the first female fighter pilot in the Israeli Air Force. Since then, Roni has flown her F-16 in defense of the Jewish state and in 2004 her excellence as a fighter pilot was recognized when she was asked to become a flight instructor at the Israeli Air Force fighter pilots' course. The Israeli Air Force forbids publication of photos of its fighter pilots and Roni refuses to speak to the press but it is clear that she carries with her the legacy that Zivia and Antek passed down to her. It is the determination and resolve of young fighters like Roni Zuckerman that ensures "Never again!"

Shortly before the Warsaw ghetto uprising, Pavel Frankel, commander of the zzw, told friends, "We will die young here, but we will not sentence ourselves to obscurity. Jewish children in the Jewish state that will arise will yet learn of our struggle." Roni Zuckerman is a symbol of those children who not only have learned the story of their grandparents' struggle during the Holocaust, but who have also made the commitment to ensure that never again will Jews be taken helplessly to the slaughter. Roni, like her grandmother Zivia Lubetkin, is a true *Eshet Chayil* – a Woman of Valor. Their story is a microcosm of Jewish history. Out of the ashes of the Warsaw ghetto rose a Jewish people – strong and determined and rooted in their own soil. Today the Israel Defense Forces stand on guard protecting the Jewish people and homeland. As Zivia Lubetkin once said, their pride and courage is rooted in their education, in their knowledge of the past and in their commitment to Israel's future.

HANNAH SENESH
ANSWERING THE CALL

Hannah Senesh (1921–1944)
- Born in Budapest; made Aliyah to Israel in 1939
- Became *halutzah* (pioneer); Hebrew poetess and fighting partisan
- March 1944 Parachuted into Nazi-occupied Yugoslavia to rescue Jews
- Captured, tortured and executed on November 7, 1944
"Blessed is the match consumed in kindling flame..."

Hannah (Aniko) Senesh was born in Budapest, Hungary, on July 17, 1921. Aniko, as she was known as in Hungary, was the daughter of Katrina and Bela Senesh and grew up in a well-to-do, assimilated Jewish home. Her father, Bela, was a distinguished playwright who died when Hannah was only six. Hannah dreamed of being worthy of her father as a writer and dictated her first poem to her grandmother shortly after Bela's death. At the age of thirteen Hannah began to keep a diary and from it we learn much about her personality and life. Until the age of seventeen, Hannah seems to have been an intelligent but frivolous young girl who worried more about what color dress to wear to a party than about events in the world around her. Hannah attended a prestigious Protestant private school in Budapest, even though Jews had to pay triple the regular tuition.

An outstanding student, she was elected secretary of the school's literary society but Nazi Germany's anti-Semitic policies were already

influencing Hungary and Hannah's school informed her that only
Protestants could hold school office. Sent home in shame, Hannah
began to delve into her own Jewish identity and found a new strength
and pride in Judaism. At the age of seventeen she made the following
entry in her diary:

> October 27, 1938
>
> I don't know whether I've already mentioned that I've
> become a Zionist. This word stands for a tremendous number
> of things. To me it means, in short, that I now consciously and
> strongly feel I am a Jew, and am proud of it. My primary aim is to
> go to Palestine [pre-State Israel], to work for it.... I am going to
> start learning Hebrew, and I'll attend one of the [Jewish] youth
> groups. In short, I'm really going to knuckle down properly. I've
> become a different person, and it's a very good feeling.
>
> One needs something to believe in, something for which
> one can have whole-hearted enthusiasm. One needs to feel
> that one's life has meaning, that one is needed in this world.
> Zionism fulfills all this for me.... I'm convinced Zionism is
> Jewry's solution to its problems and that the outstanding work
> being done in Palestine is not in vain.[29]

Hannah felt deserted by her native Hungary and decided to immigrate
to her people's historical homeland, Eretz Yisrael (the Land of Israel). In
1938 almost one quarter of Budapest's population was Jewish but very
few contemplated leaving the comfortable city known as the "Paris of
the East." A year later, Hannah made Aliyah to Israel and enrolled at
the Girls' Agricultural School in Nahalal where she prepared for a life
as a farmer on a kibbutz. Hannah's mother asked her why she was going to a farm school and suggested she enroll at the Hebrew University
in Jerusalem but Hannah told her there were too many intellectuals
in Palestine and what Eretz Yisrael needed was workers and farmers.

---

29. Hannah Senesh, Marge Piercy, et al., *Hannah Senesh: Her Life and Diary, The
First Complete Edition* (Woodstock, VT: Jewish Lights Publishing, 2004), 67.

Hannah toured the length and breadth of Israel and learned to master the Hebrew language. She began to write beautiful poems in her adopted tongue and one of her first, written in 1940 in Nahalal, read:

Our people are working the black soil,
Their arms reap the gold sheaves,
And now when the last ear its stalk leaves,
Our faces glitter as with gilded oil.

From where comes the new light and voice?
From where the resounding song at hand?
From where the fighting spirit and new faith?
From you, fertile Emek [Israel's Jezreel Valley],
    from you, my Land.[30]

Hannah fell in love with Eretz Yisrael and felt that hard work on its soil would help bring the Jewish people's redemption. When Hannah graduated from the Girls' Agricultural School in Nahalal, she was accepted as a member on Kibbutz Sedot Yam, located next to ancient Caesarea. Hannah worked hard on the kibbutz and spent her free time walking along the Mediterranean's sandy beaches. Fearing the rising anti-Semitism in Europe and worried about her mother in Hungary and all of Europe's Jews, Hannah wrote a poem-prayer as she walked along the beach one day to Caesarea. It called out to God to save the Jewish people. Its words are sung by millions today:

God – may there be no end
To sea, to sand,
Water's splash,
Lightning's flash,
The prayer of man.[31]

30. Quoted in Maxine Rose Schur, *Hannah Szenes: A Song of Light* (Philadelphia: Jewish Publication Society, 1986), 47.

31. Translated from the Hebrew by Ziva Shapiro; quoted in Hannah Senesh, Marge Piercy, *et al.*, *Hannah Senesh: Her Life and Diary*, 304.

As reports reached Israel of the horrors of the Nazi Holocaust, Hannah became restless. On January 8, 1943, she recorded this entry in her diary:

> I was suddenly struck by the idea of going to Hungary. I feel I must be there during these days in order to help organization youth emigration, and also to get my mother out. Although I'm quite aware how absurd the idea is, it still seems both feasible and necessary to me so I'll get to work on it and carry it through.[32]

In one of her poems called "At the Crossroads," Hannah writes, "A voice called and I went." Hannah truly felt she had a calling and she was ready to answer with her actions and deeds. Around that time Hannah learned that the Haganah, the Jewish underground army in Israel, was organizing a group of Jewish fighters to parachute behind enemy lines in Nazi-occupied Europe. The purpose of the mission was to rescue downed Allied pilots as well as to organize Jewish rescue and resistance. This was her chance to carry out her idea and she volunteered for the elite unit and went through rigorous commando and paratroop training with the British army in preparation for the mission. Altogether, thirty-two parachutists were chosen including Hannah Senesh.

On the day before her departure, Hannah learned that her beloved brother, Giora, was arriving in Israel as a new immigrant and she was able to spend her last day in Israel with him. In March 1944 she parachuted into Nazi-occupied Yugoslavia and met up with local partisans. Five days later she learned that the Nazis had taken over Hungary. On one of those nights in the Yugoslavian forest she wrote a tragic, prophetic poem called "Blessed Is the Match." When she showed it to Reuven Dafne, one of her fellow Israeli parachutists, he was angered by its pessimism and crumpled up the paper and threw it in the bushes. Later that night, he regretted his behavior and spent

---

32. Hannah Senesh, Marge Piercy, *et al.*, *Hannah Senesh: Her Life and Diary*, 155.

hours looking for the poem, which he eventually found and brought back to Israel. It read:

Blessed is the match consumed in kindling flame.
Blessed is the flame that burns
in the secret fastness of the heart.
Blessed is the heart with strength
to stop its beating for honor's sake.
Blessed is the match consumed in kindling flame.[33]

In June 1944 Hannah Senesh crossed the Yugoslavian border into Hungary. She carried with her a top-secret radio transmitter and hoped to infiltrate into Budapest and rescue her mother and other Jews. Sadly, Hannah was captured almost immediately and turned over to the Nazis. She was held prisoner for several months in a Gestapo jail in Budapest. During this time she was tortured and severely beaten but she did not betray her comrades nor give the Nazis the information they sought about her unit or the radio transmitter.

When the Nazis discovered that Hannah's mother, Katrina, was still living in Budapest, they arrested her and brought her to the prison where she was shocked to learn that her daughter was not safe in Palestine but behind bars in Budapest. The Nazis threatened to kill Mrs. Senesh unless Hannah talked but the young heroine would not be broken. She embraced her mother in tears but said she could not divulge any information about her mission. The Nazis demanded that Mrs. Senesh make her daughter talk, but the brave woman had faith in her daughter and her mission. Mrs. Senesh said that if Hannah was refusing to divulge information to the Nazis, there must be a good reason and she would not try to pressure her. The two were incarcerated in the same prison and on several occasions made contact by hand signals across the prison courtyard. Other Jewish prisoners testified that Hannah taught them about Zionism and Hebrew in the prison.

---

33. Ibid., 306.

On November 7, 1944, after being sentenced to death by a Hungarian fascist court, Hannah was placed before a Nazi firing squad. She refused to be blindfolded and told the Hungarian Nazis, "I am not afraid of you and I am not afraid of death!" With her head held high and her eyes uncovered, Hannah Senesh was executed. She was buried in Budapest and after the war the people she inspired won Israel's freedom and independence. In 1950 her coffin was flown to Israel and she was reburied with full military honors in the National Military Cemetery on Mount Herzl in Jerusalem where she rests today.

Hannah Senesh once wrote: "There are stars whose radiance is visible on earth though they have long been extinct. There are people whose brilliance continues to light the world though they are no longer among the living. These lights are particularly bright when the night is dark. They light the way for Mankind."[34] Hannah Senesh was one of these stars. In her life she brought a message of hope and freedom, and in her death she became an eternal light for our people. Her life and sacrifice left a legacy that will hopefully inspire each and every one of us to answer the call when we hear it.

---

34. Ibid., 1.

VICTOR "YOUNG" PEREZ
A JEWISH CHAMPION,
IN AND OUT OF THE RING

Victor "Young" Perez (1911–1945)
- Tunisian-born world flyweight boxing champion
- Arrested by French Nazis and sent to Auschwitz
- Forced to box for Nazi camp commandant; smuggled food to fellow prisoners
- 1945 Murdered by Nazis on death march
    "We live in order to help!"

"A psalm of David: Blessed be the Lord, my Rock, Who teaches my hands to battle and my fingers to fight."
– Psalm 144

Boxing is arguably the greatest Jewish sport. Daniel Mendoza, the famous English Jewish champion, invented scientific boxing in the late 1700s and gave persecuted Jews in Great Britain a reason to walk with pride among their gentile countrymen. His fellow Anglo-Jewish pugilist, Dutch Sam Elias, invented the uppercut punch. Legend even has it that the most basic boxing term "jab" is an acronym for Jewish Anglo Boxer!! Benny Leonard, the great Jewish lightweight champion is considered, pound for pound, one of the best boxers to have ever entered the ring. Barney Ross became the first champion to win world titles in two divisions and later, as a u.s. Marine, won the Silver Star for his bravery in World War II. Ross, a proud Jew and Zionist, also helped smuggle guns to Israel during the 1948 War of Independence. Many Jews held world boxing titles in the 1920s, '30s and '40s. The Star of David often adorned their boxers' trunks as these Jewish ring-warriors earned the pride and respect of the world. In the 1930s one of the greatest world boxing champions was a Tunisian Jew named Victor "Young" Perez. His heroism both in and out of the ring made him a modern-day Maccabee.

Victor "Young" Perez was born on October 18, 1911, in Hafsia, a working-class neighborhood in the North African city of Tunis in Tunisia. The feisty and handsome young Jew weighed 110 pounds and stood only five foot one but was an outstanding athlete. Victor Perez began a career as a professional boxer in Tunis and eventually moved to Paris, where on October 26, 1931, he knocked out the American champion Frankie Genero in the second round of their bout to win the World Flyweight Boxing Championship. Victor "Young" Perez at twenty-one years old became the youngest Frenchman ever to win a world boxing title. In the 1930s champion boxers were the world's superstars and "Young" Perez became rich and famous. He loved to party and enjoy life and was frequently seen in the company of beautiful women including the famous French actress Mireille Balin.

Perez fought 133 professional bouts and his record was 92 wins (28 knockouts), 26 losses and 15 draws. He lost the world flyweight title a year later to the Englishman Jackie Brown in Manchester. Perez then moved up into the bantamweight class and in 1934 fought Panama's Al Brown for the world championship but lost on a fifteen-round decision. One of Perez's last bouts was in 1938 in Berlin where he was booed by the Nazi crowd but still proudly wore the Star of David on his trunks.

Perez swore that he would only return home to Tunis after regaining the world boxing title, and tragically he was caught in Paris when World War II broke out. "Young" Perez was arrested in 1943 by the Milice Française, the collaborationist French Nazi police force that specialized in rounding up Jews and French freedom fighters. In October 1943 Perez was deported from Drancy, France, with a thousand other French Jews on the infamous Convoy 60 to the Nazi concentration camp of Auschwitz. Perez was assigned to Auschwitz Camp III, Monowitz, or as the prisoners called it, "Buna."

Auschwitz III was a slave labor camp based around the German I.G. Farben synthetic rubber factory and its prisoners were worked near to death and then sent to the gas chambers in Auschwitz II-Birkenau. The Nazi commandant of Auschwitz III was not only a mass-murderer and sadist but he also was an aficionado of boxing. At Monowitz the commandant organized a cadre of prisoners who had been amateur and professional boxers and ordered them to put on biweekly boxing exhibitions for the enjoyment of the camp's staff. Among these Auschwitz boxers were the former Greek champions Salamo Arouch and Jacko Razon, on whose lives the film *Triumph of the Spirit* was based, and of course, the former world champ Victor Perez, who was the commandant's favorite.

The boxers were given two special benefits: each week they were given a day off from their duties as slave laborers so they could train and each night they received an extra bowl of soup. Perez fought his first fight in the camp against a former German heavyweight champ who was a foot taller than "Young" and weighed fifty pounds more than him. Perez scored a lightening knockout and went on to fight twice weekly for the next fifteen months in the camp, winning 140 straight bouts.

What really made him a champion however, was his behavior and heroism outside of the ring. At Auschwitz III Victor Perez was assigned to work in the camp kitchen. Each night he stole a fifty-liter container of soup and gave it out to starving prisoners. Never afraid to risk his life for others, he took special care of his fellow Jewish prisoners from France and North Africa. He kept scores of his fellow Jews alive for months with the stolen food rations. When friends warned him that he would be hanged if caught, he answered, "Human beings were created in order to help others. We live in order to help!"[35]

A real fighter at heart, Perez tried to escape from Auschwitz but was captured and tortured for two weeks in the infamous "standing

---

35. Famed Israeli journalist, Holocaust survivor and *Exodus* crewman Noah Klieger was a prisoner and boxer at Auschwitz with Victor Perez. I have heard him speak many times, and I base much of my account of Perez's experiences in Auschwitz and on the death march on Noah Klieger's eyewitness testimony.

bunker," a tiny cell with no space to lie down, in which inmates were made to spend the night while carrying on their usual backbreaking labor in the daytime.

By 1945 the Soviet Red Army was advancing west and the Nazis decided to evacuate Auschwitz. Over fifty-seven thousand survivors of Auschwitz were forcibly marched for months by foot through the freezing Polish winter towards Germany. Among these prisoners was Victor Perez, who was one of only thirty-one survivors of the original group of a thousand Jewish prisoners sent from France on Convoy 60 back in 1943. In all, fewer than twenty thousand prisoners survived the deadly trek that became known as the "death march." (The annual "March of the Living," held in our own times, is in many ways the Jewish people's answer to the 1945 Nazi death marches.)

On January 21, 1945, the fourth day of the death march, the starving, exhausted and freezing Jewish prisoners were stopped outside the Gleiwitz concentration camp near the Czech border. "Young" Perez snuck away from the group and entered the abandoned German camp and found a large sack of bread in the kitchen. Perez put the sack on his shoulders and rushed back to feed his friends. As he approached the group and stood in front of a small ditch, a German guard pointed his machine gun at Perez and ordered him to halt. Victor tried to explain to the guard, "These are my friends and they are starving. I'm just bringing them some bread," but the Nazi insisted Perez not move. "Young" ignored the ss guard and leaped across the ditch hoping to give the sack of bread to his starving friends but the Nazi aimed his machine gun at Perez and fired several shots, killing the former champion instantly. Victor "Young" Perez, at the age of thirty-three, lay dead in the snow.

Victor "Young" Perez died as a true champion and hero. In 1986 he was inducted into the International Jewish Sports Hall of Fame located at the Wingate Sports Institute in Netanya, Israel. This great champion's example both inside and outside the ring will be an inspiration for generations to come.

BARNEY ROSS
CONTINUING THE FIGHT

Barney Ross (1909–1967)

- World boxing champion in three divisions
- U.S. Marine in WWII; hero of battle at Guadalcanal
- Active in Bergson Group to save European Jews during Holocaust

"There is no such thing as a former fighter. We all must continue the fight."

Dov-Ber ("Beryl") Rosofsky was born on December 23, 1909, in New York's Lower East Side. His father, Isadore Rosofsky, was a Talmudic scholar from Brest-Litovsk, Belarus, who came to America like so many other Jews in those years, seeking a better life and freedom from pogroms and anti-Semitism. Isadore and his wife, Sarah, were unable to make a decent living in New York and moved to Chicago's Jewish ghetto around Maxwell Street in 1911. The Rosofskys rented a two-and-a-half-room apartment for their family of five children and opened a tiny grocery store across the street from their humble home. Isadore was a proud religious Jew and sought to pass on his people's ancient traditions to his children. He hoped his son, Dov-Ber ("Beryl"), would become a Talmudic scholar and Hebrew teacher but destiny had a different mission for the young Chicago Jew.

When Dov-Ber was fourteen years old, two young hoodlums entered his father's grocery store brandishing pistols. They emptied the cash register of its meager coins and then angrily shot and killed Isadore. The Rosofsky family was devastated by this tragedy. Sarah had a nervous breakdown and had to be cared for by relatives; the younger children were placed in an orphanage. Disillusioned and filled with anger, young Dov-Ber turned to the streets and even tried to join Al Capone's gang but was rejected when the famed mobster gave him a twenty-dollar bill and told him that a rabbi's son should look for another line of business.

Dov-Ber became a tough street kid and learned to fight with his fists. Soon he became known as "Beryl the Terrible." Resolved to earn enough money to bring his family back together, seventeen-year-old Beryl began appearing in the local amateur boxing ring where he was an instant success. Beryl fought sometimes five or six times a week and pawned his victory medals off for three dollars apiece, earning badly needed money to pay for his mother's medical bills and to help his siblings. Rosofsky fought over 250 amateur bouts and in 1929 won the Intercity Golden Gloves Featherweight title. Beryl decided to turn pro but was afraid his beloved mother would disapprove of his career as a "buxfiyteh" (the name Yiddish-speakers in America gave to a boxer) so he changed his name to Barney Ross and won his first professional fight against Virgil Tobin in Chicago.

During the next four years Ross fought his way up the ranks and on June 23, 1933, Barney Ross earned a shot at both the world lightweight and junior-welterweight titles in a bout against Tony Canzoneri in front of thirteen thousand at Chicago Stadium. Barney Ross was too fast and aggressive for Canzoneri and became the first boxer in history to win two world titles simultaneously in one bout. Ross also won the rematch against the former champ three months later in New York in a fifteen-round slugfest. Though he now had worldwide acclaim, Ross's greatest joy was earning enough money to take his younger siblings out of the orphanage and reunite his family.

His mother, who at first was opposed to his boxing career, became his biggest fan and attended his fights, sometimes walking five miles to a boxing match on Saturday so as not to desecrate the holy Sabbath. She told him, "There are no more orphans in our family. Pa is looking down on you now and he is very proud of you!" Ross regained his faith in Judaism and put on tefillin and said his morning prayers. After winning his rematch with Canzoneri, Ross went to his shul on Saturday and was given an Aliyah to the Torah. As he said the Hebrew blessing, the rabbi cried in joy and remarked, "You've come back!"

In 1934 Barney Ross decided to move up in weight class and fought the popular Irish-American world champion Jimmy McLarnin, who was infamous for defeating Jewish contenders. Ross and McLarnin fought on May 28, 1934, in front of forty-five thousand fans at New York's Madison Square Garden Bowl. Ross was knocked down in the ninth round for the first time in his career but came back to knock down the baby-faced Irishman and win the world welterweight title by decision. Barney Ross became the first boxer in world history to hold three world titles simultaneously. He fought McLarnin two more times, losing a disputed rematch four months later but winning a decisive unanimous decision in May 1935, thus regaining the world welterweight title.

Ross became a symbol of courage and pride for Jews everywhere. Jewish delicatessens and shops around the country put Ross's picture in their window with the words "OUR BARNEY." Ross felt like he was fighting not only for the title but for his Jewish people and carried the burden proudly on his strong shoulders. When his mom learned that the championship bout was broadcast worldwide, she remarked,"Hitler will know about it then. Maybe he'll learn something from it about our people. He should know that he can kill millions of us but he can never defeat us!"[36] Barney Ross defended his welterweight title successfully several times until he was finally defeated in May 1938 by Henry Armstrong. He retired with an impressive professional record of 74 wins, 4 losses, 3 draws and 1 no-decision.

---

36. Quoted in Peter Levine, *Ellis Island to Ebbets Field: Sport and the American Jewish Experience* (New York: Oxford University Press, 1992), 178.

The loss to Armstrong would end Ross's boxing career but not his destiny as a great Hebrew warrior. After Pearl Harbor was attacked on December 7, 1941, thirty-three-year-old Barney Ross volunteered for the U.S. Marines, wanting to contribute to the war on fascism. Ross was sent into battle on Guadalcanal and was trapped in a bloody foxhole with three wounded marines. Single-handedly Ross fought off an entire Japanese battalion, killing twenty-two enemy soldiers, in spite of sustaining terrible wounds himself. Ross was promoted to sergeant and won both the Silver Star and the Distinguished Service Cross along with a presidential citation from Franklin Delano Roosevelt.

Barney, however, was hospitalized with malaria, dysentery and terrible wounds from the battle. Well-meaning medics gave him large doses of morphine to ease his pains but the great hero became addicted to the drug. Barney Ross became a junkie and for four years he sought out drugs to ease his fix in dark alleys from pushers. Finally, the great champion decided to beat his addiction. He checked himself into a hospital in Kentucky in 1946 and went through ten days of hell and then six months of voluntary hospitalization before finally defeating his addiction. Barney Ross died of throat cancer on January 17, 1967, at the age of fifty-eight. He was inducted into the Boxing Hall of Fame in 1956 and in 1979 he was enshrined in the Jewish Sports Hall of Fame at Wingate Institute in Israel.

If this article ended here, Barney Ross's place as one of the great boxing champions and as a great American hero would be preserved, but perhaps his greatest accomplishments were for the Jewish people and Israel. In 1944, after returning from Guadalcanal, Ross became active with the Emergency Committee to Save the Jewish People of Europe, known also as the "Bergson Group." The committee, led by Peter Bergson, a great Jewish hero from pre-State Israel, used full-page newspaper ads, public rallies, and Capitol Hill lobbying to pressure the Roosevelt administration to rescue Jews from Hitler. While much of American Jewry remained silent in those days of holocaust and destruction, Barney Ross joined the brave Jews and Gentiles working with the Bergson Group to save our people.

Bergson's real name was Hillel Kook and he was the nephew of the chief Ashkenazi rabbi in British Mandate Palestine, Rav Kook. Peter Bergson was a follower of Zionist leader Zeev Jabotinsky, who taught that silence in the face of challenge and threats is filth. Bergson, with the help of non-Jews like comedian Bob Hope and Congressman Will Rogers Jr., along with committed Jews like famed screenwriter Ben Hecht and Barney Ross, helped save thousands of Jewish lives in the Holocaust.

Bergson also organized another committee to help support the efforts of the Zionist movement in Palestine. It was called the American League for a Free Palestine and Barney Ross became an active member. He spoke at rallies and raised funds for the Zionist movement and even helped smuggle guns to the Jewish state during Israel's War of Independence. In one of the Bergson Group's ads, Barney Ross's picture appeared along with his heartfelt message: "There is no such thing as a former fighter. We must all continue the fight!"

Barney Ross continued the fight for Jewish honor and pride throughout his life. He fought for his people in the streets of Chicago, in the boxing rings of New York, in the foxholes of Guadalcanal, in a Kentucky hospital room and, most importantly, in the pages of Jewish history. He was a true champion in and out of the ring. Barney Ross will forever remain an inspiration and a light. He will never be counted out.

DOV GRUNER
THE ROAD TO THE GALLOWS

Dov Gruner (1912–1947)
- Underground Fighter in Etzel
- Arrested and sentenced to death by British
  for role in attack on police station
- Hanged in Akko Prison on April 16, 1947

*"I swear that if I had the choice of starting again I would choose
the same road, regardless of the possible consequences to me."*

Sir,

I thank you from the bottom of my heart for the great encouragement you have given me in these fateful days. You may rest assured that whatever happens I will not forget the teachings on which I was weaned, the teachings to be "proud and generous and strong" [from the Betar hymn written by Ze'ev Jabotinsky] and I shall know how to stand up for my honor, the honor of a fighting Hebrew soldier....

Of course I want to live. Who does not? ...[But] the right way, to my mind, is the way of the Irgun [Etzel], which does not reject political effort but will not give up a single yard of our country, because it is ours.... That should be the way of the Jewish people in these days; to stand up for what is ours and be ready for battle even if in some instances it leads to the gallows. For the world knows that a land is redeemed by blood.

I write these lines forty-eight hours before the time fixed by our oppressors to carry out their murder, and at such moments one does not lie. I swear that if I had the choice of starting again I would choose the same road, regardless of the possible consequences to me.

Your faithful soldier,

Dov[37]

Dressed in the crimson garb of those on death row, Dov Gruner sat in his prison cell and composed the above letter to Menachem Begin, commander of the Etzel. The Etzel, sometimes called the "Irgun," was one of the three Jewish underground organizations that fought the British for Israel's independence in the 1940s. (Etzel is a Hebrew acronym for Irgun Tzva'i Leumi, the National Military Organization. Menachem Begin went on to become Israel's sixth prime minister.) Two days after writing the letter, thirty-four-year-old Dov Gruner was hanged by the British in Akko Prison. The date was April 16, 1947.

The road to the British gallows began for Dov Gruner in a small Hungarian village near Budapest where he was born on December 6, 1912. Dov learned in yeshivas until the age of eighteen and received an excellent Jewish education. Later, he studied engineering and mastered six languages, including Hebrew. Early in his youth, Dov joined Betar, the Zionist youth movement founded by Ze'ev Jabotinsky, and it was there that the sparks of Jewish nationalism were ignited in him.

Dov Gruner made Aliyah to Israel in February, 1940, arriving aboard an "illegal" immigrant ship. The British had closed the gates of Palestine to Jewish immigration in 1939.Though he quickly found employment as a civil engineer, news of the Holocaust in Europe left Dov restless. Determined to fight the Nazis, he enlisted in the British army, where he served for the next five years. Dov was wounded twice

---

37. Quoted in Levi Soshuk, Azriel Louis Eisenberg, eds., *Momentous Century: Personal and Eyewitness Accounts of the Rise of the Jewish Homeland and State, 1875–1978* (New York: Cornwall Books, 1984), 198–99.

and his British officer remembered him as "the finest, bravest and most disciplined soldier" in the unit. While serving in Europe, Dov learned that except for his sister, his entire family had been wiped out by the Nazis. There, amongst the ruins of his home, he swore to avenge his fallen brethren and to do everything in his power to bring about an independent Jewish state. Gruner, like most Betar members, joined the Etzel, and while still in Europe he helped organize clandestine Jewish immigration to Israel.

When World War II ended with the defeat of the Nazis, the Etzel directed all their efforts towards liberating the land of Israel from the British. In the spring of 1946, Gruner was discharged from the British army and returned to Israel. Two weeks later, he was to take part in one of the Etzel's most daring operations: the attack on the British police headquarters in Ramat Gan.

The raid took place on April 23, 1946, with the major objective being the capture of arms and ammunition from the police arsenal. Gruner and the other Etzel rebels gained entrance to the police station by disguising themselves as British soldiers bringing in Arab prisoners caught stealing. Once inside the fortress, the "prisoners" along with their "guards" pulled out Sten guns and in a matter of moments, the police station was theirs.

Quickly the Etzel soldiers blew off the doors to the armory and began loading heavy boxes of rifles and ammunition onto their truck waiting outside. Meanwhile, a British policeman in the station succeeded in radioing for help to the nearby Petah Tikvah police station. As British reinforcements arrived, a fierce battle broke out. The Etzel fighters finished loading the truck and successfully made their getaway but three of their men were killed in the crossfire and Dov Gruner was shot in the face and taken prisoner. Dov lay in a hospital in excruciating pain for eight months and underwent several operations on his shattered jaw. The British did not want him to look deformed for his trial.

In January 1947, Dov was brought before a British military court, but he refused to accept the services of a lawyer. In a statement before the tribunal, Gruner said that the British were given the Mandate over Israel in 1922 to bring about a Jewish national home and had now abandoned that obligation and sought to transform the country into one of their military bases. Therefore, Dov stated, he refused to recognize the legitimacy of a British court in Israel. When the judge chastised Gruner and warned him that he faced a possible death sentence, Dov replied: "You will not frighten Jews with hangings and trials in our homeland!"

The outcome of the trial was a foregone conclusion. Gruner was sentenced to death by hanging. When his sentence was read, he rose to his feet and called out to the judge in Hebrew, "*B'dam va'esh Yehuda naf-la, u'b'dam va'esh Yehuda takum!*"[38] The translator explained the words in English to the judge: "In blood and fire Judea fell and in blood and fire Judea shall rise again!" This was the motto adopted by HaShomer, from the poem written by Tchernikovsky. The judge's face became pale at hearing the translation and he quickly left the courtroom.

Dov Gruner was immediately transferred to the British prison in Jerusalem and dressed in the red burlap uniform of the condemned. Gruner was soon joined by three more Etzel soldiers, Yehiel Dresner, Mordechai Alkahi and Eliezer Kashani, who had also been sentenced to death, and later all four were transferred to the central British prison in Akko.

Protests and appeals for clemency on behalf of Dov Gruner poured into British embassies across the world and the British, seeking to buy time and quiet, tried to get Gruner to sign a request for clemency. Dov was mistakenly directed to sign the appeal believing it was Etzel orders but later learned that the Etzel had given him freedom of choice in this matter of conscience. Dov did not recognize the right of the British to put him on trial in the Land of Israel and he immediately rescinded his signature on the appeal. On February 13, 1947, Dov's sister, Helen Friedman, arrived in Israel from the USA. She was Dov's only surviving relative. Everyone else in his family had been murdered in the Holocaust.

---

38. Quoted in Yosef Nedava, *Sefer olei hagardom* [Book of those who mounted the gallows] (Tel Aviv: Sefarim Shelah, 1952), 138.

Helen met with Dov and led a campaign to win his freedom. The British, meanwhile, lost no time in preparing the gallows in Akko.

At four a.m. on Wednesday morning, April 16, 1947, Dov Gruner was awakened from his sleep by British commandos. They ordered him to rise. Realizing that the hour of his execution had arrived, Dov defiantly refused. The soldiers beat him and dragged him to his feet. There was to be no last meal, no final request, no last visitor and no rabbi to offer consolation. One by one, Dov Gruner, Yehiel Dresner, Mordechai Alkahi and Eliezer Kashani were taken to the gallows. Each sang "Hatikvah," the Jewish national anthem, and within forty-three minutes, their voices were heard no more. In less than one hour the British had hanged four Jews at Akko Prison.

Early that morning, the British came to Tel Aviv to escort Helen Friedman to Akko to see her brother for the last time. On the way up north, the convoy she was traveling in suddenly veered east and took her to Safed. Helen Friedman was told that her brother had been executed that morning and that she could now part with him...at his funeral.

Shortly before he was executed, Dov Gruner celebrated the festival of Passover in his tiny prison cell. He offered the only chair to the British guard in keeping with the Jewish custom of hospitality. As he carried out the traditional Passover Seder, Dov smiled and read one line with particular emotion: "This year we are slaves – next year we will be free people!"

Although his execution was only days away, Dov was happy because he knew that very soon his people would be free. Dov Gruner died a hero and his sacrifice was not in vain. On May 14, 1948, the British left "Palestine" and the Jewish people declared an independent State of Israel.

POSTSCRIPT: Almost twenty years ago I was teaching the story of Dov Gruner to a group of my students from the Alexander Muss High School in Israel at Akko Prison with my friend and colleague David Sprung. A young American college student approached me and asked if he could join in on the lesson. I told him that we would be honored to have him join us. We shared the story of Dov Gruner in the actual gallows room at Akko Prison where Gruner was hanged. At the end of the story we all sang "Hatikvah" in Dov's memory. As we left the gallows room, the college student approached me with tears in his eyes and asked to thank me for the privilege of sharing the experience with us. I told him that it was our pleasure. He responded by telling us that he was Helen Friedman's grandson – Dov Gruner's grandnephew – and that this was his first visit to Akko Prison. He told us that he thought that only he knew about his great uncle and that he was so touched to see a group of American teens learning about and honoring the sacrifice of this great hero, his relative Dov Gruner.

BARAZANI AND FEINSTEIN
DIGNITY IN THE SHADOW
OF THE GALLOWS

Moshe Barazani (1928–1947)
Member of Lehi underground

Meir Feinstein (1928–1947)
Member of Etzel underground

- British captured both boys and sentenced them to death by hanging
- Were to be first Jews to be hanged in Jerusalem by British
- April 22, 1947 Blew themselves up with a grenade hours before their execution

"It is better to die with a weapon in hand than to live with your hands raised."

BARAZANI   FEINSTEIN

"Moshe Barazani, you will hang by your neck until you die!"
"Meir Feinstein, you will hang by your neck until you die!"

Moshe Barazani and Meir Feinstein were both sentenced to death by a British military court in Mandatory Palestine in March 1947. Though both were raised in Jerusalem it was only in a British prison that they met for the first time. In their lives and backgrounds they were so different but in their deaths they were to become as brothers, carrying together the banner of Jewish liberation and Israel's independence.

91

Moshe Barazani was born in Kurdistan (northern Iraq) and made Aliyah with his family to Israel in the 1920s. Moshe and his parents and five brothers settled in a one-room apartment in Jerusalem where they led lives of bitter poverty. Moshe's father, Rabbi Avraham Barazani, was a kabbalist and spent his time in the Beth El Synagogue in the Old City of Jerusalem searching the pages of the *Zohar* for the secret of Jewish redemption. Once Moshe saw his parents crying and when he asked why, they replied that they were sorry to have brought their children to lives of poverty in Israel. Young Moshe retorted: "Mother and Father, don't be sad. We must be happy, even if we only have dry bread to eat! We are in the Land of Israel!"

Moshe's love for Israel brought him to join the Jewish underground group called Lehi. Lehi is a Hebrew acronym that stands for Lohamei Herut Yisrael (Freedom Fighters of Israel). It was one of three Jewish underground organizations that fought for Israel's independence during the British Mandate period in the 1940s.

On March 9, 1947, Moshe Barazani was walking on the streets of Jerusalem late at night when he was surprised by a patrol of British soldiers. He was stopped and interrogated by them and, in the course of searching him, they found a hand grenade in his pocket. Lehi members were commanded to always carry arms with them after their leader, Yair Stern, was murdered by British detectives from the CID in 1942. In a trial that lasted only ninety minutes Moshe Barazani was sentenced to death by hanging. Barazani refused to be represented by a lawyer and read the Tanakh (Hebrew Bible) throughout the trial. When his sentence was pronounced he shouted back to the British court:

The Hebrew nation sees in you an enemy, a foreign regime in its homeland. We, the Fighters for the Freedom of Israel [Lohamei Herut Yisrael, Lehi], are fighting you to free the homeland. In this war, I have fallen your prisoner, and you do not have the right to judge me. With hangings you will not frighten us, and to destroy us you will not succeed! My people, and all peoples oppressed by you, will fight your empire until its destruction.[39]

Meir Feinstein was different in ethnic background and in political affiliation. He was born in Jerusalem's Old City on Yom Kippur Eve, 1928. His father had made Aliyah to Israel from Lithuania in Eastern Europe. As a youth Meir studied at the Etz Hayyim Yeshiva in Jerusalem and worked as a farmer. He dreamed of one day being a Hebrew writer. In 1944 he joined the British army to fight the Nazis and served with distinction. When he was discharged after World War II he returned to Israel and joined the Jewish underground group called Etzel, the Irgun Tzva'i Leumi (National Military Organization). The Etzel was led by Menachem Begin, who years later, was elected prime minister of Israel and won the Nobel Peace Prize.

On October 30, 1946, Meir took part in an Etzel attack on the railway station in Jerusalem which served as the central arrival point for British soldiers. Feinstein was driving the getaway car and drew British fire. The bullets shattered the windshield and hit his left arm, badly mutilating it. He was captured and later, at a British prison hospital, his left arm was amputated. On March 25, 1947, he was sentenced to death by hanging. As his sentence was pronounced he, just as Dov Gruner had done, shouted, "In blood and fire Judea fell and in blood and fire Judea shall rise again!"[40]

The two boys were transferred back and forth between several British prisons and eventually became cellmates in the British Central Prison in Jerusalem, located in the Russian Compound. After Dov Gruner and three other Etzel fighters were hanged by the British on April 16, 1947, in Akko Prison, Moshe and Meir decided to act. Barazani

---

39. Zev Golan, *Free Jerusalem: Heroes, Heroines and Rogues Who Created the State of Israel* (Jerusalem: Devora Publishing Company, 2003), 276.

40. Yosef Nedava, *Sefer olei hagardom* [Book of those who mounted the gallows] (Tel Aviv: Sefarim Shelah, 1952), 257.

and Feinstein were to be executed on April 22, 1947, in the Jerusalem prison, but they chose to rob the British of their designs. The inspiration for their plan came from their common Biblical hero, Samson, who died crying out, "*Tamot nafshi im Pelishtim* (Let me die with the Philistines)!" (Judges 16:30). Over a period of several days Barazani and Feinstein had parts of a grenade smuggled to them inside the peels of oranges. They decided they would throw the grenade on their captors at the gallows, dying like Samson who pulled down the pillars of the Philistine temple and died with his enemies.

On Monday, April 21, the night before the execution, Jerusalem's Rabbi Goldman came to the prison to console the two boys. He spent many hours with them and before he left he told them:

> The rabbis of old used to say that each man is brought into this world for the purpose of fulfilling some task. Some men fulfill what is given them to do in twenty years, some in seventy, and others never at all. For those who never fulfill it and go on living, life no longer has any purpose. That, too, is a kind of death. But in lives such as yours, my sons, death can get no footing at all, for even your death is turned into life.[41]

Rabbi Goldman then promised Barazani and Feinstein that he would return to be with them the next morning at the hour of their execution. The boys were shocked by this news and tried to dissuade the rabbi from returning, but to no avail. They could not tell Rabbi Goldman about their intentions for fear of compromising him and would not risk his life so they thanked him and bid him farewell. The boys sang the liturgical hymn "Adon Olam" with the rabbi before he left:[42]

---

41. J. Bowyer Bell, *Terror out of Zion: The Fight for Israeli Independence* (Piscataway, NJ: Transaction Publishers, 1996), 199.

42. Zev Golan, *Free Jerusalem: Heroes, Heroines and Rogues Who Created the State of Israel* (Jerusalem: Devora Publishing Company, 2003), 278.

Adon olam asher malach b'terem kol yetzir nivrah.... B'yado afkid ruchi, b'eit ishan v'a'irah! V'im ruchi geviati Hashem li v'lo ira. (Master of the universe, Who ruled before any creation came into being.... Into His hand I will entrust my spirit when I go to sleep – and I will wake up! And with my soul and my body, God is with me and I shall not fear.)

Now that Barazani and Feinstein could not carry out their plan as intended they were forced to make a fateful decision. Dressed in the crimson garb of the condemned, they sat facing each other in their small prison cell. While other Jewish underground fighters had been hanged in Akko, the British planned to make Barazani and Feinstein the first two Jews to be executed in the holy City of Jerusalem. The boys were determined not to let that happen! One-armed Meir Feinstein awkwardly embraced his cellmate Moshe. Barazani returned the embrace with one arm while in his other hand he held the grenade between their two hearts.

At twenty minutes before midnight, Moshe lit the fuse and the grenade went off, killing both instantly. The two heroes ensured that no Jew would ever be hanged in Jerusalem. They were buried in the holiest Jewish cemetery in the world: the Mount of Olives in Jerusalem. When Menachem Begin, former Etzel commander and later prime minister of Israel (1977–1983), died in 1992, his last request was to be buried next to his heroes: Moshe Barazani and Meir Feinstein. Today the three lie at rest on the Mount of Olives.

Shortly before the two boys took their own lives, Meir Feinstein gave a gift to one of the British guards in their prison, Thomas Goodwin. Apparently Goodwin had treated the boys kindly. The gift was an illustrated Tanakh (Hebrew Bible). After Feinstein gave him the Bible, the boys asked him to leave the area of their cell so they could pray in private. Goodwin left and shortly afterwards the explosion from Barazani and Feinstein's cell was heard. They apparently didn't want Goodwin to get hurt. Goodwin passed away in 2005 and before his death asked his son to see that the Bible was returned to Feinstein's family in Israel. Today it is on display in the Underground Prisoners Museum in Jerusalem, site of the former British prison where Barazani and Feinstein died. In the inside cover of the Bible, Meir Feinstein wrote a dedication in Hebrew and English. It said:

> In the shadow of the gallows, 21.4.47. To the British soldier as you stand guard. Before we go to the gallows, accept this Bible as a memento and remember that we stood in dignity and marched in dignity. It is better to die with a weapon in hand than to live with hands raised.
>
> –Meir Feinstein[43]

These two heroes died in dignity and helped Israel achieve its independence but there was irony in their deaths. Moshe Barazani's father was a Kabbalist who spent his whole life searching for the secrets to Israel's redemption, not knowing that his own son would be among those who would bring about that very redemption. Meir Feinstein dreamed of being an author, not knowing that the history of Israel would be written in his own blood.

---

43. Etgar Lefkovits, "'The Good Jailer'" Returns Irgun Hero's Bible Sixty Years Later," *Jerusalem Post*, April 19, 2007.

MURRAY GREENFIELD
AND *HATIKVAH*

Murray Greenfield (1926–)
- American Merchant Marine in World War II
- Volunteered to help sail Holocaust survivors to Israel past British blockade
- Set sail on Haganah boat *Tradewinds* (later renamed *HaTikvah*)
- Captured and imprisoned in British camp on Cyprus
- Later made Aliyah to Israel where he built a family and a life

"A dangerous mission with no pay?! I'm in!!"

On November 2, 1917, the British government issued the Balfour Declaration declaring that "His Majesty's government view with favour the establishment in Palestine of a national home for the Jewish people, and will use their best endeavours to facilitate the achievement of this object..." Just a month later, the British conquered Palestine from the Ottoman Turks, and in 1922 they were given the official mandate over that land by the League of Nations. The Mandate clearly stipulated that "...the Principal Allied Powers have also agreed that the Mandatory [the British] should be responsible for putting into effect the declaration originally made on November 2, 1917 [the Balfour Declaration]." In other words, the legal establishment of the British Mandate formally included the assumption that Britain would work towards turning the Mandatory territory into a Jewish homeland.

Despite these moral and legal obligations to the Jewish people and the Zionist movement, the British Mandate authorities soon began to placate Arab anti-Zionists and turn their backs on the Jews. British white papers (official British government laws or enactments) issued from 1922 onward removed 75 percent of the British Mandatory territory from consideration for Jewish settlement by turning it into the new Arab country of Transjordan (today called Jordan) and put severe restrictions on Jewish land settlements and Jewish immigration to Israel (which is called *Aliyah* in Hebrew, meaning "going up" – a term with both physical and spiritual connotations).

The culmination of this British stab in the back came in 1939 with the issuance of the 1939 MacDonald White Paper stipulating the limiting of Jewish settlements in Israel, limiting Aliyah to 75,000 over the next five years (precisely the years of the Holocaust, when six million Jews were to be slaughtered because they had no home to go to) and declaring that Palestine would not become a Jewish state but it would become a bi-national state with a two-thirds Arab majority. David Ben-Gurion, leader of the Jewish community in Israel, declared in response that "We will fight the war as if there is no White Paper, and we will fight the White Paper as if there is no war."

The great Zionist leader Zeev Jabotinsky wrote an article in 1939 called "The National Sport" in which he called on all young Jews to fight the British White Paper and help smuggle their brethren into Israel. While young Americans played baseball, Jabotinsky felt that young Jews should get involved with "Aliyah Bet" – clandestine immigration to Israel or, as the British called it, "illegal immigration." The Jews believed that it was not illegal for them to return to their ancestral home. In the article Jabotinsky wrote:

> The Jewish national sport is helping to break through a barrier which stands in the way of millions of hungry souls; it is helping to win a country for a homeless rabble and to make the rabble a nation. Other sports are, after all, not more than just a game; our sport is sacredly serious...[44]

---

44. Quoted in Joseph B. Schechtman, *The Vladimir Jabotinsky Story* (New York: T. Yoseloff, 1961), 425.

Aliyah Bet was carried out by two separate bodies in the Zionist movement between 1930 and 1948: Zeev Jabotinsky's Betar youth movement and the Zionist Labor movement's underground army called the
Haganah. The Haganah had created a wing in 1938 called the Mossad
Le'Aliyah Bet (Institution for clandestine immigration), led by Shaul
Avigur. Together, during the years 1930 to 1948, Betar and the Haganah brought over 107,000 clandestine *olim* (new immigrants) to Israel.
These "illegals" (in British terminology) were called *maapilim* in Hebrew,
which translates as "ascenders." During Israel's War of Independence
(1947–1949) there were 600,000 Jews in Israel; more than one-sixth had
come on Aliyah Bet. It is clear that without Aliyah Bet and the people
it brought, there might not have been a Jewish state!

A little-known story connected to Aliyah Bet is the role played by
North American Jews in this heroic operation. Over thirty-two thousand *maapilim* traveled from Europe to Israel on boats purchased in
the United States and manned by American volunteer sailors – mostly
Jews but several non-Jews as well. One of the most moving stories of
the American volunteers is that of Murray Greenfield, an unsung hero
from Far Rockaway, New York.

Murray was born on September 11, 1926, in the Bronx to Jewish
parents who had immigrated to the USA from Poland. He grew up in
Far Rockaway and graduated from Far Rockaway High School in the
summer of 1944. Like most of the young men in his generation, Murray enlisted in the U.S. Armed Forces. He joined the Merchant Marines,
whose job it was to ensure the safe transfer of military hardware, food
and supplies to U.S. troops abroad. He trained at the New York State
Maritime Academy and received his Able Bodied Seaman certification.
When training took Murray out to sea, he chose to remain on mission
on his ship rather than return to the academy.

In 1946 Murray was honorably discharged from the Merchant
Marines and decided to attend Hunter College, formerly an all-girls
school…now gone co-ed for the first time. One need not have too active
an imagination to figure out Murray's reasoning for applying to Hunter

College. His path to a productive and joyous college career seemed all but paved, when during one Saturday morning he had a destiny-changing conversation at his synagogue's Sabbath prayer services. (Murray was an ardent shul-goer and loved attending synagogue services.) At services that Sabbath, Murray met a young American Zionist activist who told him that the Haganah was looking for some brave American Jews with naval training to sail Holocaust survivors to Eretz Yisrael (the Land of Israel) as part of Aliyah Bet.

Murray was intrigued by the idea of serving his people and agreed to meet one of the Haganah's "Shu-Shu" boys – a term American Jewish volunteers used for Haganah agents who were so secretive that they were always telling others, "Shu-Shu! (Hush-Hush!)" At the secret interview the Haganah emissary explained to Murray all about the mission and asked if he had any questions. Murray had two: "Is the mission dangerous?" and "How much do you get paid?" The Haganah agent replied that it was a dangerous operation to rescue Jews who had survived the Holocaust and bring them home to Israel past the British blockade and that there was no money available to pay the American volunteers. Greenfield smiled and replied, "Those are the answers I was hoping for! I'm in!" Murray then told his mother that he was deferring his college career, which angered the Jewish matriarch who dreamed of sending her son to college, but when he told her that it was to do something good, but secretive, for the Jewish people, she gave her proud approval.

Murray Greenfield's heroic voyage began in February 1947 when the crew of American volunteers met their boat, the *Tradewinds*, in Miami, Florida. The *Tradewinds* was a former ice-breaker on the Saint Lawrence River. It had served as a Coast Guard cutter in World War II tracking down German submarines. Like the rest of the Aliyah Bet boats, the *Tradewinds* was not fit to carry its cargo of fourteen hundred refugees, but the Haganah was determined to do the best it could with the supplies and crew available. The *Tradewinds* sailed up the u.s. coast and after running into tough weather, put into the port of Charleston. The crew members had to shower in shifts at the local YMCA so as not to draw attention to the large number of Jewish males on the boat, which might alert authorities to the *Tradewinds'* true mission.

From Charleston the boat sailed to Baltimore where the volunteers caught a glimpse of their fellow Haganah ship the *President Warfield*, a Chesapeake Bay River boat about to become famous as the *Exodus 1947*. Then the *Tradewinds* set sail across the Atlantic with its unique crew of volunteers. While some of those aboard, like Murray, had naval training, many of the Zionist volunteers had never sailed before and had no maritime experience. Murray relates that once, out in the mid-Atlantic, the Navy veterans told the un-seaworthy Zionists that they should prepare letters for family and friends back at home, as they would soon be passing the "Mid-Ocean Mail Buoy." The Zionist volunteers wrote for hours and prepared scores of letters only to learn that they were the brunt of a practical joke.

In Lisbon, the crew met their Haganah commander, Yehoshua Baharav, who used the name "Captain Diamond" as a cover and claimed he was working for the United Fruit Company. He had the volunteers build sleeping racks in the boat's hold, telling the local authorities that the racks were for bananas. Anyone having seen the Nazi concentration camps quickly recognized that the beds on board looked like those in the Nazi camps, but with one big difference: these beds were built to bring Jews to their freedom. The *Tradewinds* continued on its journey, passing through Gibraltar and Marseilles, and eventually pulled into Portovenere on the northwest Italian coast. There, and at Bogliasco on the Italian Riviera, fourteen hundred *maapilim*, having survived the Holocaust, boarded the boat.

After about one week at sea, a British Royal Air Force plane buzzed the ship from above and discovered the "illegals." Soon British destroyers appeared and surrounded the *Tradewinds*, which defiantly declared its new Hebrew name: *Hatikvah* (the hope – the name of the Jewish national anthem). The British commander demanded to speak with the *Hatikvah's* captain. The Haganah officers displayed their contempt for the British by dressing a ten-year-old boy up in an admiral's hat and having him announce from the bridge, "I am the captain." The Royal Navy was not amused. They rammed the refugee boat and began to board it with Royal Marines. The Jewish refugees fought back with their fists and by hurling food cans but they were violently subdued by British tear gas, billy clubs and guns.

On May 17, 1947, the *Hatikvah* was towed into Haifa harbor and all of the Jewish *maapilim* and most of the twenty-six American volunteers, including Murray Greenfield, were sent to British detention camps on the island of Cyprus. There, the young American volunteers learned not only of the terrible trials the *maapilim* had faced in the Holocaust, but more importantly of the strength and spirit of a people who had faced the Third Reich and the British Empire and could not be broken. Murray would later say that the *maapilim* were the true heroes, not him!

In Cyprus, the Jews ran life inside the British prison camps. They taught the *maapilim* Hebrew and trades and prepared them for life in the Jewish state that would soon arise. Murray and the American volunteers played an active role in the Hebrew Resistance Movement (comprising the Haganah, IZL and Lehi) and helped the Haganah dig escape tunnels in the camps and even prepared gelignite pipe bombs that were used to blow up one of the British deportation prison ships, the *Empire Lifeguard*. Several months later in the summer of 1947, the American volunteers were released from Cyprus and Murray Greenfield returned home to America. He went on a speaking tour for the United Jewish Appeal (UJA) and on one occasion was the "bagman" for a large donation made to the emerging Jewish state by well-intentioned Jewish gangsters. It turns out that the "bad boys" had a poker game going with a pot of thousands of dollars. They decided to donate all their winnings to the Jewish homeland and somehow got hold of Murray Greenfield, who was "asked" to bring the big bag of bucks to Israel, which he kindly consented to do.

Murray was back in the USA but he began to feel that home was in Israel. He had been so inspired by the people he met from the Haganah and on the *Hatikvah* and in the camps on Cyprus. Murray Greenfield eventually moved to Israel where he met and married Hana Lustig, a Holocaust survivor from Czechoslovakia; they had three children. Hana, like Murray, has opened her heart to young people from around the world and shares her own moving story in speeches and in her writings.

In Israel, Murray got involved in the Palestine Economic Corporation (PEC), founded by luminaries like Justice Louis Brandeis. The PEC was in effect a precursor to Israel Bonds and funneled millions of dollars of investments into the new country. Greenfield got involved in helping supply mortgages to new immigrants and helped found the Association of Americans and Canadians in Israel (AACI). Eventually, he and his wife founded Gefen Publishing House, now run by their son Ilan.

One of Murray's greatest loves is speaking to students and adults about Aliyah Bet and the many heroes he has met on his life's journey. What those students quickly understand is that one of the most inspiring heroes they will ever meet is the sweet, smiling man standing in front of them: Murray Greenfield. Murray has a great sense of humor, but more importantly a deep sense of responsibility to his people's history and destiny. As a young American Jew he heard an inner voice calling him to action and he has been responding ever since.

DAVID MARCUS
AMERICAN JEW –
HERO OF ISRAEL

David Marcus (1902–1948)
- 1924 Graduated U.S. Military Academy at West Point
- 1944 World War II hero
- 1947 Recruited by Haganah to help Jewish army in Israel's War of Independence
- 1948 Opened "Burma Road" and saved New Jerusalem; tragically killed

"There were many who could have come to help, but only one came."

Colonel David Marcus was a real American success story. He rose out of the slums of New York City to become an All-American athlete, a Rhodes Scholar and an officer in the United States Army. After completing night law school, David went on to become a successful attorney and later a respected judge with a bright future. In 1948 David Marcus left all the comforts and promises of life in America to join the Jewish people struggling for independence in Israel. It was there that he would attain his greatest achievements – and meet a tragic death in the hills of Jerusalem.

David "Mickey" Marcus was born on Washington's birthday (February 22) in 1902, the fifth child of poor Jewish immigrants from Rumania. The family lived on Hester Street in New York's Lower East Side and later moved to Brooklyn. Mickey's parents had high hopes for him and he seemed destined from an early age to fulfill their wishes. David Marcus graduated at the top of his high school class and was voted Best Athlete. He received high school letters in track, basketball, baseball and football. A member of the scholastic Honor Society, Mickey could have gone to any college in America, but his inner convictions led him to a decision that shocked his family and friends. In 1920 David Marcus became one of the few Jews to enter the United States Military Academy at West Point.

Cadet Marcus showed an exceptional aptitude for the military sciences and excelled in all his studies. During his junior year Mickey took up boxing and went on undefeated to take the u.s. intercollegiate boxing championship. In his senior year Marcus concentrated on gymnastics and won several national titles as well as an invitation to try out for the 1924 u.s. Olympic team. Mickey graduated from West Point in 1924 at the top of his class and was offered a Rhodes scholarship to Oxford University in England. He declined the offer in order to be near his sweetheart, Emma, whom he married in 1927.

After getting married, Mickey left the army and completed night law school. He quickly made a name for himself as a competent lawyer, first serving the u.s. Attorney General's Office and later on the New York State Commission of Correction. In 1936 he was appointed to the bench and in 1940 Mayor Fiorello La Guardia named him commissioner of corrections. It was in that capacity that Mickey made national headlines with his successful war on organized crime and corruption.

When World War II broke out David Marcus temporarily left his promising career to reenlist in the army. As a West Point graduate, Colonel Marcus was appointed commander of the Rangers training school in Oahu. On D-Day he volunteered to parachute into Normandy with the 101st Airborne despite the fact that he had never received any training as a paratrooper. His courage and heroics won for him several major United States and British decorations including the Distinguished Service Medal. In May 1945 Colonel Marcus took part in the liberation of Dachau Concentration Camp and it was there that he witnessed the horrors of the Nazi Holocaust. Haunted by what he had seen, Marcus became convinced of the need for a Jewish homeland in Israel. In 1947 Mickey retired from the army and resumed his legal practice in New York.

On November 29, 1947, the United Nations voted in favor of establishing an independent Jewish state in Palestine. The very next day Arab terrorists opened fire on a Jewish bus traveling to Jerusalem, in effect beginning the War of Independence. Palestinian Arabs sought to isolate and harass Jewish settlements, including Jerusalem, in anticipation of the British evacuation several months away. Then, they hoped, Arab regular armies would invade and destroy the newborn Jewish state. David Ben-Gurion, leader of the Jewish Yishuv (the Jewish community in pre-state Israel) in Israel and later the state's first prime minister, understood the gravity of the situation. The Jewish army was outgunned, outmanned and ill prepared.

Ben-Gurion sent an emissary to the United States to recruit an American Jewish army officer who would be willing to help build a new, strong Israeli armed force capable of securing and maintaining independence. As Ben-Gurion later said, "There were many who could have come but only one came!" That man was David Marcus. Leaving a comfortable life, a promising career and a devoted wife behind, Marcus arrived in Israel in January 1948 under the nom de guerre Mickey Stone. Serving as Ben-Gurion's personal military advisor, Mickey quickly perceived the special spirit and needs of the new army. He prepared vital military manuals, improved training procedures and made important observations and recommendations. Using his vast military expertise, David Marcus helped mold Israel's scattered underground forces into a modern army.

After a brief visit to the U.S., Mickey returned to Israel in May of 1948. Minutes after declaring independence on May 14, Israel was invaded by five Arab armies. The most critical battle areas proved to be in the south (Negev) along the Egyptian line of invasion up the coast and in the Judean Hills where the Arab Legion laid siege to Jerusalem.

Mickey devoted all of his energy and talent to relieving those two fronts. In the Negev Mickey organized a special mechanized unit that fought out of jeeps and armored half-tracks, known as the "Beasts of the Negev." The unit succeeded in halting the Egyptian advance and helped raise the fighting spirit of the Jewish troops. Marcus's greatest challenge, however, was to be in the hills of Jerusalem.

On May 28 the Jewish Quarter in the Old City of Jerusalem surrendered to the Arab Legion. At the same time Arab soldiers succeeded in cutting off the road to the New City of Jerusalem, in effect, putting a stranglehold on eighty-five thousand Jews. Physically isolated but spiritually inseparable from the rest of Israel, Jerusalem held the key to the young state's future. Realizing the need for strong and united leadership, Ben-Gurion appointed David Marcus supreme commander of the Jerusalem front with the rank of "aluf" (Hebrew for general). Marcus became the first Jew since Judah the Maccabee to hold this rank in Israel.

Aluf Marcus knew that his primary objective was to break the Arab siege of Jerusalem but charred armored vehicles lining the road to the Holy City stood as grim reminders of those who had failed in previous attempts. Aware of this, Mickey turned his attention towards finding an alternative route.

In late May three Israeli soldiers on leave descended on foot from Jerusalem to Tel Aviv and discovered an old goat path that ran parallel to the blocked main highway. Marcus began to infiltrate troops and supplies by foot along this trail and speculated that the path might be widened to enable vehicles to pass through. With a United Nations truce days away, Marcus brought in hundreds of laborers from the coast, who began clearing boulders and dynamiting rock sidings. If the road was not completed by June 11 (the day the truce went into effect) no further work would be permitted and Jerusalem would starve. Under Mickey's brilliant leadership the "Burma Road" was completed and on June 9 the first trucks loaded with water, food and supplies entered Jerusalem. There, they were greeted by thousands of the city's grateful citizens. David Marcus had saved Jerusalem.

Sadly, Mickey's heroic life was to have a tragic ending. Several hours before the truce went into effect Mickey was waiting outside his headquarters near Abu Ghosh. On the watch for Arab terrorists, the Jewish sentry challenged the figure in the dark. When Mickey answered in English, the frightened sentry fired a shot killing Marcus instantly. Mickey was the last casualty on the Jerusalem front before the truce began on June 11.

David Marcus, the American Jewish hero of Israel, was buried at West Point's military cemetery with full military honors. He is the only soldier buried there who died fighting for another flag. His unique gravestone is made of Jerusalem stone and carries the inscription "Colonel David Marcus – a soldier for all humanity." At the bottom of the gravestone is a memorial plaque from the Israel Defense Forces. After Mickey's tragic death, Israel's prime minister, David Ben-Gurion, sent Marcus's widow, Emma, a telegram expressing the Jewish nation's debt of gratitude in straightforward, simple words. Ben-Gurion wrote of David Marcus, "He was the best man we had."

ELI COHEN
THE SPY WHO SAVED A NATION

Eli Cohen (1924–1965)

- Early 1960s Israeli espionage agent in Damascus, Syria
- Rose to prominence in Syrian government
- Supplied Israel with vital intelligence that helped it win the 1967 Six-Day War
- 1965 Captured, tortured and executed by Syria

"Against the Arabs you mustn't defend yourself.
You have to attack..."

"I would like to have been like all other children. I would have liked my father to be a simple man and not a hero. Then he would be alive today and I would have a father who lived with us like all the other fathers. I have read everything about my father's life and what he did for our country. I have collected all the books, articles and photographs but I have hesitated to talk about him until now because I know that it still hurts my mother when his name is mentioned. I will now make my vow. I promise you, Father, that in my life I will never fail you. I will do my duty with all my strength and devotion for the Nation of Israel. I will be a faithful son of an admired hero. I will try to be like you, Father. That is my pledge."

With these moving words, thirteen-year-old Shai Cohen concluded his bar mitzvah speech on July 29, 1977. He, along with one hundred other thirteen-year-old boys whose fathers had fallen in Israel's wars, celebrated his bar mitzvah that day at Kfar Chabad near Tel Aviv in Israel. There, every year, a communal bar mitzvah ceremony for Israeli war orphans is held. Twelve years earlier, on May 18, 1965, Shai's father, Eli Cohen, was hanged in Damascus as an Israeli spy. He was one of the greatest heroes in Israel's history and was a spy who saved a nation.

Eli Cohen was born on December 6, 1924, in Alexandria, Egypt, and lived there until he was thirty-two years old. His father emigrated in 1914 from Aleppo, Syria, to Egypt where Eli was born and received a rich Jewish education. As a young boy, he dreamed of being a rabbi and teaching in the local synagogue but he was destined to serve the Jewish people in a different way.

Like many young Jews in Egypt during that period, Eli was active in the local Zionist movement. In 1954 he was contacted by the Mossad, Israel's intelligence organization, and asked to give assistance to an Israeli spy ring operating in Egypt, which Eli willingly did. The Israeli spy ring was caught in 1955 and Eli was also arrested and interrogated by the Egyptian police. Two of the Israelis, Shmuel Azar and Moshe Marzuk, were tortured and subsequently executed but Eli was released for lack of evidence. In 1957 Eli Cohen was expelled from Egypt and made Aliyah to Israel. Two years later he married a beautiful Sephardic woman named Nadia and began to work as an accountant for Hamashbir Hamerkazi (a wholesale supplier), but after several months he was laid off from his job. All this time, without him knowing it, the Mossad had been keeping an eye on him.

Eli Cohen's potential as a Mossad agent was enormous. He had lived all his life in an Arab country and spoke fluent Arabic. He was bright and had rudimentary training in intelligence work from his days in Egypt. The Mossad was in need of an espionage agent to infiltrate the upper echelons of the Syrian army and government and turned to Eli Cohen. Eli accepted the mission and immediately began a year of arduous training with the Mossad. He had to erase his identity as an Egyptian Jew and as an Israeli and adopt a new one as a wealthy Syrian

Moslem businessman. His new name was to be Kamal Amin Tabet and, according to the biography prepared for him by the Mossad, he was born in Beirut to Syrian parents who immigrated to Buenos Aires, Argentina, where there existed a large Syrian community. The plan was for Eli to move to Syria from Argentina with the Syrian connections he had made in Buenos Aires and this meant that he had to learn Spanish as well as the Syrian dialect of Arabic.

In early 1961, he finished his training and arrived in Buenos Aires where he set up a successful import-export business which prospered with the financial help of the Mossad. Soon Eli had influential friends in the Argentinean Syrian community including important members of Syria's ruling Baath Party. They were impressed with the handsome and charismatic Kamal Amin Tabet (Eli) and the patriotic way in which he spoke of his "beloved" Syria. These Syrian VIPs convinced him to return to the "fatherland," telling him that Syria needed loyal sons like him.

In January 1962, Eli arrived in Damascus and went right to work on his dangerous secret mission. He rented an apartment near the Syrian military command and for the next three years transmitted vital information nightly to Israel. (Proximity to Syrian army headquarters in Damascus was dangerous but also gave excellent cover to his nightly radio transmissions which were undetected in the radio-busy neighborhood.)

Using his unique capabilities, Eli befriended leading Syrian army officers and politicians. He invited them to swinging parties at his home and used his new friends to gather important information. When the Syrians planned to divert the waters of the Jordan River so that Israel would be pumped dry, it was Eli Cohen who relayed to the Mossad every detail of their deadly plan. This intelligence data was immediately translated into Israeli military action which on November 13, 1964, destroyed the Syrian diversion project.

Eli discovered and revealed to Israel the precise nature and caliber of all new Soviet weapons received by Damascus, the number of Syrian pilots capable of flying Russian Migs, the exact hour that Syrian pilots ate breakfast and were not sitting battle-ready in their planes, and the precise Syrian order of battle; and he accurately reported and predicted the upheavals and events in Syrian politics. Cohen even sent a letter bomb to Franz Rademacher, a Nazi war criminal living in Syria who had been an assistant to Adolf Eichmann in the Holocaust. Perhaps his most important contribution was the sketching and photographing of the entire Syrian fortifications on the Golan Heights. It was this very data that enabled Israel in the 1967 Six-Day War to conquer the seemingly impregnable Golan Heights and free northern Israel from years of Syrian shelling.

Among Eli's closest friends were the commander of the Syrian forces on the Golan Heights and a Baath political leader he had met in Argentina, Amin al-Hafez, who on March 8, 1963, became Syria's president. Eli was sent by President Hafez on important political missions and there was talk that perhaps one day he would replace Hafez as Syria's president. Eli Cohen, the Israeli spy, was just a heartbeat away from becoming the next president of Syria. No espionage agent has ever risen so far in the ranks of the enemy country he was spying on.

In October 1964, Eli returned to Israel for a short vacation to see his family and to be present at the birth of his son Shaul (Shaul was originally named for Eli's father; he was renamed Shai or "gift" after Eli's execution as he was Eli's last gift to Nadia). He promised his wife, who believed he was working as an arms procurer for the Israeli Ministry of Defense in Europe, that he would make only one more trip abroad. His words would tragically prove to be prophetic. Eli returned for one last time to Syria but, by then, the Syrians knew there was a clever spy working in their midst. In January 1965, using advanced Soviet electronic tracking devices, the Syrians located the elusive spy during one of his transmissions to Israel. They burst into his apartment and were shocked to learn that the spy they were searching for was Kamal Amin Tabet – Eli Cohen.

Eli was arrested and went through months of long interrogations and horrible torture but revealed nothing to his captors. His trial was a farce and at the end he was sentenced to death. On Tuesday, May 18, 1965, Eli was hanged in Damascus before a crowd of over ten thousand. His last words were the "Shema Yisrael" prayer. In a final letter to his beloved wife, Nadia, Eli sent his love and kisses and asked her to remarry and to go on with her life, but she never remarried, remaining faithful to the memory of her late husband.

Sadly, Cohen's remains were never returned to Israel and his family continues to long for the day when they can say "Kaddish" by his grave. Two years after Cohen's execution, the State of Israel was threatened with extinction by the combined armed forces of Syria, Egypt, Jordan and Iraq, but Israel won a lightening victory in what became known as the 1967 Six-Day War. Israeli pilots destroyed most of the Syrian Air Force on the first day of the war at the exact hour Eli had suggested. Israel climbed and liberated the Golan Heights in just two days of fighting despite estimates by western military sources that Israel could not take the strategic heights. It was the information supplied to Israel years earlier by Eli Cohen that enabled Israel to achieve this miraculous victory.

One of Eli's greatest accomplishments in the early 1960s was convincing the Syrian military on the Golan Heights to plant trees around top-secret Syrian gun emplacements and bunkers as camouflage against Israeli attacks. In 1967 these trees were the beacons that led the Israel Defense Forces to their objectives. Israel was saved from annihilation in 1967 by the work of one man – perhaps his nation's greatest hero – Eli Cohen. He was the spy who saved a nation.

Twelve years after his father's execution and ten years after Israel's amazing victory in the 1967 Six-Day War, Shai Cohen would read his bar mitzvah speech to a select crowd at Kfar Chabad – an audience that included newly elected prime minister Menachem Begin. The young boy proved to be no less heroic than his father when he pledged to do everything he could for his people and his country. No nation has ever faced greater threats to its existence than the State of Israel but heroes like Eli Cohen and his son, Shai, ensure that Israel's future is even brighter than its glorious past.

To learn more about Eli Cohen and to sign a petition asking the Syrian government to return Eli's remains to Israel, go to www.elicohen.org.

JACOB BIRNBAUM AND NATAN SHARANSKY
"LET MY PEOPLE GO"

Jacob Birnbaum (1926–)
- Father of movement to liberate Soviet Jewry
- 1964 Founded Student Struggle for Soviet Jewry (SSSJ)

Natan Sharansky (1948–)
- Soviet Jewish refusenik and Prisoner of Zion
- Spent nine years in Soviet gulag (labor camp)
- Feb 11, 1986 Released by Soviets; made Aliyah to Israel
  "Fear no evil."

SHARANSKY

During the 1960s and 1970s, there lived over three million Jews in the Soviet Union, making up one quarter of the world's Jewish population. At that time, the Soviet Union was one of the most powerful empires in world history. It singled out its Jewish population for a state-sponsored war of spiritual and national annihilation. What the Romanov Czars had begun with anti-Semitic laws and pogroms would now be completed with Soviet persecution and oppression.

As a thirteen-year-old Jewish student in 1969, I was cognizant of the suffering of my Soviet Jewish brothers and sisters but could not imagine that one day, the great Soviet Empire would be brought to its knees by proud, courageous Jews on both sides of the Iron Curtain. Yet, in 1989 the Berlin Wall collapsed and two years later, in December 1991, the Soviet Union was dissolved. Three million Soviet Jews were now free and during the 1990s over one million immigrated to their ancestral homeland in Israel, where they now live in freedom and dignity. Two of the greatest heroes in this story are Jacob Birnbaum from Manchester, England, who in 1964 founded the Student Struggle for Soviet Jewry (SSSJ) – perhaps the most successful protest movement in history – and Anatoly (Natan) Sharansky, who became a Soviet prisoner of conscience in 1977 but through determination and persistence won his freedom and moved to Israel in 1986.

Jacob Birnbaum was born in Hamburg, Germany, in 1926. His grandfather, Natan, helped Theodore Herzl organize the first Zionist Congress in Basel in 1897 and even coined the term *Zionism*. Jacob disdained assimilation among Western Jews and was drawn to the Jewish communities of Eastern Europe. Jacob's father moved to London in 1933 and eventually worked for the British government's national censor. In that position he came across scores of letters written by European Jews facing extermination under Hitler, but he was unable to help his dying brothers. Jacob later wrote of his father's work during the Holocaust, "He tried to do what he could but his helplessness seared itself into my soul."

In the 1960s the Soviet Union sought to finish Hitler's work. Jews were denied almost all expressions of national and religious identity. Hundreds of synagogues were shut down and the few that remained open were controlled by the Soviet secret police, the KGB. Jews requesting to immigrate to Israel (called refuseniks) were expelled from universities and jobs, arrested, imprisoned and tortured in Soviet gulags (labor camps). Jacob Birnbaum was determined that helplessness would not be his legacy. In 1964 he turned to the one Jewish community in the world that he felt had the resources and connections to help save Soviet Jewry: the American Jewish community. In the early spring of 1964, Jacob Birnbaum appeared on the campus of Yeshiva University in Manhattan and began knocking on dormitory doors, soliciting help for the noble cause of saving Soviet Jewry. He felt, "New York is the largest center of Jewish life in the world and from New York we can generate pressure on Washington."

On April 27, 1964, Birnbaum convened the founding meeting of the Student Struggle for Soviet Jewry (sssj), comprised of committed student activists from Yeshiva University, Stern College, the Jewish Theological Seminary, Columbia University and Queens College, among others. Many of the sssj's founding members were ashamed of the cowardly silence of their parents' generation in the face of the Holocaust in the 1940s. They were determined that American Jews would be silent no more!

Three days later, on May Day, May 1, 1964, the sssj held its first protest rally in front of the Soviet Mission to the United Nations in Manhattan. Over one thousand students protested for four hours carrying placards with the slogan "Let My people go!" During the rally, the large crowd remained absolutely quiet so as to mirror the enforced silence of their Soviet brethren. A veteran of the u.s. civil rights movement, Glen Richter, joined Birnbaum and became the sssj's national coordinator. Conservative movement rabbi Abraham Joshua Heschel spoke at sssj rallies and supported the movement, lending it legitimacy, although most American Jewish leaders still remained silent on the cause.

A major turning point in the attitude of both Soviet and American Jews was the 1967 Six-Day War in Israel. Jews around the world braced for a second holocaust as Arab nations threatened Israel with destruction. Instead, the tiny Jewish state defeated its murderous neighbors in six miraculous days of fighting, culminating in the liberation of the Old City of Jerusalem and the Kotel (the Western Wall, Judaism's holiest site). Thousands of Soviet Jews were energized by Israel's victory and found the courage to stand up and face the Kremlin. Zionist clubs and groups were organized across the ussr.

One Moscow university student, Yasha Kazakov, courageously wrote a long letter to the Kremlin in 1967, ending it with the statement, "I renounce Soviet citizenship, and I demand to be freed from the humiliation of being considered a citizen of the Union of Soviet Socialist Republics. I demand to be given a possibility of leaving the

Soviet Union."[45] The letter was smuggled out to the West and was published in the *Washington Post*. A few days later, Kazakov was given a visa to Israel, proving that publicity in the West about Soviet Jewry's plight helped their cause.

Shortly afterwards a Jewish engineer from Kiev, Boris Kochubiyevsky, penned his own rebellious words to Soviet officials, stating, "As long as I live, as long as I am capable of feeling, I shall devote all my strength to obtain an exit permit for Israel. And even if you should find it possible to sentence me for this – I shall anyway, if I live long enough to be freed, be prepared even then to make my way even on foot to the homeland of my ancestors."[46] Kochubiyevsky was sentenced to three years in prison and became a "Prisoner of Zion" (the official title the Soviets gave to anyone who promoted Zionism or Jewish culture) in a Soviet gulag.

The sssj could now put a face on the victims of Soviet persecution. Young American Jewish teenagers hung posters of Boris Kochubiyevsky's letter on their bedroom walls. The courage and resolve of Soviet Jews inspired their free brethren around the world to heightened action and commitment. In the ussr, the Jewish holiday of Simchat Torah in particular became a symbol of identification with Judaism, and was used as an occasion for both celebration and protest; thousands of Soviet Jews demonstrated against Soviet persecution in front of synagogues in Moscow and Leningrad. Tens of thousands of Soviet Jews began to study Hebrew and Judaism and many applied for visas to Israel. The Soviet government's response was not uniform. Some Jews were given visas to Israel but others were imprisoned or harassed by kgb agents.

The plight of Soviet Jewry was also brought to the forefront with the publication of Holocaust survivor and Nobel Peace Prize laureate Eli Wiesel's book *The Jews of Silence*.

In December 1970, the Kremlin placed eleven Soviet citizens (nine of them Jews) on trial for attempting to hijack an airplane to

---

45. Quoted in Leonard Schroeter, *The Last Exodus* (Seattle: University of Washington Press, 1979), 90.

46. Ibid., 47.

freedom in Israel. The "Leningrad Trial," as it became known, caused international outcry when two of the defendants were sentenced to death on Christmas Day. The Soviet government was forced to commute the sentences and once again the effectiveness of public protest was proven. The cause of Soviet Jewry began to make the headlines of leading world newspapers. In the early 1970s the Soviets began to allow a few thousand Jews to leave the USSR, hoping to deplete the ranks of the dissident movement. This action had the reverse effect, as the arrival of the "Refuseniks" in Israel energized the Soviet Jewry movement on both sides of the Iron Curtain.

The 1970 Leningrad Trial shocked organized American Jewry and led to the creation in June 1971 of the National Council on Soviet Jewry, which began to organize massive rallies across the USA in the 1970s and '80s. Jacob Birnbaum's SSSJ had become a catalyst for a massive new campaign adopted by the organized American Jewish community. This eventually led to the U.S. Congress passing the Jackson-Vanik Amendment in 1974, tying the Soviet Union's human rights behavior to its attainment of most-favored-nation trading status with the United States. U.S. Senator Henry "Scoop" Jackson from Washington State became one of Jewry's most effective and dedicated proponents. His amendment fit in perfectly with the policies of the Reagan administration, which saw the Soviet Union as an evil empire.

Jacob Birnbaum saw the vindication of his beliefs and remarked, "In one decade I went from knocking on dormitory doors at Yeshiva University to knocking at doors in Congress." On the eve of a summit between U.S. president Ronald Reagan and Soviet premier Mikhail Gorbachev, a mass demonstration was held in Washington, DC, on December 6, 1987, attended by more than 250,000 Jews demanding that the USSR "Let My people go!" The protests of American Jewry and the courage of the Russian Jewish Refuseniks would help bring down both the Iron Curtain and the Soviet Union. The man who, more than any other, symbolized the struggle of Soviet Jews for their freedom and the right to make Aliyah to Israel was Natan Sharansky.

Natan was born Anatoly Borisovich Sharansky on January 20, 1948, in Donetsk, in Soviet Ukraine. He was the son of Jewish parents and graduated from the Moscow Institute of Physics and Technology with a degree in applied mathematics. In 1973, Sharansky applied for a visa to Israel but was refused on the grounds of national security. He then became active in the Soviet human rights movement, working as an English translator for prominent Soviet physicist and dissident Andrei Sakharov. Sharansky became the most famous Soviet Jewish Refusenik and brought worldwide attention to the struggle of Soviet Jewry. In March 1977 he was arrested by the KGB and charged with treason and spying for the United States. He was sentenced by a Soviet kangaroo court to thirteen years of forced labor in a Soviet gulag.

Sharansky spent sixteen months in confinement, at times in a special torture cell, at Moscow's infamous Lefortovo Prison before being transferred to a Siberian gulag called "Perm 35," where he served the next nine years. A childhood chess prodigy, Sharansky kept his mind sharp in prison by playing games of chess in his head. (Later he would beat world chess champion Garry Kasparov in a simultaneous exhibition held in Israel!) Sharansky's imprisonment became a cause of great embarrassment to the Soviet authorities and an international campaign spearheaded by Sharansky's wife Avital eventually bore fruit.

Avital met Anatoly in 1973 outside the Moscow synagogue at a demonstration for Soviet Jewish freedom. The couple fell in love and were married on July 4, 1974, under a huppah in an illegal Jewish religious ceremony. The next day Avital received her visa to Israel but Anatoly was refused his visa. He encouraged her to leave for Israel immediately and promised to join her soon afterwards. Anatoly would not see her for thirteen more years. During that time, Avital left no stone unturned, vigorously campaigning on behalf of her imprisoned husband and all Soviet Jews. She met U.S. presidents, European prime ministers and many celebrities. Eventually the Soviets agreed to release Sharansky on February 11, 1986, in return for two Soviet spies.

Famed for his resistance in the Soviet gulag, Sharansky disobeyed the Soviets until the end. He was released in East Germany and was ordered to walk straight across the Glienicke Bridge to freedom in West Berlin. Instead, Sharansky walked in a zigzag as a final act of defiance. When he reached the border line between East and West Germany on the bridge, he joyfully leaped across to his hard-won freedom. When he finally was reunited with his beloved Avital in Frankfurt, the couple tearfully embraced and Anatoly whispered to her in Hebrew, "*Sliha she'eiharti ketzat* (Sorry, I'm a little late)."

Anatoly Sharansky immigrated to Israel where he adopted the Hebrew given name of Natan. He was greeted by Israeli prime minister Shimon Peres, who declared, "We receive here a great and heroic man, made of unbreakable material, unbreakable spirit."[47] Natan Sharansky immediately traveled to the Kotel in Jerusalem, carrying with him the tiny book of Psalms Avital had given to him back in Russia. The book had served as an amulet through his darkest days in prison. At the Kotel he held the precious book in his hand and offered up the Hebrew prayer, "*Baruch...matir asirim* (Blessed is He Who liberates the imprisoned)."

In Israel, Sharansky founded and became the first president of the Zionist Forum, an umbrella organization dedicated to helping new immigrants in Israel and educating veteran Israelis about absorption issues. He was awarded the U.S. Congressional Gold Medal and, in 2006, President George W. Bush awarded him the Presidential Medal of Freedom. Natan Sharansky helped found the Yisrael B'Aliyah political party and was elected to the Knesset in 1991. From 2002 to 2005 Sharansky served as a cabinet minister in the government of Ariel Sharon but resigned in May 2005 in protest to the ruling Likud Party's decision to withdraw Israeli communities from the Gaza Strip. In 2009, Sharansky was nominated by Prime Minister Benjamin Netanyahu to be the next

---

47. Quoted in Elinor Slater, Robert Slater, *Great Jewish Men* (Middle Village, NY: Jonathan David Publishers, 1996) 292.

head of the Jewish Agency. Natan and Avital live in Jerusalem and have two married daughters.

When Natan Sharansky was sentenced to thirteen years in prison back in 1978, he made the following closing statement to the Soviet court:

> Five years ago, I submitted my application for exit to Israel. Now I am further than ever from my dream. It would seem to be cause for regret. But it is absolutely the other way around. I am happy. I am happy that I lived honorably, at peace with my conscience. I never compromised my soul, even under the threat of death.... For more than two thousand years the Jewish people, my people, have been dispersed. But wherever they are, wherever Jews are found, every year they have repeated, *"Next year in Jerusalem."* Now, when I am further than ever from my people, from my wife, facing many arduous years of imprisonment, I say, turning to my people, *"Next year in Jerusalem."* Now I turn to you, the court, who were required to confirm a predetermined sentence. To you I have nothing to say.[48]

The Soviet Union tried to crush its Jewish community, but Russian Jews, along with their supporters around the world, stood strong and in the end brought the USSR to its knees. Jacob Birnbaum founded a protest movement that helped win a revolution and bring freedom to his Jewish brethren. This year, Natan Sharansky and over one million Jews from the former Soviet Union are free in Jerusalem, in Israel. Jacob Birnbaum and Natan Sharansky, two of the greatest heroes in modern Jewish history, have left their people a legacy of courage and commitment.

48. Quoted in Noam Zion, Barbara Spectre, *A Different Light: The Hanukkah Book of Celebration* (Jerusalem: Devora Publishing, 2000), 54.

AVIGDOR KAHALANI
AND ZVIKA GREENGOLD
HEROES OF YOM KIPPUR

Avigdor Kahalani (1944–)
- Commander of 77th Tank Battalion in 1973 Yom Kippur War
- Stopped Syrian onslaught at battle of the Valley of Tears
- Won Israeli Medal of Valor

Zvika Greengold (1952–)
- Born on Ghetto Fighters' Kibbutz to Holocaust survivors
- Formed and commanded "Force Zvika" during Yom Kippur War
- Won Israeli Medal of Valor for his heroism

"As a boy I had heard much about Zionism, about building my country, and about defending it. Today, I feel I am part of all of these things – as every scar on my body will attest." –Avigdor Kahalani

KAHALANI GREENGOLD

At 1:55 p.m. on Saturday, October 6, 1973, the State of Israel was surprise attacked by the armed forces of Syria and Egypt. The date chosen for the attack was no coincidence. It was Yom Kippur, the holiest day in the Jewish calendar. Over forty thousand Egyptian infantry commandos poured across the Suez Canal, and attacked the mere 450 Israeli soldiers positioned in the fortified bunkers of the Bar Lev Line (Israel's fortified bunkers on the eastern bank of the Suez Canal). Israeli tanks rushing to the aid of their beleaguered comrades along the Suez Canal were picked off by deadly Sagger anti-tank missiles fired by well-trained Egyptian commandos. All but one of the Israeli positions along the canal fell to the Egyptians.

In the Golan Heights things were no less grim. Over fifteen hundred Syrian tanks invaded the Israeli Golan with only 177 Israeli tanks defending. By the end of the first day the Syrians had taken much of the Golan and were within one mile of the Kinneret (Sea of Galilee) and the Jordan River. The situation was so severe on the second day of the war that it was reported that the Israeli minister of defense, the famed eye-patched General Moshe Dayan, told Prime Minister Golda Meir, "This is the end of the Third Temple" – symbolically referring to the State of Israel. The Israeli chief of staff, David "Dado" Elazar, was one of the few to keep his cool and orchestrated the holding battles, organizing the counterattacks that would change the tide of the war. In a press briefing he defiantly promised to break the bones of Israel's enemies.

In the Sinai Desert, one of the largest tank battles in history took place, with over two thousand Egyptian and Israeli tanks engaged. In that battle 264 Egyptian tanks were decimated compared to only ten Israeli tanks knocked out of action. Israeli general Ariel "Arik" Sharon, with an elite force of tanks and infantry, secretly built a pontoon bridge and crossed the Suez Canal into Africa, effectively surrounding and incapacitating the Egyptian Third Army with its over twenty thousand soldiers. The tide also began to turn against the Syrians after forty-eight hours and soon Israel had recaptured all of the Golan Heights and was well on the way to threatening the Syrian capital of Damascus. During the initial three days of battle in the Golan Heights on October 6–9, 1973, many great Jewish heroes performed miraculous acts of courage that helped saved the Jewish state. Perhaps the two most remarkable stories are those of Avigdor Kahalani and Zvika Greengold.

Avigdor Kahalani was born on June 16, 1944, to Yemenite parents in Kerem HaTeimanim (the Yemenite Quarter) of Tel Aviv. His father had immigrated to Israel with his family from Aden in the 1920s and Avigdor grew up in the Israeli city of Nes Ziona. When he was eighteen years old, Kahalani was drafted into the Israel Defense Forces and was assigned to the Armor Corps. In the spring of 1963 he was sent to Israel's "West Point," the Haim Laskov Officer Candidate School (OCS), at Bahad 1 (Bahad is the acronym for *basis hadracha*, meaning "training base"), but shortly after his arrival, Kahalani was removed from the course. His ejection form stated: "Poor familiarity with the subject matter. No command leadership ability. Unfit to be an officer in the IDF." Most likely it was Kahalani's dark skin and Yemenite background that most worried his Ashkenazi (European-background) commanders.

Luckily their mistake in judgment was corrected when Armor Corps Commander David "Dado" Elazar, a Sephardic Jew himself, sent Kahalani to armored officers' training school, skipping over the OCS, with the approval of IDF Chief of Staff Yitzhak Rabin. Kahalani became an exceptional tank commander and officer and during the Six-Day War of 1967 he was awarded the Distinguished Service Medal for his heroism. During one of the battles in Gaza, his tank was hit by Egyptian fire and Kahalani was almost killed. He sustained third-degree burns on 60 percent of his body and ended up in a hospital fighting for his life.

Kahalani warmly remembered a physiotherapist at his hospital burn ward named Jeanette, who tried to motivate the wounded soldiers through painful rehabilitation exercises and even offered to let one soldier touch her body if he would only lift and move his burnt hands. An intense will to survive pulled Kahalani through rehabilitation and against all odds he was soon back in the IDF and eventually rose to be commander of the 77th Battalion, known as Oz 77. (*Oz* is Gematria for 77 but also means "strength" in Hebrew). It was in that role that Avigdor Kahalani entered the Yom Kippur War in 1973.

The Syrians invaded the Golan Heights on Yom Kippur 1973 with 1,650 tanks. Only 177 Israeli tanks were there to hold the line and many were destroyed within the first forty-eight hours of the war. Ninety percent of the Israeli soldiers on the front line with Syria were killed or wounded on those first two days. Avigdor Kahalani's 77th Tank Battalion led the holding battle against the Syrian onslaught for three days and nights of nonstop fighting. By October 9, 1973, Avigdor Kahalani was left with only eight tanks, holding the line at Hermonit in the northern Golan. They had little ammunition left, no food and little water and were totally exhausted.

During the previous night, Kahalani noticed a suspect tank within his unit's formation. Unlike the Syrians, the Israelis had no night-vision scopes and were unable to see in the darkness. Kahalani gave orders to all his tanks to dim their lights and all but the suspect tank responded. Kahalani still thought it might be one of his tanks whose radio had been knocked out. He ordered one of his tanks to put a projector light on the tank next to him and quickly saw his intuition was correct: it was a Syrian tank. Kahalani ordered his gunner to fire. The soldier asked at what range and Kahalani barked, "Zero range – fire!" The gunner moved quickly and efficiently and finished off the enemy tank that had mistakenly joined the Israeli battalion in the confusion of the night.

Suddenly, however, hundreds of fully armed Syrian tanks moved on Hermonit and Kahalani's men realized they were facing suicide. Divisional Commander Rafael Eitan asked Kahalani to hold on for another half hour. Kahalani, realizing that his men were in shock facing the overwhelming enemy force, called out on the radio in code, "All POLICEMAN [77th Battalion] stations – this is POLICEMAN [battalion commander]. Look at how the enemy fights bravely! He takes his positions and looks us in the eye. What about us? What the hell is happening to us? We are stronger than they are! Start advancing! I'm moving forward. OUT." Kahalani rushed forward to retake the ramparts overlooking the valley below.

Inspired by Kahalani's personal example and courage, the Oz 77 tanks joined him and opened fire. They caught the Syrians in the valley and unleashed all they had. When the smoke lifted, over 260 Syrian tanks were left destroyed in the plain that became known as the "Valley of Tears." The remaining Syrian force retreated back into Syria and many of them were picked off by a fresh force of Israeli tanks that had just arrived, led by Yossi Ben-Hanan. Yossi, who flew back to Israel from his honeymoon in Nepal to defend his country, would be wounded and left behind in enemy lines. As Syrian commandos closed in to capture him, he called out on the radio for help. A brave Israeli reconnaissance officer named Yoni Netanyahu rushed into Syrian territory and rescued Ben-Hanan, who later named his daughter Yonit, after the man who saved his life. Netanyahu was wounded in the rescue and was decorated for his bravery. He would later die heroically in the 1976 Entebbe rescue mission. His brother, Benjamin, was elected prime minister of Israel in 1996 and again in 2009. As the battle at the "Valley of Tears" ended, divisional commander Rafael "Raful" Eitan called the soldiers of the 77th Tank Battalion and told them, "You have saved the nation of Israel!"

Later brigade commander Colonel Avigdor "Yanush" Ben-Gal called Kahalani aside and told him that for several days he had kept very sad news from him. The news that he was now sharing was shocking for Kahalani. His beloved brother, Emmanuel, had fallen heroically in battle in the Sinai Desert and his wife's younger brother, Ilan, had been killed while crossing the Suez Canal. Avigdor broke out in tears and rushed home to sit shivah for his brother and brother-in-law.

After the war, Avigdor Kahalani was awarded the Medal of Valor, Israel's highest military decoration, for his supreme courage and leadership in battle. He would rise to become a general in the IDF, a member of Knesset and a cabinet minister from 1996 to 1999. Avigdor Kahalani authored two best-selling books on his life: *The Heights of Courage: A Tank Leader's War on the Golan*, about the Yom Kippur War, and his autobiography, *A Warrior's Way*, both of which have become mandatory reading in military colleges around the world including West Point. Kahalani closes his autobiography with the words, "As a boy, I had heard much about Zionism, about building my country, and about defending it. Today, I feel I am part of all of these things – as every scar on my body will attest."[49]

While Kahalani was earning his scars at Hermonit, Lieutenant Zvika Greengold was fighting for the life of his people and for his own life in the central Golan. Greengold was a kibbutznik from Kibbutz Lohamei HaGhettaot. His parents were Holocaust survivors who had fought the Nazis and taught their son that only a strong Israel could ensure that never again would a holocaust attempt to destroy the Jewish people. In 1973 Zvika was an officer in the Israeli Armor Corps and at the beginning of October he was given a two-week leave from the army in preparation for the company commanders' course. While marking the Yom Kippur holiday on his kibbutz he heard that war had broken out. Zvika grabbed his uniform and hitchhiked up to the Golan Heights HQ of Nafakh where he intended to report for duty.

As he arrived at the base, four Israeli tanks pulled in from the desperate battle – three suffering from enemy hits. Zvika organized new crews and took command of the new unit, reporting that "Force Zvika" was in action. He went into action along the tapline, the Israeli section of the twelve-hundred-mile oil pipeline running from the Persian Gulf across the Golan to Lebanon, and began to knock out Syrian tank after Syrian tank. Each hit was accompanied with the report that, "Force Zvika has knocked out an enemy tank."

Zvika was fighting superior enemy forces that outnumbered him fifty to one. When his radio was knocked out by an enemy shell, Zvika switched tanks and continued to fight, taking out three Syrian tanks. The three Israeli tanks fighting alongside him were all hit, and Zvika was forced to continue the rest of the war on his own in a single tank, which he still called "Force Zvika." A half hour later Zvika ran into a Syrian force of thirty tanks and took out the lead tank from twenty yards away. He played a cat and mouse game with the enemy, popping up from behind hills, blowing away ten Syrian tanks, and fooling them into thinking they

---

49. Avigdor Kahalani, *A Warrior's Way: Israel's Most Decorated Tank Commander Relives His Greatest Battles* (New York: SPI Books, 1994), 423.

were up against a formidable Israeli force. Zvika's tank was then hit by a Syrian shell and burst into flames. Zvika jumped out of the burning tank and rolled around in the dirt putting out the flames. He climbed into another tank and reported, "Force Zvika back into action!"

Meanwhile the Golan HQ at Nafakh was being overrun by Syrian tanks and commandos. An Israeli officer at the base, Lieutenant Colonel Pini, was defending the base but ran out of ammo. A Syrian tank saw him and turned its turret to fire. Lieutenant Colonel Pini prepared to die, when at the last second "Force Zvika" appeared and destroyed the Syrian tank. In the next few hours Zvika blew up ten more Syrian tanks, eventually reaching a kill total of thirty Syrian tanks. By then, Zvika was exhausted, wounded and his clothes were burned. His blonde hair and fair skin were all blackened from burns and wounds.

Zvika pulled back into Nafakh and climbed out of his tank murmuring, "I can't anymore!" and fainted. When he came to, he was in an Israeli hospital ward surrounded by doctors and nurses tending to his wounds. A general at his bedside praised his courage and resolve and wished him a speedy recovery. The general then asked about the rest of "Force Zvika," as HQ had lost connection with them. Zvika apologized and said that his tank was hit and some of his crew was killed. The general responded that he knew about Zvika's tank but that he had lost communications with the rest of the amazing force that had stopped the Syrian onslaught in the central Golan. Zvika said, "General, you don't understand. My lone tank was 'Force Zvika'!" Like Kahalani, Zvika was later awarded the Israeli Medal of Valor.

The Yom Kippur War took place in 1973 when sophistocated weaponry already existed. Yet, what saved Israel in this war was the dedication and sacrifice of individuals. Within the Jewish people, what each and every one of us does affects the path of our history. In 1973 Avigdor Kahalani and Zvika Greengold saved their nation with raw courage and determination. Their heroism will never be forgotten.

❖ ❖ ❖

MORRIS KATZ
LETTER FROM A FALLEN SON

Morris Katz (1952–1973)

- Scottish Jew; made Aliyah to Israel in 1971
- Fought in 1973 Yom Kippur War
- Fell in battle along Suez Canal after writing to family in Scotland

"Only when more people will come here will Israel's future be secure."

"*Yizkor*," the Hebrew word for "remember," is also the name of a set of volumes published by Israel's Ministry of Defense. The books contain the names, photographs and biographies of all the fallen in the ranks of the Israel Defense Forces (IDF, or, in Hebrew, Tzahal) during the wars for Israel's independence and survival. Several volumes have already been published, and sadly, more are being prepared to include the fallen from the recent wars. *Yizkor* is not sold in bookstores but is given to the bereaved families of Israel's war dead. While most of the thousands of names and stories remain unknown to all but a few family members and friends of the fallen, each page of *Yizkor* tells a story of Jewish heroism and sacrifice. It was while glancing through those pages that I came across the story of Morris Katz, of blessed memory. While we share the same last name, we are not directly related, although it was this similarity that first drew my attention to his story.

Morris (Moshe) Katz was born on April 17, 1952, in Edinburgh, Scotland. He was the son of Sylvia and Andre Katz. Morris attended public schools in Edinburgh and was active in the local chapter of Bnei Akiva, a religious-Zionist youth movement. It was in Bnei Akiva that Morris developed his deep love for Torah and Israel. When he finished high school, Morris elected to attend Bnei Akiva's year-long program in Israel located on Kibbutz Lavi. There Morris worked in the fields, toured the length and breadth of the country, studied Torah and spent hours wrestling with questions of Jewish identity and commitment. When the program ended, Morris returned to Scotland and informed his parents that he had decided not to attend the University of Edinburgh, as originally planned, but that he had chosen to make Aliyah to Israel.

Morris arrived in Israel in 1971 and a year later was drafted, as are all Israeli citizens of appropriate age, into Tzahal, the Israel Defense Forces. He volunteered for an elite airborne division of the Nahal, an infantry brigade of the Israel Defense Forces which combines military service with pioneering work on new border settlements. After basic training, Morris attended parachute jump school and then squad-commanders course, graduating as the company's outstanding soldier.

In the summer of 1973, Morris asked the army for permission to visit his parents in Scotland and was told that in October he would be permitted to go on a short leave for the said purpose. His plans had to be postponed when the Yom Kippur War broke out on October 6, 1973. On the holiest day in the Jewish calendar, Israel was surprise attacked by Egypt and Syria. Over eighty thousand Egyptian soldiers poured across the Suez Canal with only 436 Israeli soldiers positioned on the other side in defense. Morris took part in the heroic holding battles on the first days of the war along the Suez Canal but on October 19, 1973, he was killed instantly when his position took a direct hit from an Egyptian

Katyusha rocket. He was buried on Kibbutz Lavi and was survived by his parents and a sister, Sharon.

Shortly before his death, Morris wrote a letter from the Sinai battle-field to his "adopted" father on Kibbutz Lavi, Simha Shulkovski. Morris enclosed in the envelope a second, sealed letter and asked Shulkovski to forward it to his parents in the tragic event that he was killed in the war. When Simha received word of Morris's death, he sent the letter to the Katz family in Scotland. It read:

Dear Mother and Father,

You will be reading this letter only if something has hap-pened to me. I want you to know that I have no regrets about what I have done and if I could live my life again I would choose the same path. I am sorry for what I have done to you, breaking your hearts, but I did what I felt I had to do.

I am proud of what I have done and I know that you are too. The State of Israel needs people and only when more people will come to live here will Israel's future be secure. I hope that all that I have done will convince you and others to come to live in Israel. I want you to know that I love you and that I'm sorry we haven't seen each other since I made Aliyah. For the sake of my sister Sharon, and for your sake and mine, please don't be sad. Be proud, smile and hold your heads up high!

It's strange but I don't know how to end this letter. It's not the type of letter one writes every day and I'm not sure about the etiquette of such letters. Maybe it's better if I don't end it at all! I'll just write: Much Love… Your Son, Morris

Today, few people in Israel or throughout the Jewish world know the name Morris Katz, yet it is anonymous heroes like him who have given us a Jewish state on a silver platter. There are over twenty-two thousand heroic stories like his in the pages of *Yizkor*. It is our hope and prayer that no new pages be added to this encyclopedia of modern Jewish heroism. As Morris requested in his final letter, we should hold our heads up high and be proud Jews. And may his life be an inspiration to us all.

> "Yizkor – may the loyal and valiant heroes of freedom and victory be sealed forever within the heart of Israel." (From the *Yizkor* prayer for the fallen of the Israel Defense Forces)

YONI
A HERO IN WORDS AND DEEDS

Yonatan (Yoni) Netanyahu (1946–1976)
- Israeli soldier and commander of Sayeret Matkal
  (top Israeli commando unit)
- Hero of 1976 Entebbe rescue mission
- Personal letters collected and published in *Self-Portrait of a Hero*
  *"Tzahal is the only thing that stands between us
  and the slaughter of our people as in days gone by."*

"I remembered we stormed in two groups, Yoni's on the right and mine on the left. When I reached the top of the hill, I saw a kind of crevice farther ahead where several Syrians were firing at us. I shouted to Yoni to cover us so we could attack the position but before I could move, Yoni had already taken his men and in a matter of seconds stormed the position. I had nothing left to do but to cover him and the picture I always remember is that of Yoni running ahead of his eight men and destroying the enemy force. When I arrived I saw ten Syrian commandos; they were all dead."[50]

This is how an Israeli army officer remembers one of the decisive battles in the Golan Heights during the 1973 Yom Kippur War. The hero in that battle was Yonatan (Yoni) Netanyahu – a man of both words and deeds.

---

50. Jonathan Netanyahu, *Self-Portrait of a Hero: The Letters of Jonathan Netanyahu, 1963–1976* (New York: Ballantine Books, 1980), 224.

Yoni was born on March 13, 1946, in New York City, where his parents, Benzion and Cela Netanyahu, were working as emissaries of the Zionist movement trying to create a Jewish state in Israel. In 1948 the family returned to their homeland in Israel and Yoni grew up in Jerusalem. Yoni was active in the Israeli scouting movement and in eleventh grade he was elected president of his high school's student council. At the age of seventeen Yoni returned to the United States with his family. His father, a professor of Jewish history, was the editor of the *Encyclopedia Judaica* and came to the United States on sabbatical to teach at Dropsie College in Philadelphia. Yoni lived in the affluent Elkins Park suburb of Philadelphia and studied at Cheltenham High School where he was a classmate of former New York Yankees star Reggie Jackson. In the summer of 1963 Yoni worked as a camp counselor at Camp Young Judea in New Hampshire. It was during this period in his life that Yoni began to write letters to his friends and family back in Israel. We learn much about Yoni's heart and soul from these letters. In one he writes to a friend:

> [...] I live outside Philadelphia. My school has about 1,500 students who don't know what they're doing there. It looks more like the Tel Aviv Sheraton than a school (beautiful even by American standards, brand new, and it cost 6.5 *million* dollars to build). My house is "terribly" nice, surrounded by lawns and trees and empty, meaningless life.
>
> The only thing people talk about is cars and girls. Life revolves around one subject – sex; I think Freud would have found very fertile soil here. Bit by bit I'm becoming convinced I'm living among apes and not human beings.[51]

Perhaps Yoni was a bit harsh on his fellow students but one of his Cheltenham High School classmates told an interviewer: "All we cared about in high school were cars, parties and football games, but Yoni

---

51. Yonatan Netanyahu, *The Letters of Jonathan Netanyahu, the Commander of the Entebbe Rescue Force* (Jerusalem: Gefen Publishing House, 2001), 10.

had broader horizons. We just didn't understand Yoni's depth at the time. So we dismissed him as different."[52]

On his return to Israel, Yoni was drafted into Tzahal (the Israel Defense Forces) where he volunteered for the elite paratroops unit. Yoni became an outstanding soldier and was sent to officers' training school where he graduated at the top of his class. During the 1967 Six-Day War, Yoni took part in several battles in the Sinai and in the Golan Heights and on the last day of the war he was wounded in his arm, while reaching out to help a wounded comrade. He managed to crawl back to the Israeli lines, and upon reaching them, fainted. Yoni was evacuated to a hospital, where he was operated on twice and released from the army as a disabled veteran. His left elbow remained permanently disabled.

Like his father, Yoni was a scholar by nature. He was accepted to Harvard University as a philosophy major and excelled in his studies. It was during this time, however, that the PLO terrorist organization began to carry out murderous terrorist attacks against innocent Jewish civilians. Yoni felt compelled to return to Israel and reenlist in the army. He prayed for the day when he could return to his studies but for now he had to lend a hand in the defense of his people. In a letter to his father, Yoni explained his reasons for leaving his studies at the university and reenlisting in the army:

> I am not at all reconciled to being a civilian. Not only am I restless, but I feel that by continuing with my present way of life I'm being untrue to myself. I have been torn between my desire to go on with my present life and my conviction that my duty to my country, to my people, and above all to myself dictates that I go back to serve in the army. It would be an evasion in the full sense of the word if I went on with my current way of life, an evasion well camouflaged by all kinds of considerations and arguments. Not that these considerations

---

52. "Loner in the Class: Classmate Remembers Hero of Entebbe," *Philadelphia Inquirer*, November 30, 1983, A23.

and arguments are groundless. They may have a solid enough foundation, but to me they don't constitute sufficient reason not to rejoin Zahal. I won't be faithful to myself, and I will betray that inner summons that calls me forward, if I fail to do so. Your argument, Father, that if they needed me they'd call me is wrong. You have no idea how badly Zahal *needs* good officers now. Things have come to such a pass that in the newspapers and even in the cinema newsreels appeals are made for young men to reenlist for active service.

When I talk about this with friends, they all agree that we ought to enlist, but most don't do so. How can I also say that, and yet not do anything about it?!

[...] Zahal is the *only thing* that stands between us and the slaughter of our people as in days gone by. Our state exists and will go on existing as long as we can defend ourselves. I feel that I must lend a hand in this defense *by force* against the Arab states. In two years I'll know where to turn. I hope with all my heart that I'll be able to resume my studies. Perhaps there won't be any need for me to stay in the army. It is essential for us to have educated people in all spheres, and in the future they'll be the ones who will determine the direction of our country; but at this moment, now, the problem is far more fateful. It's a question of life or death, and I opt for life!

I hope you'll understand me. I'm not listing all the reasons that have brought me to this decision. I deliberated hard for months before reaching the conclusion that I must return to the army. It will be hard for you to imagine the sense of relief that came over me when I finally arrived at this decision. I know I'm doing the right thing![53]

Yoni joined the elite Israeli commando unit "Sayeret Matkal" and served there with his two brothers, Benjamin (who would eventually become

---

53. Ibid., 173–74.

Israel's prime minister) and Iddo. He later would become the unit's commander and his missions behind enemy lines remain classified till this
day. On October 6, 1973, Israel was surprise attacked by Egypt and Syria
on the holiest day in the Jewish calendar in what became known as the
Yom Kippur War. Yoni took an active part in the fighting in the Golan
Heights. During a fierce tank battle with the Syrians, an Israeli tank commander, Yossi Ben-Hanan, was wounded behind enemy lines. When Yoni
heard Ben-Hanan's radio call for help he rushed into action, fought Syrian
commandos and rescued the Israeli officer. Netanyahu was awarded the
Israeli Medal of Distinguished Service for this action and Ben-Hanan later
named his daughter, Yonit, in honor of the man who saved his life.

Though Yoni was a hero long before July 4, 1976, it was the raid he
led on that date which brought his name and legend out in the open.

On Sunday, June 27, 1976, an Air France plane en route from Tel
Aviv to Paris was hijacked by a group of PLO terrorists with 256 passengers aboard. On June 28, the plane landed in Entebbe Airport in
Uganda where the terrorists were greeted by Ugandan dictator Idi Amin.
The Christian passengers were freed and the 106 Jewish passengers and
crew aboard were held as hostages. The terrorists demanded the release
of fellow terrorists being held in Israeli jails, or they would kill all the
hostages. When no nation in the world would lift a finger to help these
Jewish hostages, the Israeli government decided to act. On July 4, 1976,
the Israel Defense Forces (Tzahal) mounted the most remarkable rescue
mission in history.

Flying thousands of miles over hostile territory, Israeli commandos
took off from Sharm el-Sheikh, at the southern tip of the Sinai Desert,
heading for Africa in four Hercules transport planes. Yoni's unit was
flown in three of these planes, with the lead plane carrying Yoni and
his initial assault party of twenty-nine men. At the stroke of midnight,
Ugandan time, on July 4, 1976, the first plane landed at Entebbe Airport.
Yoni and his men, driving in a black Mercedes and two Land Rovers,
which were camouflaged to look like Idi Amin's limo and Ugandan
military cars, got off the plane and proceeded to the Old Terminal,

where the hostages were held. A battle developed with the Ugandan soldiers and the Arab terrorists, following which the terrorists in the building were killed and the hostages freed. The hostages say they will never forget the voice of an Israeli officer telling them, "We are Israelis and we've come to take you home!"

During the battle, Yoni was hit in the chest, as he commanded the action, and lay critically wounded outside the main hall where the hostages were held. The efforts of the medical team to revive Yoni were unsuccessful and he died at the entrance to the evacuation plane, as the hostages were being herded aboard. Yoni was the only man of the rescue force to die in the battle. (Three out of the 106 hostages were killed during the exchange of fire and a fourth, seventy-four-year-old Dora Bloch, was later murdered by Idi Amin's men.) Yoni's body was placed inside the plane, which then took off to safety in Kenya. From there it proceeded to Israel. Only a few of the hostages may have realized that the fallen soldier lying at the front of their plane was the commander of the force responsible for saving their lives.

Yoni died as he had lived, at the head of his men, leading by example. He saw himself as an inseparable link in the chain of Jewish history, an heir to the Maccabees and Bar Kokhba. His life was dedicated to ensuring Israel's independence and Jewish freedom. When Yoni was a teenager at Cheltenham High School in Philadelphia, he wrote a letter to a girlfriend back in Israel on the occasion of her sixteenth birthday. He closed that letter with a reflection on life that would prove to be prophetic:

Death – that's the only thing that disturbs me. It doesn't frighten me; it arouses my curiosity. It is a puzzle that I, like many others, have tried to solve without success. I do not fear it because I attribute little value to a life without a purpose. And if I should have to sacrifice my life to attain its goal, I'll do so willingly.[54]

---

54. Ibid., 13.

Yoni lived and sacrificed his life for his ideals and values. He died defending his people and nation and left a legacy that would inspire generations to come. In 1978, just two years after Yoni fell in Entebbe, I made Aliyah to Israel and a dear friend gave me a book of Yoni's personal letters as a going-away gift. The book, entitled *Self-Portrait of a Hero: The Letters of Jonathan Netanyahu*, became the most inspiring book I would ever read in my life. It gave me a window into Yoni's soul and enriched mine beyond description. Lovers of freedom everywhere should make it their second Bible. Yonatan Netanyahu lies at rest now in the National Military Cemetery on Mount Herzl in Jerusalem. His memory and legacy will forever light our way through the darkest nights. He was a hero in his words and, most importantly, in his deeds.

RAFUL AND *THE OC*
MOURNING A MODERN
MACCABEE

Rafael "Raful" Eitan (1929–2004)
- Israeli soldier and eleventh chief of staff of Israel Defense Forces

"If we hadn't stopped the Syrians on the Golan Heights, then the State of Israel would have been destroyed. And do you know who held back the Syrians? You did...the soldiers of this division. All of you! This division saved Israel from defeat, from catastrophe! ...I am not a writer or a poet, but anyone who can understand plain speech can understand the meaning of the words."

On November 23, 2004, Raphael "Raful" Eitan, the eleventh chief of staff of the Israel Defense Forces, was laid to rest after a drowning accident at the port of Ashdod on Israel's coast. That same day, "Seth Cohen," a fictional character on Fox Broadcasting Company's hit TV series that year, *The OC* (Orange County), walked along the California coast and pondered his "world of insecurity and paralyzing self-doubt." These two Jewish role models – the former real and unique and the latter fictional but quite common in the real American Jewish scene – could not have been more different.

"Seth Cohen" was one of the lead characters on *The OC*, Fox network's hit TV series between 2003 and 2007. Seth was described on the network's official website as a "socially awkward, friendless misfit" who was the son of Sandy Cohen, a socially conscious Jewish public defender, and Kirsten, a wealthy "California shiksa goddess." The hit series, which ran in the USA and around the world including in Israel, proved to be the early twenty-first century's answer to *Beverly Hills 90210* and *Melrose Place*. The basic story line was that do-gooder Sandy Cohen brought home from juvenile court one day a tough delinquent with a good heart named Ryan who was then adopted by the family. Seth, the quintessential Jewish dork, was excited to finally have a cool friend and the show followed their exploits together in affluent Orange County, California.

In an episode entitled "The Best Chrismukkah Ever," Seth, wearing a sweater festooned with reindeer, explained to Ryan that he didn't need to choose between the birth of Jesus and the eight days of light because in the Cohen home they celebrated "Chrismukkah"! Seth explained how this combined festival was a "super-holiday" of gifts and presents. In another episode, Ryan, who knew how to fight to protect his honor and often did, promised Mrs. Cohen that he wouldn't get into any more fights. Later in that show, he kept his promise when an altercation broke out and he refused to defend himself. As Ryan lay beat up on the floor, Seth ran over to comfort his "step-brother" and said, "You just got the crap beat out of you and you didn't fight back…now you're a real Cohen!"

Halfway around the world from Newport Beach, in Israel's Jezreel Valley, Raphael Eitan, 75, was laid to rest on November 23, 2004, after he died in a drowning accident at the Port of Ashdod, where he was supervising the building of a new pier. "Raful," as he was known to everyone in Israel, would not have passed Seth Cohen's test for entry into *The OC*'s Cohen clan. Eitan was a fearless fighter and a Hebrew warrior who never doubted the Jewish people's right to a national homeland and dedicated his life to winning and defending Israel's independence.

Raful was born in 1929 on Moshav Tel Adashim in the Jezreel Valley where he was weaned on the love of Zionism and Jewish labor. Throughout his life he remained a farmer rooted in the soil of the Hebrew homeland as well as an accomplished carpenter. At the age of sixteen he joined the Palmach, the elite commando unit of the pre-

Jewish State Haganah underground and fought in Israel's 1948 War of Independence.

It was during the battle of San Simon in May 1948 that Raful learned one of his most important lessons. One hundred twenty Jewish fighters faced thousands of Iraqi and Arab soldiers in a battle that would decide the fate of the New City of Jerusalem and perhaps of the entire Jewish state. Holed up in a Greek monastery, the Palmach fighters lost forty comrades and had sixty wounded in the fierce battle. Unable to evacuate the wounded and facing capture and mutilation in enemy hands, the Palmach soldiers contemplated a Masada-like suicide. However, a fellow officer named Benny Marshak convinced his comrades to fight on with the words, "When it rains, not only you get wet!" Eventually the Arabs broke and retreated and the battle was won, saving the New City of Jerusalem and perhaps all of Israel. Raful learned that whenever you're caught up in a tough battle, the enemy is also having a tough time and whichever side perseveres will win. Perseverance and determination in battle, called *d'veikut* in Hebrew, became Raful's greatest legacy.

In the 1956 Sinai campaign against Egypt, Raful served as a paratroop officer in Tzahal (Israel Defense Forces) and courageously lead the country's only parachute drop into battle. The soldiers who fought under his command said that he was fearless in battle and always led by personal example. Raful, wounded four times in combat, fought bravely in the 1967 Six-Day War and in 1968 led a gutsy commando raid on the Beirut Airport in retaliation for Arab terrorist hijackings. During that attack, Raful is said to have entered a Beirut Airport coffee shop, where he calmly ordered and drank a cup of coffee and paid the bill in Lebanese currency...all in the midst of the battle!

In 1973 during the Yom Kippur War, Raful was divisional commander in the Golan Heights and using the lesson learned at San Simon in 1948 he helped his soldiers persevere and push back the Syrian onslaught. Raful would lead Israeli forces to within twenty-five kilometers of Damascus and he brought Israel victory in a war that, at first, almost saw Israel's destruction. In 1978 Raphael Eitan was appointed the eleventh chief of staff of the Israel Defense Forces and in that capacity directed the controversial 1982 Lebanon War during which Yasser Arafat and thousands of PLO terrorists were ousted from Israel's northern border.

General Eitan believed in strict military discipline yet he had a soft spot in his heart for the underprivileged youth of Israel. He loved his people no less than he loved his homeland! As chief of staff he initiated a special program in Tzahal called Na'arei Raful (Raful's boys), to help these young men enlist in the army and integrate successfully into Israeli society. Raful's home was always open to Israel's youth and today thousands of graduates of Na'arei Raful mourn the death of a fearless warrior whose caring heart gave their lives hope and a brighter future.

After leaving the army, Eitan served in the Israeli Knesset for almost sixteen years as Knesset member, minister of agriculture and deputy prime minister. A man of few words but many deeds, he fought against political and religious corruption in Israel, led the war on drug abuse, lobbied to strengthen the Jewish settlements he felt were vital to Israel's security and demanded that all Israel's citizens serve in the Israel Defense Forces. He quit politics in 1999 and returned to his home in the Jezreel Valley to harvest olives. He became project manager for a new breakwater being built in Ashdod. It was there that he met his death during the stormy weather of November 2004. It is perhaps fitting that no enemy, except nature itself, could ever defeat this fearless Hebrew centurion in battle.

Two thousand years ago, our people faced religious persecution and extinction at the hands of the Seleucid Greeks. Judah the Maccabee, a great Jewish warrior, won our people their freedom and independence back then. We mark that victory every year by celebrating the Festival of Lights known as Chanukah. Judah the Maccabee was a Cohen by family clan but I'm sure he would have been ashamed to meet real-life assimilated Jews like "Seth Cohen," who desecrate our most meaningful traditions and pride themselves on their weakness and cowardice. It has

been proud, strong Jews like Judah the Maccabee and Raphael Eitan
that have always illuminated our people's way and given us true role
models to emulate. When Chanukah comes around next, Jews would
do well to seek inspiration in the light of Jewish heroes like Raful and
not be blinded by the lights of assimilation and *The OC.*

MENACHEM BEGIN
"TO DIE OR TO CONQUER THE MOUNTAIN"

Menachem Begin (1913–1992)
- Commander of Etzel underground that fought for Israel's independence
- 1977 Elected Israel's sixth prime minister
- 1978 Won Nobel Peace Prize for signing peace treaty with Egypt

"You will see in our days the return to Zion and the restoration of Israel."

"We shall fight; every Jew in the homeland will fight. The God of Israel, the Lord of Hosts, will aid us. There will be no retreat. Freedom – or death…. 'The fighting youth will not flinch from tribulation and sacrifice, from blood and suffering. They will not surrender until they have renewed our days as of old, until they have ensured for our people a Homeland, freedom, honour, bread and justice. And if you will give them your aid you will see in our days the Return to Zion and the restoration of Israel."[55]

Speaking these words on February 1, 1944, Menachem Begin, then commander of the underground army Irgun Tzva'i Leumi (known as the Etzel, the Hebrew acronym for National Military Organization), began the Jewish revolt against the British Empire for liberty

---

55. Menachem Begin, *The Revolt* (Tel Aviv: Steimatzky Agency, 1977), 43.

and independence in Eretz Yisrael. This four-year struggle against the might of the British army, reminiscent in many ways of the American Revolution for its freedom from England, ended in victory when the British withdrew from Israel and an independent Jewish state was declared on May 14, 1948.

Leading such a courageous revolt and achieving the two-thousand-year-old dream of Jewish independence would alone have reserved for Menachem Begin an honored place in the annals of Jewish history. Yet this remarkable man, a great leader but always modest, a fighter and a scholar, would eventually be elected Israel's sixth prime minister and in that capacity win the Nobel Peace Prize for signing the historic peace treaty with Egypt in 1979. When Menachem Begin died of a heart attack on March 8, 1992, the Jewish people lost one of its greatest heroes.

Menachem Begin was born on August 16, 1913, in Brisk (now Brest-Litovsk), then part of the Russian Empire. His birth occurred on "Shabbat Nachamu," the first Shabbat after Tisha b'Av. It is customary to read on that Shabbat the Haftorah from Isaiah which begins with the words, "Be comforted, be comforted, my people." While Tisha b'Av commemorates the destruction of the First and Second Jewish Temples and the loss of Jewish sovereignty, "Shabbat Nachamu" has always been an occasion for comfort and Jewish hope. Menachem, the youngest of three children born to Zev Dov and Hassia Begin, was named for that Shabbat and in his heart always carried the hope and desire for the restoration of Jewish independence.

Begin was raised in an enlightened yet religious home where Jewish nationalism was an integral part of Jewish tradition. Zev Dov instilled in his children a fierce Jewish pride that was backed up by action and commitment. Menachem remembered once seeing his father bravely attack Polish anti-Semites who were brutally cutting off the beard of an elderly rabbi. Begin never forgot his father's courage and later said of him, "I have never known a man braver than him.... I shall never forget how my father fought to defend Jewish honor."

The Begin family was forced to flee their home during World War I but returned to Brisk, then part of a new independent Poland, at the end of the war. Menachem attended a Polish high school and excelled in his studies though he never forgot his Jewish identity. Once he received an "F" in Latin for refusing to take a test on Shabbat. In fact, Begin remained a traditional observant Jew throughout his life. He put on tefillin and "davened" (prayed) daily, kept kosher, studied Tanakh and, as prime minister, walked to Anwar Sadat's funeral because it took place on Shabbat. Menachem Begin graduated from high school and enrolled in 1931 in Warsaw University, which four years later granted him a law degree.

It was in the 1930s that Begin became active in the Jewish-Zionist youth movement Betar, founded by Zeev Jabotinsky. The goal of Betar was to prepare Jewish youth for the struggle to create an independent Jewish state in Eretz Yisrael. Jabotinsky warned the Jews of Europe that unless they left the "Galut" (the Jewish Exile or Diaspora) the "Galut" would liquidate them! Sadly, Jabotinsky's prophetic words went unheeded by most European Jews. Begin, however, was moved by Jabotinsky's teachings of Jewish pride and action and eventually, in 1939, became head of Polish Betar, one of the most influential positions of Jewish leadership in pre-Holocaust Europe. Jabotinsky would remain Begin's mentor throughout his life. Begin later wrote of him, "To those of us who were his pupils, he was not only our teacher, but also the bearer of our hope." When Jabotinsky died in 1940, it was Begin who kept that hope aflame among the members of Betar.

At the outset of World War II Menachem Begin encouraged the emigration of thousands of Polish Jews to Israel, yet precisely at that time the British Mandatory government shut the gates to the Jews' "Promised Land." Begin never forgot that as the Nazi Holocaust began, the British were crushing the Jews' last hope for salvation. In 1940 Begin was arrested by the Soviet secret police for his Zionist activities and sent to a Siberian prison. He was forced to endure nine long months in a Soviet gulag, suffering tortures by his Russian captors and anti-Semitic attacks from his Polish cellmates. Throughout this ordeal, which Begin describes in his book *White Nights*, his spirit never broke. Menachem was released from prison in 1941 and eventually made his way to Israel via Iraq in the ranks of the Polish army-in-exile. In Israel he was reunited with his wife, Aliza, whom he had married in 1939. It was also at that time that he sadly learned that both his parents and older brother had been murdered by the Nazis in the Holocaust.

Shortly after his arrival in Israel, Begin was asked to assume command of the Irgun Tzva'i Leumi (Etzel) and in that capacity he led the Jewish underground's struggle for independence. Begin turned the Etzel into a highly organized and effective underground fighting force. He drafted strategy manuals, procured arms and in 1944 declared the Jewish revolt against the British occupation of Israel. The British tried to hunt Begin down and offered a ten-thousand pound reward for his capture, dead or alive. The Etzel commander, however, succeeded in outsmarting the British army and secret police by disguising himself as an Orthodox rabbi and hiding in a secret attic of a modest Tel Aviv apartment. Throughout this ordeal his courageous wife, Aliza, stood ever by his side.

In attempts to crush the Etzel's revolt, the English turned to floggings and even hangings but under Begin's leadership the Jewish underground's determination grew only stronger. Among the most famous of the Etzel's actions were the blowing up of British headquarters located in the King David Hotel in 1946 and the Akko Prison break in 1947, where scores of Jewish underground prisoners were freed from a seemingly impregnable British fortress. These and other Etzel exploits (along with the actions of the much larger Haganah and smaller Lehi underground armies) caused worldwide sensation and dealt serious blows to British prestige. Eventually the British were forced to withdraw from Eretz Yisrael and on May 14, 1948, the independent State of Israel was declared.

Following the establishment of the Jewish State, the various underground armies were merged together forming Tzahal, the Israel Defense Forces. Begin turned to politics, forming the Herut ("Freedom") political party with his former Etzel comrades. Menachem Begin made a major contribution to Israeli democracy by forging his political party into a tough but loyal opposition to Prime Minister David Ben-Gurion's ruling Labor Party. Begin was famous for his brilliant speeches and provided the Israeli Knesset with drama and high standards of parliamentary performance. In May 1967, on the eve of the fateful Six-Day War, Menachem Begin played an instrumental role in creating a national unity government in Israel and served in the cabinet as a minister without portfolio. In times of peace he was a fierce opponent to the ruling Labor Party but during national emergencies Begin's party always joined hands with their rivals in support of the country's welfare and security. Under Begin's leadership, Herut merged with several smaller factions in 1973 creating the Likud Party. On May 17, 1977, the Likud defeated Labor for the first time since the establishment of the State and Menachem Begin became Israel's sixth prime minister.

Upon taking office Begin told the Knesset, "Our main aim is to avert a Middle East war. I appeal to King Hussein, and to Presidents Assad and Sadat, to meet me, either in their capitals or in neutral territory.... Too much Jewish and Arab blood has been shed in this region. Let us put an end to the bloodshed that we [all] abhor." A series of secret meetings was soon organized between Israeli and Egyptian officials and on November 9, 1977, Anwar Sadat answered Begin's challenge and offered to come to Jerusalem to talk peace. Two days later Begin issued the formal invitation and on Saturday night, November 19, President Sadat arrived in Israel to a full state reception. Though Egypt was still technically at war with Israel, Begin stretched out his hand in peace.

Sixteen months of tough negotiations followed between the two countries, eventually leading to the Camp David Accords and the Israeli-Egyptian Peace Treaty signed on the White House lawn in Washington, DC, on March 26, 1979. Begin, the rebel who fought for independence in the 1940s, showed the same determination in struggling for peace in the 1970s. In December 1978, Menachem Begin and Egyptian President Anwar Sadat were jointly awarded the Nobel Peace Prize.

Menachem Begin was a self-taught scholar who spoke nine languages (Hebrew, Yiddish, Polish, Russian, English, German, French, Spanish and Latin). He had a great love for Jewish history and the Tanakh (Hebrew Bible). After his election as prime minister, Begin instituted a weekly Bible-study session at his house, held every Motza'ei Shabbat, attended by rabbis and other Jewish scholars. During one of these meeting in June 1981, Begin spoke about his admiration for Joshua as a military leader. The prime minister, who was also serving concurrently then as defense minister, said that Joshua's success as a general was due to his bold, imaginative and unpredictable strategies.

Just days later, Begin ordered the successful Israeli Air Force bombing of Iraq's Osirak nuclear reactor outside of Baghdad. Though world leaders condemned the Israeli action, Jews in Israel gave thanks to their prime minister for his courageous decision. Today, in the aftermath of the Gulf War, the entire world owes Menachem Begin its gratitude for ensuring that Saddam Hussein was not equipped with nuclear weapons. In retrospect, the rabbis who attended that June 1981 Tanakh study session must have wondered what had been Menachem Begin's inner thoughts when he spoke about Joshua that night. Inspired by such heroes of the past, Begin proved capable of meeting the challenges of his day and ensuring a secure future for his people.

One of Begin's greatest achievements as prime minister was on the domestic front. Menachem Begin will always be remembered as the Israeli leader who helped bridge the social gap between Ashkenazic and Sephardic Jews in Israel. Begin opened the doors of the Israeli establishment to the country's Sephardic Jews, who had felt like second-class citizens under the previous Labor governments. Begin initiated Project Renewal whereby Jewish communities around the world joined Israel's war on poverty and neglect in its poor neighborhoods and towns. While Begin's domestic policies paid off at the polls, his motivation came from a warm Jewish heart and the sincere desire to right an injustice that threatened the fabric of Israeli society.

Once during Begin's administration, the Israeli government discussed raising the prices of basic food commodities such as milk and bread. When Begin came home for lunch, his cleaning maid told him that such price rises would severely hurt the nation's poor, especially large families with many children. That afternoon, Begin returned to his cabinet and ordered the cancellation of the price rises. Begin respected, listened to and cared for the common man and, as with King David, the common people loved him. It should also be remembered that it was Menachem Begin who initiated the movement to rescue Ethiopian Jewry that led to "Operation Moses" and successfully culminated in "Operation Solomon."

Begin was reelected prime minister in June 1981 and his second government was soon forced to confront rising Arab terrorism from Lebanon. Terrorist attacks planned in Lebanon soon hit Israeli and Jewish targets around the world while Katyusha rockets fired from Lebanon rained down on Israeli towns and settlements in the Galilee. In June 1982, Israeli troops invaded Lebanon in "Operation Peace for the Galilee" with the goal of destroying the PLO infrastructure there. Though the 1982 Lebanon War did achieve some of its goals and an Israeli security zone in southern Lebanon ensured years of peace for Israel's Galilee settlements, the price Israel paid was considered by many to be too high. Hundreds of Israeli soldiers fell in battle and many Israelis questioned the conduct of the war. Debate over the Lebanon War caused a great rift in Israel. This and the loss of Israeli lives sorely pained Begin.

In November 1982, Begin was invited to Washington, DC, for top-level talks with President Reagan. The prime minister hesitated in accepting because his beloved wife, Aliza, was very ill, but when her condition improved temporarily, she convinced him to attend the important summit and Begin flew off to the United States. While preparing to address an important gathering in Los Angeles, Menachem Begin was informed of his wife's sudden death. He was not only bereaved by her death, he was pained by the fact that he had not been by her side in her last hours. Less than a year later, On September 15, 1983, a grief-stricken Menachem Begin submitted his resignation as prime minister, many believing the loss of his wife and the high number of Israeli casualties in Lebanon had broken his heart and his spirit to rule the country.

Begin spent his remaining years in seclusion, alone with his thoughts and family, and succumbed to a heart attack at the age of seventy-eight. He was buried on the Mount of Olives in a simple religious funeral with no official ceremony as requested in his will. His funeral, attended by tens of thousands of the common people who loved him, ended with his family and former comrades in arms singing the Betar anthem, which closes with the words "to die or to conquer the mountain!" These words poetically express the values of sacrifice and determination, love of Am Yisrael (the people of Israel) and commitment to Eretz Yisrael (the Land of Israel) that Menachem Begin personified in his life.

NAOMI SHEMER
"...FOR ALL YOUR SONGS"

Naomi Shemer (1930–2004)
- One of Israel's greatest songwriters
- 1967 Wrote "Yerushalayim shel Zahav"
"Jerusalem of gold and of copper and of light, behold,
I am a harp for all of your songs."

Naomi Shemer, one of Israel's greatest songwriters, was born on July 13, 1930, in Kvutzat Kinneret, a small kibbutz by the Sea of Galilee that her parents helped found. Naomi took piano lessons at an early age and proved to be extremely talented. When drafted into the Israel Defense Forces (IDF), she served in a Nahal entertainment troupe. Shemer later continued her music studies at the Rubin Academy of Music and eventually moved to Tel Aviv where in 1956 she wrote the words to the successful musical *Hamesh-Hamesh* (Five-five). At that time she married her first husband, the actor Gideon Shemer, and gave birth to a daughter, Lali. In 1957 she wrote the words for the first show of the highly popular Batzal Yarok troupe.

Naomi Shemer's songs are imbibed with her own love of the land and scenery of Eretz Yisrael (the Land of Israel). In 1960 her song "Hoopa Hey," written for the IDF Central Command entertainment troupe, won "Best Song" at an international song festival held in Italy and in 1963 she wrote her moving ballad "Hurshat HaEkaliptus" (The eucalyptus grove) to mark the jubilee year of her home, Kvutzat Kinneret. In the mid-60s Naomi and her husband got divorced and in 1969 she married an attorney named Mordechai Horowitz, and gave birth to a son, Ariel.

It was an event in May 1967, however, that was to crown Naomi Shemer as the "First Lady of Israeli Song." That year the annual Israel Song Festival took place in Jerusalem in honor of Israel's Independence Day. Each year a song contest was held in which the "Song of the Year" was chosen. The contest used to generate much interest and excitement but as time passed, the Song Festival became boring and was kept going only by inertia. In May 1967 fourteen mediocre songs registered for the contest and Teddy Kollek, mayor of Jerusalem, thought of an idea to rescue the event. He turned to five renowned poets and asked if they would write songs about Jerusalem to be played at the contest's intermission. Shemer's four colleagues were intimidated by the request and refused to take part in the project but Naomi Shemer reluctantly agreed.

Naomi labored diligently in search of a message to share in her song about Jerusalem. Suddenly she remembered a beautiful Talmudic story she had learned in her kibbutz school from two wonderful teachers, Aminadav and Shoshana Yisraeli from Kibbutz Deganya Bet. The story was about Rabbi Akiva, a poor, ignorant man who had fallen in love with Rahel, daughter of Kalba Sabua, the richest Jew in Jerusalem. The couple married to her father's chagrin, and Kalba Sabua disowned his daughter, evicted her from his home and disavowed her from his property. Rahel loved Akiva with all her heart and one day cut off and sold her long, beautiful hair to pay for lessons for him at a yeshiva (Talmudic Academy).

Akiva, who was forty years old, had never studied a day in his life. Using the money that Rahel gave him, Akiva studied at a prestigious yeshiva for twenty-four years and eventually became one of the greatest rabbis in Jewish history. When he finally graduated from the school he had twenty-four thousand students who came to honor him, but he told his students that all that he had accomplished was thanks to his beloved wife, Rahel. It was then that Rabbi Akiva presented Rahel with a priceless token of his gratitude. It was a gold broach shaped like the crown that once adorned the Beit Hamikdash (the Temple) in Jerusalem. The broach, called "Yerushalayim shel Zahav" (Jerusalem of gold) was an expression of Akiva's love for Rahel as well as the couple's love and longing for Jerusalem. The story made a lasting impression on Naomi Shemer and she titled her love song for Jerusalem "Yerushalayim shel Zahav." It read:

> Mountain air as clear as wine and the scent of pine
> Borne on the evening wind with the sound of bells,
> And in the slumber of trees and stone,
>   imprisoned in her dream
> Is the city which dwells alone, a wall within her heart.
>
> Jerusalem of gold, of copper, of light,
> Behold, I am a harp for all of your songs.
>
> But when I come today to sing unto you
>   and bind garlands for you,
> I become smaller than the youngest of your sons
>   or the least of your poets.
> For your name burns the lips like the kiss of a seraph,
>   If I forget thee, O' Jerusalem, that is all of gold.

Naomi spent the night writing the song, which originally had two verses. In the morning she showed her draft to a friend, the entertainer Rivka Michaeli, who asked why the Old City wasn't mentioned. Shemer said that the first verse mentioned "a wall within her heart," which referred to the Kotel. Michaeli replied that her father was born in the Old City, and though exiled from it in 1948 when it was captured by the Jordanians, he dreamed of it every night. Shemer realized that Am Yisrael (the Jewish people) not only loved Jerusalem but longed for it, as if for a lost lover. She added in the second stanza:

How the cisterns dried out, the market square is empty.
None go up to the Temple Mount in the Old City.
Through caves in the rocks the winds howl.
None go down to the Dead Sea by the way of Jericho.

Naomi was now finished writing the song and was asked by Teddy Kollek to find a famous singer to perform it at the festival. Kollek told Shemer that the festival was a big deal and that the song needed to be sung by a big name but Shemer adamantly refused his request. She told the mayor that she had heard an Israeli female soldier named Shuli Natan singing on the radio and felt that the unknown performer could best represent the song's message. Shuli was reluctant to accept the heavy burden of the task but in the end agreed to sing "Yerushalayim shel Zahav" at the intermission of the song festival.

The event was held on May 15, 1967, at Binyanei HaUma (Jerusalem's convention center) and fourteen boring songs were performed that night before the moment for Shuli to appear arrived. Small in stature with long, dark hair, Shuli Natan came on stage alone, dwarfed by her folk guitar, and began to sing. The bright spotlights blinded her and as she finished the song, she waited for the polite applause. None came. Shuli immediately thought that she had failed Naomi and her song of love for Jerusalem, and was about to run off the stage in tears. Suddenly, the spotlights went off and Shuli Natan saw that the entire audience was in tears. Her rendition of Naomi Shemer's song had touched their hearts and souls and when the audience regained its composure, they rose to their feet and gave a standing ovation for eleven minutes.

Teddy Kollek asked Shuli Natan to sing an encore and as she did the entire audience joined in, having instantly memorized the lyrics. In effect, Naomi Shemer had unlocked the feelings bound up inside of the Jewish people's soul for over two thousand years. Israel Defense Forces chief of staff Yitzhak Rabin was in attendance at the festival but had to leave immediately upon learning that Egyptian president Gamal Nassar had closed the Straits of Tiran to Israeli ships – an international act of war.

Naomi Shemer's song gave strength to the soldiers and people of Israel in those days before the 1967 Six-Day War. Her song was played non-stop on the radio and became a second national anthem. (After the war, an Israeli member of Knesset, Uri Avnery, recommended that "Yerushalayim shel Zahav" should replace "Hatikvah" as the national anthem but the motion was rejected. Naomi Shemer was touched by the gesture but remarked that she liked "Hatikvah" and that it was not replaceable!) On June 4, Naomi Shemer drove down to the Negev to sing to the Israeli troops assembled along the border with Egypt. When she arrived, the commander, General Arik Sharon, told Shemer that war was imminent and that she could not sing as the troops had gone on high alert. Shemer felt she had arrived too late and had failed her people, but General Sharon told her that her presence had strengthened the troops and that they were carrying her song with them into battle.

The Six-Day War broke out on Monday, June 5, 1967, and on June 7 Israeli paratroopers broke into the Old City through the Lion's Gate and fought their way to the Kotel. As Israeli soldiers ran down the ancient alleyways, a female soldier suddenly appeared and said, "Soldiers, look up – it's the Kotel!" Jerusalem was free for the first time in two thousand years. IDF chief rabbi Shlomo Goren blew the shofar as the battle-weary paratroopers cried and kissed the holy Wall. Then, all of a sudden, the Israeli soldiers at the Kotel began to sing in their coarse voices a song. It was "Yerushalayim shel Zahav." Naomi Shemer listened to the historic moment live on radio and as the soldiers sang her ballad, tears rolled down her cheeks.

That night Naomi Shemer added a fourth and final stanza to her song, expressing the new, miraculous reality. She told the soldiers before whom she was appearing, "I shall sing for you a stanza I have just added to 'Yerushalayim shel Zahav,' because when I first wrote the song, Jerusalem was just a beautiful dream for all of us, but now it belongs to us!" The new stanza read:

We have returned to the cisterns,
to the market and to the square.
The shofar calls on the Temple Mount in the Old City,
And from the caves in the rocks,
a thousand suns glow again.
We will go down to the Dead Sea by the way of Jericho.

That year "Yerushalayim shel Zahav" was chosen as the "Song of the Year" and Shuli Natan won the "Kinnor David" (David's Harp) Prize as Best Singer in Israel. On Israel's fiftieth jubilee anniversary, "Yerushalayim shel Zahav" was chosen as the best song in Israel's first fifty years.

Even after 1967, Naomi Shemer continued to be the "First Lady of Israeli Song." In 1973 during the Yom Kippur War she penned the song "Lu yehi," an Israeli adaptation of the Beatles' hit "Let It Be." "Lu yehi" became the theme song of the Yom Kippur War and expressed the nation's feelings at the battlefront and home front. Then in 1980, Shemer wrote "Al kol eileh" (All of these) to encourage her recently widowed sister, but the song gained added significance when its line "Al na ta'akor natu'a (Do not uproot that which is planted)" became the slogan for those who were opposed to the evacuation of Yamit and the Sinai settlements.

In 1983, Naomi Shemer was awarded Israel's most prestigious civilian award, the Israel Prize. The judges wrote: "The Israel Prize is awarded to Naomi Shemer for her songs, which everyone sings, because of their poetic and musical merit and the wonderful blend of lyrics and music, and also because they express the emotions of the people." In 1994 the Hebrew University of Jerusalem awarded Shemer an honorary doctorate and in 2001 she received one from Tel Aviv University. Her final piece, *Ilan,* composed just three weeks before her death, was a tribute to Israeli astronaut Colonel Ilan Ramon (1954–2003), who died in the explosion of the space shuttle Columbia on February 1, 2003.

Naomi Shemer died from cancer on June 26, 2004, in Tel Aviv. She was buried at her birthplace, Kvutzat Kinneret, near the grave of the famous Hebrew poetess Rahel. In fulfillment of her last request, the mourners at her funeral gave no eulogies but sang three of her songs instead. After her death, Israeli prime minister Ariel Sharon said, "Using marvelous lyrics and melodies, she succeeded in connecting us to our roots, to our origins, to the beginnings of Zionism. Today, as we bid farewell to Naomi Shemer, we bow our heads with sorrow and are grateful for the wonderful gift Naomi gave us." Naomi Shemer left a legacy in Hebrew poetry and music that will forever touch the Jewish people's hearts and souls. She, like her songs, will never be forgotten.

BRIAN BEBCHICK
THE RED BERET

Brian Bebchick (1972–)
- Born in Bethesda, Maryland
- Made Aliyah to Israel in 1994 and joined
  Israeli Paratroopers Brigade
- Became observant after meeting hesder yeshiva soldiers in IDF
  "If Israel is ever attacked, I'll be there in a second!"

BEBCHICK ON RT WITH AUTHOR

In a medieval crypt at the Belvoir Crusader fortress, Brian Bebchick made his bold declaration. The high school junior from Bethesda, Maryland, announced to his twenty classmates that if Israel was ever attacked and needed volunteers, he would leave his college or job in America and come to the aid of the Jewish homeland. Several of the students in the discussion circle scoffed that Brian was just trying to impress his teacher with his Zionist declaration but Brian retorted that he meant what he said and that one day soon he would fulfill his obligation to Am Yisrael (the people of Israel) by making Aliyah and serving in the Israeli Paratroopers Brigade.

This discussion was one of many that take place with our students at the Alexander Muss High School in Israel (AMHSI), where I have been teaching Jewish history since 1980. The aim of the two-month program is to take American Jewish high school students on a four-thousand-year journey through Jewish history, using historical sites in Israel as their classrooms. Our goal is to strengthen the connection and commitment of young American Jews to the Jewish people, Israel and Jewish tradition. We teach that every individual can make a difference; we present students with stories of heroes and heroines of Jewish history to inspire them to help meet the challenges facing our people today. Many AMHSI students return home to the United States and play important roles in all levels of life and leadership in the American Jewish community. The program is accredited in America by the Middle States Association of Colleges and Schools and has been honored by the president of Israel as an outstanding study experience. The curriculum of this unique program runs chronologically, beginning with Abraham and ending eight weeks later with current events in the modern Jewish state.

Thus, it was in the third week of studies that I traveled with my class to the Belvoir Crusader fortress overlooking the Jordan River Valley. After literally attacking (in simulation, of course) and reconnoitering the fortress, we sat down to discuss the Crusades and their effect on Jewish history. Later we tried to analyze why the Crusaders, representing the might of Christian Europe, were defeated by the Muslims after only one hundred years. Among other important factors, it seems that Christian Europe lost interest in the Crusades and support for the Crusaders waned. I told my class that some modern Arab leaders have viewed Israel as a contemporary Jewish version of the Crusader Kingdom. They are convinced that, like the Crusader Kingdom, so too will the Jewish state fall within a hundred years.

The class played "point-counterpoint." How are we similar to the Crusaders and how do we differ? Do American Jews see Israel as their national, cultural and spiritual homeland or just as a distant, exotic holy land? In times of crisis for Israel, what would American Jews do? It was at this point in the discussion that Brian made his personal avowal.

When the eight-week program ended, Brian returned home and graduated from high school. He enrolled at Brandeis University where he became an activist on behalf of Jewish and Zionist causes. He became a leader of the Sigma Alpha Mu fraternity which, contrary to the *Animal House* stereotype of many college frats, became a hotbed of Jewish activism and commitment. On one occasion the Brandeis *Justice* (the Brandeis college newspaper) published an ad from a neo-Nazi group denying the Holocaust. The *Justice*'s editors felt they had an obligation to freedom of the press. Brian felt he had an obligation to the six million martyrs in the Holocaust and to the Jewish people. Along with some of his frat buddies, Brian confiscated all the copies of the Brandeis *Justice* with the offensive ad, before they were distributed. Brian was suspended from college for his actions but later reinstated after Harvard law professor Alan Dershowitz took up his case.

I next saw Brian on January 20, 1991. It was the fourth day of the Persian Gulf War and the fourth consecutive day of Iraqi Scud missile attacks on Tel Aviv. Israel was empty of tourists and even many Jewish leaders canceled their visits of solidarity. That night there was a knock on my door. There was my former student, Brian Bebchick, with a backpack and an Israeli gas mask slung over his shoulder. "Shalom, Yossi," he said, "I was in the Virgin Islands on college break when I heard that Israel was attacked, so I got on the first plane to Tel Aviv, and here I am! Do you remember what I said in our discussion at Belvoir two years ago? Well, I really meant it! By the way, can I use your phone – I had better call my parents and tell them I'm here."

Brian stayed in Israel for several weeks, volunteering and setting a personal example of courage and commitment that inspired many. My neighbors still recall with fondness and gratitude the young American Jewish hero who came when others faltered.

Brian, meanwhile, had returned to the United States, completed his degree at Brandeis University and in May 1994 made Aliyah to Israel. When drafted into Tzahal (Israel Defense Forces), Brian volunteered for the elite paratroops, dreaming of wearing the coveted silver wings and red beret. After long months of rigorous training, Brian achieved his goal, earning his red beret at the end of a torturous sixty-mile march.

Several weeks later, Brian showed up at the AMHSI campus in Hod Hasharon and asked to speak to me in private. Standing before me in dress uniform, he reminded me that "seven years ago you started me thinking about my connection to Israel and the Jewish people during our discussion at Belvoir. That morning I envisioned myself one day standing in the uniform of the Israeli paratroops. It took me seven years to get to this day and I owe it all to everything I learned at AMHSI. I want to give you my red beret as a token of my appreciation." With tears in my eyes, I told Brian how proud I was of him and thanked him for the most meaningful gift I had ever received.

During his military service in the Israel Defense Forces, Brian met many young modern-Orthodox boys serving in hesder yeshiva units. These boys combine elite combat service with study in their yeshivas and are considered to be among the finest soldiers in the IDF. Brian was so inspired by these young men and their high motivation that he soon became religious himself. Today he is a fully committed Zionist and Jew living in Beit Shemesh, near Jerusalem.

Like most Israelis, I also have served in the Israel Defense Forces and for much of my adult life spent around forty-five days a year in *miluim*, the combat reserves. My unit is called Palsar and is a reconnaissance unit in the Israeli Armor Corps. One year I was called up to reserve duty and traveled to our meeting point at the bus station in the southern Israeli town of Gedera. Suddenly I saw Brian Bebchick approaching the bus stop with his uniform and duffle bag. I asked him what he was doing there and he said he had just finished his regular army service a half year ago and now had his first call-up to the reserves. I quickly grabbed his call-up papers and couldn't believe what my eyes saw: Brian was put into my reserve unit.

For the next several years Brian, my former student, and I did our combat reserve duty together. Once again, Brian had given me a wonderful gift. It was an honor and a pleasure serving with this young hero who has become a dear soul-friend. At the age of forty-five I was honorably discharged from my unit but Brian continues to serve our people and nation. Once he was my student; now he is my teacher and inspiration.

❖   ❖   ❖

ALEX AND ADAM

Alex Singer (1962–1987)
- Made Aliyah to Israel and became combat officer in IDF
- Sept 15, 1987 Fell in battle on his twenty-fifth birthday

Adam Bier (1972–)
- Born in USA; made Aliyah to Israel in 1992
- Served in elite unit of IDF
- Left medical school in 2002 to rejoin his army unit in Operation Protective Shield

"My connection to this country [Israel] is only strengthened as my knowledge of and commitment to Judaism grows."
–Alex Singer

SINGER   BIER

Alex Singer and Adam Bier grew up not far from each other but they never met during their lives. In spite of that fact, Alex was to have a great effect on Adam's life.

Alex Singer was born on September 15, 1962, in White Plains, New York, to Suzanne and Max Singer; he was the second of four sons.[56] (His older brother, Saul, in recent years served as the editor of the *Jerusalem Post*'s editorial page and is the co-author with Dan Senor of *Start-up Nation: The Story of Israel's Economic Miracle* [New York: Twelve, 2009]). In 1973 the family traveled to Israel for a year's sabbatical but ended up staying for four years before returning home to the USA. Alex graduated from Bethesda Chevy Chase High School (BCC) in Maryland and later from Cornell University. During two summers while Alex was in college, he attended the Brandeis Camp Institute (BCI) in California. BCI is an intensive academic learning experience for young American Jews. At BCI Alex became convinced that one of the main goals of Judaism was *tikkun olam* (repairing the world) and decided to dedicate his life to that noble purpose. He spent his junior year of college in England at the London School of Economics and during that year traveled throughout Europe. While visiting in Russia, Italy, Greece and Spain, Alex sought to learn about the Jewish history of those lands and how Jews were living there today. Wherever he went he sketched and painted the places he saw and poured out his thoughts and feelings in a series of letters to family and friends.

Alex completed his senior year at Cornell and summarized the previous year's experience in his thesis entitled "Letters from the Diaspora." While doing so, Alex wrestled with the meaning of his own life and decided he wanted to move to Israel and serve in the Israel Defense Forces. Alex made Aliyah to Israel on December 31, 1984. He loved Israel with all his heart but he did not look at life in his new land with rose-colored glasses. In one of his personal letters from Israel he wrote:

---

56. Biographical information on Alex Singer in this chapter is based on the Alex Singer Project website at http://www.alexsinger.org, and is used by permission of Suzanne Singer.

This country is my home emotionally, religiously, and in every other way except for the location of my family.... I feel more "at home" here than I can describe. This is not an intellectual feeling. It is just the way it is. My connection to this country is only strengthened as my knowledge of and commitment to Judaism grows. Don't read any of the above as blind nationalism. It is not. There are many things about this country which I truly hate (others hate them enough to be driven to leave). I hate the economic idiocy; I hate the way the PLO is allowed to determine the anti-Israeli education of Arab children (this may surprise you but it is true); I hate the fact that members of parliament are exempt from all the disgusting taxes they impose on the rest of us; I hate the way talent is wasted. There is a long list. But, because I see this place as my home, I don't pile the cons on one side of the scale, and the pros on the other, and come to a conclusion about whether it was "worth" staying here. Home is home and it will take more than irritations to force me to leave. I just want to make this place better. Love, Alex[57]

Alex was soon drafted into the Israel Defense Forces (IDF) and volunteered for the elite paratroops infantry unit. He passed their tough selection test and began his eighteen-month mandatory service in February 1985. After completing his basic training, Alex's unit was assigned to protect Israel's northern border. He served on the northern front for several months and then was sent to sergeants' course and, immediately afterwards, Alex was asked to attend officers' training school. He accepted the invitation even though this meant he'd have to extend his army service by a year. In August 1986, while in officers' training school in the Negev, Alex wrote a poem about his feelings as a future officer and about what it meant to him to be a leader. Here is the poem:

---

57. Alex Singer, *Alex: Building a Life; The Story of an American Who Fell Defending Israel* (Jerusalem: Gefen Publishing House, 1996), 222.

Once in a while.
As I progress towards the course's end.
I feel a pang of fear.

Today I felt such fear.

If the war comes
When the war comes
I will have to lead men to die

But those men were not men a short time ago
Some don't even shave yet
And I will have to have the calm power
to yell to them
or to whisper

Kadima.

And,
I will have to have the calm power
to step forward myself.

Alex completed officers' training school in October 1986 and was
assigned to be an infantry instructor in the Israeli Air Force. Singer,
however, felt unfulfilled in his new position and actively started looking
for the opportunity to lead an infantry platoon. In May 1987 he got his
chance in the Givati Brigade and in August 1987 he was moved with
his new platoon to the Lebanese border next to the security zone in
southern Lebanon. In mid-September of that year, intelligence reports
were received by the IDF pointing to a planned Arab terrorist attack on
Israeli settlements along the Lebanese border. Alex's unit was sent to
stop the terrorists and protect Israel's citizens from the attack.

On September 15, Alex's twenty-fifth birthday, he and eleven other
men were dropped by helicopters onto a rugged ridge in the foothills
of Mount Hermon, about a mile into Lebanon. Their mission was to set

up an ambush and to try to intercept the Arab terrorists on their way into Israel. Alex's commander, Ronen Weissman, landed on the first helicopter, while Alex's unit came on the second chopper. Unexpectedly, the first group landed among about thirty Arab terrorists who had hidden themselves behind some of the Hermon's huge boulders. Ronen was shot and killed by the terrorists. Alex, who was second in command, was told that Ronen was not answering the radio and was given the option, on the second helicopter, to delay the mission. Alex chose to land under heavy fire, took a medic and went to help Ronen.

When Alex reached his fallen commander, he too was shot and killed. Some time later, not knowing what had happened to the two commanders, another soldier from the platoon, Oren Kamil, was sent to help them. He too was hit by enemy gunfire and fell at the same spot. Outnumbered, and without their officers, the remainder of the small Israeli force continued to return fire until reinforcements arrived. Eventually the terrorists retreated, unable to complete their mission of attacking civilian settlements in Israel.

Alex was buried on September 18, 1987, in the National Military Cemetery on Mount Herzl in Jerusalem. Thirty days later there was a memorial program for Alex at the Embassy of Israel in Washington. Family and friends read from Alex's letters and journals and some spoke of their memories of him. Saul read a letter he had written to his dead brother that expressed one of Alex's lasting messages to us all. In it, Saul said: "Your message to me is one word. 'Do.' Do as you believe and people will follow you. Do not just know what is right, do what is right. Only then will other people follow you. Only then will you have the power to affect the world."

After his death, Alex's family published a moving book of his personal letters, poems and drawings entitled *Alex: Building a Life; The Story of an American Who Fell Defending Israel.* It is a book that should be read by every Jew.

I made Aliyah to Israel in 1978 and after serving in the Israeli army, I began to work as a Jewish educator at the Alexander Muss High School in Israel (AMHSI) in Hod Hasharon. Our school teaches four thousand years of Jewish history while traveling to the sites of the actual events. Over the years I have taught thousands of wonderful young students but one of the most special was a young man named Adam Bier from Bethesda, Maryland. Adam's dad is a prominent DC physician and an ardent Zionist who had previously tried unsuccessfully to get his son to go to Israel on a high school educational program.

As previously mentioned, Alex Singer fell heroically in battle on his twenty-fifth birthday on September 15, 1987. According to Israeli army protocol, a delegation from the Israeli embassy in Washington was sent to inform Alex's family in DC of the tragic news. The Israeli military attaché at the embassy, General Amos Yaron, was entrusted with this sensitive task and brought a physician along in case of any possible emergency. The physician was Dr. Charles Bier, Adam's father. One month later a memorial service was held at the Israeli embassy in DC and Benjamin Netanyahu, who had lost his brother, Yoni Netanyahu, during the 1976 Entebbe rescue mission, gave one of the eulogies for Alex. Dr. Bier brought his son Adam to the memorial ceremony and Adam was so touched by Alex's story that he chose to come in 1989 to the Alexander Muss High School in Israel where I was privileged to be his teacher.

During the two-month session, one of our class debates focused on the question of whether the students would choose to come to Israel if the country was imperiled and needed volunteers. Most of the students said they would not leave college to come help, but Adam said that if Israel ever needed him he would be there. This was not just a worthless emotional promise to impress his teacher; Adam would one day soon prove his intentions. Bier would later write his teacher that his experience at AMHSI had changed the course of his life and he now felt he had an obligation to serve his people and homeland Israel. Adam attended the Hebrew University in Jerusalem and Boston University and in 1992 made Aliyah to Israel.

Adam was drafted into the Israel Defense Forces (Tzahal) and served with distinction in an elite unit. When injured during training, Adam was honorably discharged but refused to leave the army and underwent a painful operation and physical therapy. He fought the army's medical bureaucracy and was finally reinstated in an elite commando unit of Tzahal. The heroism of Adam and his comrades was recognized several years ago when they were awarded a citation from the Israeli chief of staff for their bravery and contribution to Israel's security. Upon completing his service, Adam was accepted into medical school at Dartmouth University. When Operation Protective Shield began in March 2002, Adam took a leave of absence from medical school and decided to fly back to Israel to rejoin his unit. When asked why he was making this sacrifice, Adam replied, "I couldn't sit back and study anatomy and watch while terrorists try to dissect our nation." Adam said that all his friends back in Israel were being called up and it was time for him to come home and fight for his people.

Alex and Adam have made this world a better place through their ideals and actions. Alex gave his life for Israel and Adam continues to live his life for it.

ILAN RAMON
A SYMBOL IN SPACE

Ilan Ramon (1954–2003)

- Israeli fighter pilot; took part in bombing of Osirak nuclear reactor in Baghdad
- 2003 First Israeli astronaut to take part in NASA space shuttle mission
- February 1, 2003 Space shuttle exploded on reentry to Earth's atmosphere

"I am kind of proof for my parents and their generation that whatever we've been fighting for in the last century is becoming true."

Ilan Ramon was born on June 20, 1954, in Tel Aviv to Tova and Eliezer Wolferman. His father, Eliezer, fought in Israel's War of Independence and his mother, Tova, was a survivor of Auschwitz. Tova's father, Ilan's grandfather, was murdered in the Holocaust along with much of his family. Ilan grew up in Beer Sheva and graduated at the top of his high school class. In 1972 he was drafted into the Israel Defense Forces and volunteered for flight school. Ilan was an outstanding pilot and not only completed the course but graduated number one in his class. He fought for Israel in the 1973 Yom Kippur War as well as in the 1982 Lebanon War. Ramon accumulated over four thousand flight hours on fighter aircraft, including over a thousand hours on the coveted F-16.

In 1981 the State of Israel faced an existential threat from Saddam Hussein's Iraq, which was in advanced stages of developing nuclear weapons. Israeli prime minister Menachem Begin made a courageous decision to bomb Iraq's Osirak nuclear reactor near Baghdad. Eight Israeli pilots flew the long, dangerous journey to Iraq and successfully completed their mission destroying the nuclear reactor. The pilots flew much of the mission tightly bunched together so as to fool the Iraqi radar operators into thinking they were seeing a large commercial airliner and not eight Israeli fighter aircraft. The youngest pilot among the eight was Ilan Ramon.

In 1987 Ilan Ramon graduated from the University of Tel Aviv with a BS degree in electronics and computers. He married Rona, a bright Sephardic woman, and the couple had four children: Asaf, David, Tal and Noa. Ilan was modest, unassuming, shy and polite. He was a real gentleman with an air of intelligence and dignity and lots of charisma.

On December 11, 1995, U.S. president Bill Clinton announced that an Israeli astronaut would be chosen to join an upcoming NASA space shuttle mission as an expression of American and Israeli strategic cooperation. Ilan Ramon was selected from an elite list of Israeli fighter pilots and in 1998 Israel's first astronaut reported for duty to the Johnson Space Center in Houston, Texas. Ilan became very involved with the local Jewish community, attending Shabbat services at a Houston Conservative synagogue and making frequent speaking engagements at the local Jewish day school.

On January 16, 2003, Ilan Ramon blasted off on the space shuttle Columbia as a payload specialist for a sixteen-day journey with six other astronauts. Ramon, though not religious, took his mission representing Israel and the Jewish people very seriously. Though previously six Jewish astronauts had flown into space (Judy Resnick, Jeff Hoffman, Ellen Biker, Jay Apt, David Wolf and Scott Horowitz), Ilan Ramon became the first astronaut to request and receive kosher food. As the space shuttle flew over Jerusalem, Ilan Ramon said the "Shema Yisrael" prayer in

Hebrew and on Friday night he made Kiddush in outer space with a special Kiddush cup he had brought along on his mission.

Ramon remarked, "I think that the people of Israel, and the Jewish people as a whole, are a wonderful people, and we have to maintain our Jewish heritage. I think it is very, very important to preserve our historical and religious traditions."[58]

Ilan Ramon understood the spiritual significance of his mission in space and carried a number of symbolic items with him on the space shuttle, such as a copy of Israel's Declaration of Independence and a microfiche copy of the Tanakh along with an Israeli Air Force flag. Ramon's mother and grandmother were both liberated from the Auschwitz concentration camp on January 27, 1945. Ilan saw special significance in being the son and grandson of Holocaust survivors. He once said, "I know my flight is very symbolic for the people of Israel, especially the survivors, the Holocaust survivors, because I was born in Israel, [and] many will see this as a dream that is come true. I am kind of proof for my parents and their generation that whatever we've been fighting for in the last century is becoming true."[59]

Ramon also took three items relating to the Holocaust with him on his journey into outer space. The first was a mezuzah made by Aimee Golant, a famous artist and the granddaughter of Holocaust survivors. The mezuzah was decorated with a Jewish star surrounded by barbed wire from a Nazi concentration camp. Ilan also took a miniature Torah scroll that had an amazing story itself. The scroll was smuggled into Bergen-Belsen concentration camp by a Dutch rabbi who gave it as a gift to a thirteen-year-old Jewish boy from Amsterdam named Joachim Yosef. Yosef was an inmate at Bergen-Belsen with the rabbi, who secretly prepared him for and carried out his bar mitzvah in the Nazi camp at four in the morning one day in 1944. The rabbi told Yosef, "Take this

---

58. Quoted in Alan Abbey, "An Israeli Journey to Jewishness," *Jerusalem Post*, Rosh Hashana 5764 Supplement.

59. Quoted in "Israeli Astronaut Carried Nation's Dreams," *BBC News World Edition*, February 1, 2003.

Torah scroll. I will not leave here alive but promise me you'll tell this story one day!"

The rabbi was later murdered by the Nazis but Joachim Yosef survived the Holocaust, moved to Israel at the end of the war and fought in Israel's War of Independence. Yosef later became a distinguished professor of planetary physics and was given responsibility over some experiments to be carried out by the Columbia space shuttle. In preparation for the experiments, Professor Yosef met Ilan Ramon and told him his personal story and about the miniature Torah. Ramon cried as he heard the moving tale and offered to carry the Torah in the space shuttle as a symbolic gesture of the triumph of the Jewish people over the Nazis. Ramon said of the Torah, "This represents more than anything the ability of the Jewish people to survive despite everything we faced during that terrible period."

Ilan Ramon also carried with him on the space shuttle a replica of a small pencil drawing made by a fourteen-year-old Czech-Jewish boy named Peter Ginz. During the Holocaust, Ginz was thrown by the Nazis into the Theresienstadt ghetto near Prague. There he secretly organized other young Jews and published an underground magazine named *Vedem*. Peter was intelligent and creative and along with his young followers, painted, sketched and wrote about all they experienced under the Nazis. Peter's drawing "Moon Landscape" depicted a view of Earth from the moon, perhaps expressing his desire to leave the planet where his people were being murdered. On September 28, 1944, Peter Ginz was deported to Auschwitz where he was murdered by the Nazis. Ramon felt that by carrying the sketch into space, he would honor Peter's memory and help the Jewish people to rise out of the ashes to new heights.

During the space shuttle's journey, each astronaut was awakened once by his or her spouse playing their favorite song over the NASA communications network with the shuttle. Rona Ramon was told that her turn would be on the mission's second morning and she chose to awaken Ilan with their favorite song, "Zemer nugeh" (A sorrowful song) by Israel's famous poetess Rahel. "Zemer nugeh" became the first

Hebrew song ever broadcast into outer space and on Israel's sixtieth anniversary, it was voted the best song in Israel's history. The poem is a song of love and longing and its words would prove to be tragically prophetic. They read:

> Do you hear my voice, my distant one?
> Do you hear my voice from where you are?
> My voice calls out in strength.
> My voice weeps in tears,
> Transcending time, commanding a blessing.
>
> The world is vast with many roads.
> Our meetings are fleeting,
> But our parting is forever.
> People seek to find what they have lost,
> But their feet always stumble.
>
> My last days are perhaps approaching
> With tears of separation
> I will wait for you till I die.
> As Rahel waited for her lover (Jacob).

It would be the last time the couple would listen to their favorite song. On February 1, 2003, the Columbia space shuttle began its reentry into the Earth's atmosphere but due to a technical failure, the space shuttle exploded instantly, killing all seven astronauts. Their remains were found scattered for miles over Texas and Louisiana; on February 10, 2003, Ilan Ramon was laid to rest in Israel's Jezreel Valley at Moshav Nahalal. Not long afterwards the Israeli Air Force flag he carried with him on his space mission was found unscathed among the shuttle's remains. Like the Jewish people, it had survived fiery trials and tribulation. Ilan Ramon, the hero who carried this symbol in space, will never be forgotten.

DAVID SPRUNG
"PROUD, GENEROUS AND FIERCE"

David Sprung (1943–)
- Early 1960s Commander of Betar youth movement in USA
- Made Aliyah and fought in 1967 Six-Day War
- Jewish educator and martial arts expert

"We all long for peace but as long as our enemies
seek our destruction we need to be strong and on guard."

Betar –
From the pit of dust and decay
With blood and sweat
A new generation will arise
Proud, generous and fierce…

Zeev Jabotinsky, the great Zionist leader and visionary, wrote the above lines in 1932 as the opening verse to his epic Betar Anthem. Betar, the militant Zionist youth movement founded by Jabotinsky in 1923, sought to create a new generation of Jews who would win the Jewish people their freedom and independence in their ancient homeland of Israel. The movement's name, Betar, has a dual symbolic meaning, referring both to the last fortress of the great Jewish general Shimon Bar Kokhba, which fell to the Romans in 135 CE; and as an acronym for *Brit Trumpeldor*, honoring Yosef Trumpeldor, the one-armed Jewish hero who was killed by Arab marauders while defending the Zionist pioneer settlement of Tel Chai in 1920. Jabotinsky saw in Bar Kokhba and Trumpeldor the perfect role models for young Betarim (Betar members) in his quest to build a new generation that would be "proud, generous and fierce."

Zeev Jabotinsky's pupils would one day help lead the Jewish

185

people out of the darkness of the ghettos into the light of freedom but, sadly, Jabotinsky would not live to see that day. Exiled from Israel by the British, he died in 1940 at a Betar training camp in the Catskill Mountains and was buried in Long Island. In 1964, at the orders of the Israeli government, Jabotinsky's body was reinterred on Mount Herzl in Jerusalem. The head of the honor guard for that ceremony was the young commander of Betar in the USA, David Sprung. Sprung, today a Jewish educator and a colleague of mine at the Alexander Muss High School in Israel, embodies all the highest ideals and values that Jabotinsky sought to inculcate in Jewish youth. He is an unsung hero of modern Jewish history and it's his story that I unfold below.

David Sprung was born on March 14, 1943, in Havana, Cuba – the son of Belgian Jews who fled from Hitler in the 1930s. Sprung's grandmother was saved from the Nazis because her two sons-in-law were famous soccer players in Belgium but, sadly, most of his family was murdered in the Holocaust. Though born in Cuba, David grew up in Manhattan near Spanish Harlem and was a champion stickball player. The Puerto Rican girls in "the hood" loved this handsome tough guy and called him "Manolito," until they saw their idol one day with a *kippah* on his head heading off to shul. As a kid, David attended a Jewish summer camp in the Catskills where he and his childhood friend, Reuven Genn, put on wrestling and martial arts exhibitions. The other campers were awed by the site of two tough Jews who could stand up and fight.

In the '50s Sprung was even accepted as the only Jewish member of the Italian street gang "The Black Diamond Joes." Sprung attended an ultra-Orthodox yeshiva in the Lower East Side and when he stirred up trouble there, his rabbi smiled and retorted, "You think you're tough; I once taught Louis Lepke!!" (Lepke was head of Murder Inc. and perhaps the most feared gangster in America in the '30s and '40s) As a teen, David joined the Betar youth movement and in 1965 become the group's national commander. It was in those days that David gathered around him hundreds of young Betarim and infused them with Jabotinsky's principals of *Hadar* and *Tagar*.

Hadar stands for Jewish pride and self-dignity, which every Betari and Jew should possess. Jabotinsky wrote in the Betar Anthem:

Hadar – Even in poverty, every Jew is a prince…wearing the crown of King David.

Tagar means "challenge" and calls on Betarim to stand up and meet every challenge facing our people, no matter what the obstacle. Jabotinsky wrote in the anthem:

Silence is filth! For the sake of the hidden glory, give up blood and soul! To die or to conquer the mountain!

David Sprung embodies all these ideals. He walks tall with Jewish pride and strength and yet always treats people with politeness and dignity. While young Americans protested the war in Vietnam during the '60s, David Sprung led an activist campaign for Jewish causes: fighting neo-Nazis like George Lincoln Rockwell, struggling to free Soviet Jews and standing up for the embattled Jewish State of Israel.

Once David was taking his mostly Orthodox Betarim on a holiday Lag b'Omer picnic across the George Washington Bridge when they were attacked by an anti-Semitic motorcycle gang who thought the religious Jewish boys were easy prey. David never lost his cool and ordered, "Betarim – remember Tel Chai! Attack!" The motorcycle gang panicked as blackjack-wielding Jews ran forward to meet their enemy. The Betarim actually knocked two of the gangsters off their motorbikes and held them, with their lives in the balance, over the bridge. David was always ready to defend the Jewish people and its honor. During these years David also bravely helped bring justice to Nazi war criminals around the world….but that story is best served by silence.

David Sprung made Aliyah (immigrated) to Israel in 1966 and joined the Nahal, an elite combat unit of the Israeli army. While on active combat duty in Israel, he read in November 1966 that eighteen of his Betarim had taken over the Syrian Mission to the United Nations in protest of that body's refusal to discuss Syrian bombing of Israel from the Golan Heights. David was so proud of his Betarim, who refused to remain silent in the face of challenge. The story made the front page of the *New York Times* and forced the UN to discuss Israel's plight, but an Israeli newspaper editor called the American Betarim "hooligans" and said if they were real Zionists, they'd move to Israel. When the Six-Day War broke out on June 5, 1967, these eighteen Betarim from New York were the first volunteers to arrive in Israel and the same Israeli editor publicly apologized to these young heroes…most of whom ended up staying in Israel permanently.

Shortly before the war, David proposed to his Israeli sweetheart and even suggested holding a military wedding on the Jordanian border to show the world that Jews could not be frightened by the Arab terror being waged in those days. Fate, however, intervened and the Six-Day War broke out before the wedding could be arranged. During the war, David fought bravely against the Jordanian Legion as a heavy machine gunner. As missiles and shells fell all around him, he called out to God and said, "God in Heaven – it's ok if I die in this war but please, before I die, let me at least know that our people will be victorious." This is the prayer of an unselfish patriot. Luckily, David survived the intense battles and was even privileged to be among the Israeli soldiers who reached the Kotel on June 7, 1967. Sprung said, "If I live another thousand years, I'll never know again the emotions I felt that day. The last Jew to experience such a moment was Judah the Maccabee two thousand years ago. How privileged I am to merit such an honor as this!"

Since the Six-Day War David Sprung has led a multifaceted life. He raised three proud sons on a farm in Binyamina where he grew grapes for Carmel-Mizrachi wines. He served as a physical education teacher (he holds an MA in the subject!) in a high school, as a detective and criminal investigator in the Israeli police department, as a tour director in Europe, as a pistol instructor at a gun range, as a Muay Thai boxing coach and martial-arts expert, as an attack-dog handler, and as an Israeli emissary to both Australia and Argentina. While in Argentina the ruling junta of fascist generals murdered many Jews. David trained local Jewish youth in self-defense but eventually, due to his work, had to flee the country.

In 2009 David Sprung celebrated his sixty-sixth birthday, but he looks at least twenty years younger. Though he is the quintessential man of iron and steel and rock, David is really a kind, gentle spirit at heart and is actually even shy. As a hobby he studies the flowers of Israel and even grows medicinal herbs in his backyard. After he got divorced from his first wife, he met his new soulmate a few years ago, a lovely divorcee named Galia. The two moved in together and though the unofficial arrangement was fine for both, David surprised Galia on her birthday by proposing marriage to her. It seems that beyond his iron muscles lies a sweet, romantic heart.

Regarding religion, David claims he is an atheist, though one suspects he is just wrestling with God and, after all, that is the true definition of "Israel." In any event, he puts on Tefillin every day and loves Hasidic music. The place that, perhaps, gives the most introspective view of David Sprung is the National Military Cemetery in Jerusalem, where he always takes his students on their last day in Israel. Standing beside the graves of heroes like Zeev Jabotinsky, Hannah Senesh and Yoni Netanyahu, David shares the stories of those who gave us our state on a "silver platter."

His final stop is by the grave of Eli Michael Solomon, who fell heroically in the 1973 Yom Kippur War. David tells his students, "I could stop in military cemeteries from Metulla to the Negev and in each and every one are the graves of comrades who fell defending our country, but this is the grave of one of my dearest friends, Eli Solomon. Eli was a Betari of mine in New York and followed in my footsteps and made Aliyah to Israel. During the Yom Kippur War in 1973 he gave his life to save one of his fellow soldiers. When I learned of his death I was devastated. Eli was married to Rena, another Betari of mine, and had two young daughters."

Suddenly, as David shares this very personal story, his voice chokes up and his eyes begin to tear. He tells his students that nothing is more

painful than losing a best friend and that every Israeli has lost a best
friend, a father, a brother or a husband in war. "None of us wants war,"
Sprung tells his students, and "the debate in Israel is not between the
peace camp and those who want war but between different Jews on
how to bring peace. We all long for and pray for peace but as long as
our enemies seek our destruction we need to be strong and on guard."
David stands ready even today.

In 1987 David Sprung was brought into my classroom at the
Alexander Muss High School in Israel (AMHSI) where I teach Jewish
history. The principal back then, Baruch Kraus, said that David had
been his commander in Betar in the '60s back in New York and that
when he heard that David was looking for a job, he asked him to try
Jewish education and come work at our school. Baruch said that David
was a natural Jewish educator and that he thought we'd get along nicely.
Nothing could have been more of an understatement. Since 1987, David
has been my colleague, my mentor and my best friend. He is the finest
Jewish educator I know.

David Sprung has inspired thousands of young American Jews
with his passionate teaching of Jewish history; he makes it come alive
and inspires his students to not only remember the past but to take
responsibility for the present and build our people's future. His students
will never forget descending Mount Gilboa with King Saul or climbing Masada with Elazar Ben-Yair, or crawling through caves with Bar
Kokhba and Rabbi Akiva, or standing in the gallows room with Dov
Gruner at Akko Prison. Most of all, they will never forget meeting this
unsung Jewish hero who is "proud and generous and fierce," a man
who embodies dignity and pride and is always ready to stand up and
fight for his people. More than David has taught his students history,
he has inspired them to make it. Zeev Jabotinsky would be proud to
know that the Jew he sought to create lives in the heart and soul of
David Sprung.

❖   ❖   ❖

ROI KLEIN
"SHEMA YISRAEL" AND
THE LEGACY OF RABBI AKIVA

Roi Klein (1975–2006)
- Deputy battalion commander of Golani Infantry Brigade
- Dived on a grenade in 2006 Second Lebanon War, saving his soldiers
- Shouted "Shema Yisrael" prayer before he died in explosion
  "Hear, O Israel, the Lord our God,
  the Lord is One!"

In the year 132 CE the great Jewish general Shimon Bar Kokhba led a three-year revolt for Jewish freedom against the mighty Roman Empire. While the immediate causes of the revolt were the Romans' outlawing of *brit milah* (circumcision) and their decision to rebuild Jerusalem as a pagan city called Aelia Capitolina, perhaps the greatest cause of the revolt was the undying Jewish desire to be a free people in their own land. General Bar Kokhba was supported by the greatest rabbi in Israel – Rabbi Akiva, whose students became his bravest soldiers. His guerilla tactics frustrated and outsmarted the Romans. Bar Kokhba liberated Jerusalem and even minted silver coins with a picture of the Jewish Temple and the words in Hebrew: "Year one for the freedom of Israel."

In the end, Rome feared slave nations around the world would be inspired by Bar Kokhba to rise up and fight for their freedom. Emperor Hadrian sent eight Roman legions from around the world including their best general, Julius Severus, who was in Britain at the time. The Romans, after three and a half years, eventually crushed the revolt killing 600,000 Jews including Bar Kokhba, who died heroically in battle at the last fortress called Betar. Hadrian then outlawed Judaism and tried to annihilate the Jewish people. He renamed Israel "Palestine," Latin for Philistines, a people that had disappeared a thousand years earlier. His goal was to make the world forget the Jews ever had a country of their own.

The ten leading rabbis in Israel, including Rabbi Akiva, were captured and executed in Caesarea. One rabbi was wrapped in a Torah scroll and burned at the stake and Rabbi Akiva was raked over with iron combs. As he was tortured he smiled and his students, who were forced to watch the execution, cried out in wonder, "Rabbi, how do you smile?" Akiva answered: "It is written in the Torah, 'You shall love the Lord your God with all your heart, with all your soul and with all your might.' I have always loved God with all my heart and all my might, but I never knew how to love God with all my soul. Now the Romans think they are killing me but they are actually helping me carry out the one mitzvah I was unable to follow in my life – to love God with all my soul…even when it is taken from me." Then Akiva, feeling his life slip away, cried out the Shema Yisrael prayer, *"Shema Yisrael, Hashem Elokeinu, Hashem ehad* (Hear, O Israel, the Lord our God, the Lord is One)." Akiva died on the word "one," but along with Bar Kokhba, left our people a legacy of courage, strength and Jewish commitment that would fuel our modern-day struggle for independence in Israel.

Two thousand years later the courage of Bar Kokhba and the spirit of Rabbi Akiva continue to live on in the soldiers of the Israel Defense Forces. On July 12, 2006, the Hizbullah terrorist organization attacked Israel across its northern border, causing the Second Lebanon War. During that campaign the common Israeli soldiers distinguished themselves with countless acts of bravery and heroism. The most moving story perhaps is of Major Roi Klein, from the settlement of Eli, who was the deputy battalion commander of the 51st Battalion of the Golani Infantry Brigade.

Major Klein grew up in Raanana but moved to Eli after studying in the Bnei David Yeshiva. He was educated on the ideals and values of love and commitment to Torah, the Jewish people and the State of Israel. He saw his service in Golani as fulfillment of his Jewish obligations. He was loved and admired by all his soldiers and was designated for promotion in Tzahal. On July 26, 2006, a day before his thirty-first birthday, Roi Klein took part with his unit in the fierce fighting in the Hizbullah stronghold of Bint Jabil. As they cleaned out terrorist gun nests in house-to-house fighting, a barrage of Hizbullah gunfire and grenades was unleashed on the Golani soldiers. Klein sent his platoon commander, Lieutenant Amichai Merchavya, with several soldiers to outflank the enemy but they came upon a high, impassable wall next to a courtyard. Intense sniper fire and grenades rained down on Merchavya and his men and Amichai was hit; he called to Klein on the radio for help.

Major Klein rushed to Merchavya's aid with several soldiers and a medic. He succeeded in placing the wounded Merchavya on a stretcher when a Hizbullah grenade was thrown at the soldiers assembled in the courtyard. It seemed that they all faced certain death, when their beloved commander, Roi Klein, dived on the live grenade and screamed, "*Shema Yisrael, Hashem Elokeinu, Hashem ehad* (Hear, O Israel, the Lord our God, the Lord is One)." Klein died in the explosion but saved the lives of the many soldiers with him. He died on the word "one," just like his teacher and hero Rabbi Akiva.

Roi Klein was a sensitive, caring soul who was loved by all who knew him. He was a brilliant and outstanding student of engineering and also played the saxophone. He is survived by his young wife Sara and his two sons, Gilad and Yoav. Klein was buried in the National Military Cemetery on Mount Herzl in Jerusalem on July 27, 2006. That day would have been his thirty-first birthday. In all eight soldiers died in the battle of Bint Jabil, including Klein and Merchavya. Posthumously, Roi Klein was awarded the Israeli Medal of Valor.

As with the Bar Kokhba revolt, Jews in Israel and abroad will debate the merits of the 2006 Second Lebanon War for years to come. There are, of course, many issues that need to be investigated and lessons that must be learned so that we can continue to preserve our freedom in Israel. While our prime minister, defense minister and chief of staff all earned poor grades for their leadership in the war, the soldiers in the field proved that they are among the finest generations of young Jews in two thousand years. It would be wise for us to honor the courage of our youth and the memories of our fallen heroes so that their legacy will never die. From Akiva to Roi Klein, it is that very legacy that has been the secret of our survival.

MICHAEL LEVIN
"AHARAI!"

Michael Levin (1984–2006)
- Born in Philadelphia; made Aliyah to Israel in 2003
- Joined Israeli paratroops, fulfilling a personal dream
- Rushed back to Israel to rejoin fellow soldiers in battle when Israel was attacked
- Fell in battle against Hizbullah terrorists on August 1, 2006

"You can't fulfill your dreams unless you dare risk it all."

Michael Levin grew up like most American Jewish kids. Born on February 17, 1984, and raised in Philadelphia, he graduated from Council Rock High School in 2002. Michael's maternal grandparents were survivors of the Holocaust and passed on to him a legacy of pride and strength in his Jewish heritage. As a teenager Michael was active in the HaGesher Region of United Synagogue Youth (USY) and attended Camp Ramah in the Poconos. He loved sports and was an avid fan of Philly teams, especially the Philadelphia Phillies.

In February 2001, Michael came to Israel for two months to study the four-thousand-year history of the Jewish people at the Alexander Muss High School in Israel (AMHSI). While in Israel Michael expressed his desire to make Aliyah (move to Israel and become an Israeli citizen) and serve in Tzahal, the Israel Defense Forces. Michael proved to be an outstanding student at AMHSI and was especially moved by the stories of Jewish heroes like Judah the Maccabee, Shimon Bar Kokhba, Rabbi Akiva, Hannah Senesh, Eli Cohen, Avigdor Kahalani and Yonatan "Yoni" Netanyahu.

The most moving moment at AMHSI for Michael was on the last day of the program when his class visited the grave of Yoni Netanyahu, hero of the 1976 Entebbe rescue mission, at Mount Herzl in Jerusalem. Michael looked up to Yoni as a role model and a hero and was touched by Yoni's words from a 1975 letter:

> By "past" I mean not only my own past, but the way in which I see myself as an inseparable part, a link in the chain of our existence and Israel's independence.[60]

Like Yoni, Michael also saw himself as a link in the chain of Jewish history, and felt an obligation to defend his people. He dreamed of serving in the Israel Defense Forces.

After graduating high school, Michael attended "Nativ," USY's year-long course in Israel, and in his "Nativ" yearbook wrote the words that would become his motto: "You can't fulfill your dreams unless you dare risk it all."

Michael was neither a daredevil nor a gambling man. He was a sweet, funny, humble, kind, loving human being who relished life and lived it to the fullest.

He simply believed that life wasn't worth living unless there was some ideal you loved so much that you'd be willing to sacrifice your life for it. For Michael, that ideal was Israel.

In 2003 Michael made Aliyah to Israel and began studying Hebrew at an ulpan (intensive course in speaking Hebrew) on Kibbutz Yavne. Like all Israelis, Michael was drafted into the Israel Defense Forces (IDF) and reported to the Army Induction Center at Tel HaShomer. As he was being processed, the officer in charge noticed his papers had not been finalized due to his new status in the country. The officer told him that he couldn't be drafted at this time. Undeterred, Michael went outside the Army Induction Center and climbed up a trash dumpster, sneaking into the second floor of the building. When the officer discovered

---

60. Jonathan Netanyahu, *The Letters of Jonathan Netanyahu: The Commander of the Entebbe Rescue Force* (Jerusalem: Gefen Publishing House, 2001), 262.

him, he hollered at Michael and said, "No one can get through the front door here without papers," to which Michael smiled and replied, "What makes you think I came through the front door?" The officer pulled some strings and arranged for Michael to be processed as an Israeli soldier. He later remarked: "I've been here at the Army Induction Center for twenty years. Some kids don't want to be here and look for ways to get out, but Michael was the first kid I ever met who 'broke in' to be inducted into Tzahal!"

Once in Tzahal, Michael volunteered for the IDF's finest combat unit, the red-bereted paratroops. During his basic training Michael learned to parachute. Small in size, five foot six and weighing only 118 pounds, Michael was blown off course on his first jump. Afterwards his officers had to tie weights to his parachute to keep him from drifting. Despite his small size, Mike was a fierce fighter with a lion's heart. At the end of their basic training the paratroops go on a ninety-kilometer (fifty-five-mile) march to Jerusalem where they receive their red berets at Ammunition Hill, a famous battle site from the 1967 Six-Day War. In 2001, while at AMHSI, Michael had learned about the heroism of the paratroops in that battle from one of the surviving veterans who spoke to his class. Now he was receiving his red beret on that hallowed ground. Michael described that day as one of the happiest in his life!

Mike was not only a brave soldier but he remained a loving son and brother. He once said, "I'm not worried about dying! I'm just worried about what it would do to my family." Michael held a special status in Tzahal called *chayal boded*, given to lone Israeli soldiers whose parents do not live in the country. Military service is tough enough for most young Israelis but they are comforted knowing they will come home on their Shabbat leaves to a warm and loving family. Michael had none in Israel, making his service that much tougher.

In June 2006, Mike received a thirty-day leave from the IDF to visit his family back in Philadelphia. Michael, who had a great sense of humor, wanted to surprise his mom and dad and worked out a cute prank with his older sister, Elisa. When he arrived in Philadelphia that summer he had Elisa put a gigantic cardboard box with real Fed-Ex markings on the front steps of their home. Michael got into the box and had his sister tape it up and ring his parents' doorbell. When Mrs. Levin saw the package, she tried to carry it into the house, but it was too heavy. Suddenly Michael jumped out of the box and screamed, "Surprise!!" This story is indicative of Michael's loving heart and playful spirit.

Michael spent quality time with his family and visited friends at Camp Ramah in the Poconos. When some friends expressed their worries to Michael about his safety in an elite combat unit of the Israeli army, he responded philosophically, "I'm doing exactly what I want to do and going exactly where I want to be, and if God should decide to call me home, I'm fine with that." During his visit to Philadelphia, Michael told his parents that if anything ever happened to him, he wanted to be buried on Mount Herzl in Jerusalem. On July 12, 2006, the Lebanese terrorist organization Hizbullah attacked Israel and kidnapped two Israeli soldiers, Ehud Goldwasser and Eldad Regev. The Hizbullah, dedicated to Israel's destruction and armed by Iran, began shelling Israel's northern cities. Michael heard that his unit was sent into battle and he promptly told his family that he had to cut his visit short to rejoin his comrades at arms. He rushed back to Israel and rejoined his unit, the 890th battalion of the Paratroopers Brigade, then fighting inside Lebanon.

Michael's unit was on a mission in the Lebanese village of Aita al-Shaab, a Hizbullah stronghold, when they came under heavy missile- and gunfire. Held up in a house, Michael fought bravely but on August 1, 2006, he was tragically killed by a Hizbullah sniper. His fellow soldier and friend, Shlomi Singer, described Michael's last moments:

I heard a round of gunfire and saw Michael lying on his stomach. I knew in my heart he was dead. I lifted him to one of the houses where I tried to revive him, but there was no chance. I said quietly in English, "I love you, Michael, and I am so sorry." He was wearing a big green *kippah* and before we went into Lebanon, I put his *kippah* on my head and said the "Shema," …praying that we all come back safely. After Michael was killed we placed his body on a stretcher and carried him for several kilometers between the cliffs and rocks to bring his body to safety. It was the final honor and respect that we could give him.

Michael's family was notified in Philadelphia of his death in battle and they immediately flew to Israel for his funeral. One of their biggest worries was whether they'd be able to find a minyan (a quorum of ten necessary for communal prayer) for the ceremony, as they had no family in the country. They arrived at Ben-Gurion Airport on August 3, 2006, and drove right from the airport to the National Military Cemetery on Mount Herzl. When the car arrived at the cemetery, the Levins saw thousands of people gathered there. Michael's father was confused by the large crowd and thought there were ten or fifteen other funerals taking place at the same time. The soldiers escorting the family told them that Michael's was the only funeral being held at this time and all the thousands of people in attendance, most of whom had not known Michael, were there to honor their fallen son. Immersed in their shock and grief but embraced by a loving and grateful nation, the Levins buried their son on the hills of Jerusalem, the city he loved with all his heart…just a few yards from the grave of his hero, Yoni Netanyahu.

Michael's mother, Harriet, at first had wanted her fallen son buried near her home in Philadelphia but her rabbi convinced her that it was Michael's last wish to be buried in the land he loved. She said that when she and her husband, Mark, saw all the people who had come to honor Michael, they knew they had made the right decision.

Harriet said that about a month after the funeral, a friend of hers from Philadelphia went to visit Michael's grave on Mount Herzl. When the friend reached the burial site, she was shocked to see there was an Israeli soldier sitting on the grave drinking a cup of coffee with a small gas burner and finjan (coffee pot) next to him. Thinking he was acting improperly in the cemetery, the woman asked him what he was doing there. The young warrior answered softly, "Michael was my best friend in the army and every Friday afternoon just before Shabbat, we'd sit down and drink a cup of coffee together and shmooze about life. Now, just like before, I come visit Michael every week just before Shabbat and drink a cup a coffee and chat with my best friend."

Harriet Levin said that if Michael had been buried in Philadelphia, probably only a handful of family would visit his grave but at rest at home in Israel, hundreds come every week to pay their respects to the young hero from Philly with the contagious smile and the heart of a lion.

Michael was buried on the afternoon of Tisha b'Av on August 3, 2006. Tisha b'Av is a fast day where we commemorate the many tragedies that have befallen our people on this black date in our history, notably including the destruction of the First and Second Temples in Jerusalem, the fall of Betar during the Bar Kokhba revolt, the expulsion of the Jews of Spain in 1492 and the transportation of over 300,000 of Warsaw's Jews to the gas chambers in Treblinka in July 1942. As a sign of mourning we do not wear tefillin during the morning service on Tisha b'Av but we do put on tefillin during the afternoon service that day as a sign that life must continue and we must move on from destruction and mourning to comfort and rebirth.

It is fitting that Michael was buried on the afternoon of Tisha b'Av and not in the morning. His death was a tragedy that tore into the hearts and souls of all who loved him; but Michael's legacy to us is one of hope and commitment. As he smiles down on us from above, his memory will best be honored not by remembering so much how he died but more importantly how he lived. The motto of the Israeli paratroops is "Aharai (Follow me)!" Michael set a dugma ishit (personal example) of how to live a life as a committed Jew with passion and pride dedicated to the Jewish people, to the Torah and to Israel. His legacy commands us all, "Aharai!"

POSTSCRIPT: Michael Levin's mother, Harriet Levin, once told this author that Michael was a normal American Jewish kid. She said he was just like you and me and added, "You know he wasn't always an angel...at times he made mistakes and could get into trouble." In many ways, though, that makes Michael even more inspiring. He wasn't a "superhero"! He was just the kid from down the block, but when his people and Israel needed him – he was there!

A moving documentary film by Sally Mitlas has been made about Michael Levin called "A Hero in Heaven." For more information on the film go to: www.aheroinheaven.com.

TAL BRODY
PUTTING ISRAEL ON THE MAP

Tal Brody (1943–)
- American Jewish basketball star
- Made Aliyah to Israel in 1970
- Played for Maccabi Tel Aviv and led them
  to European championship in 1977

*"We are on the map and we are staying on the map –
not only in sports, but in everything."*

Tal Brody was born on August 30, 1943, in Trenton, New Jersey. As a youngster, Tal proved to be a talented basketball player and when he attended the University of Illinois, he became an All-American basketball star. In 1965 he was picked thirteenth in the NBA draft by the Baltimore Bullets but that same summer, he took part in the seventh Maccabiah Games. Held every four years in Israel, the Maccabiah is the international Jewish Olympics. In 1965, fifteen-year-old swimmer Mark Spitz won four gold medals at the games, while Tal Brody led the USA to a gold medal in basketball. Brody was immediately approached by the managers of Israel's top professional basketball team, Maccabi Tel Aviv, and even the famous Israeli general with the eye patch, Moshe Dayan, spoke to Brody about staying in Israel.

The pressure soon paid off. Tal Brody completed his master's degree in educational psychology at the University of Illinois and then returned to Israel in 1966 to play for Maccabi Tel Aviv. He helped the Israeli team reach the European Cup finals that year. In 1969 Tal returned to the USA to fulfill his military obligations to his native country. Though he would soon become a proud Israeli citizen, Tal loved America and felt a debt of gratitude to the country of his birth, which he repaid with his service in the U.S. Army. He also played for the U.S. Army and armed forces all-star teams and then for the U.S.A. National Team at the 1970 FIBA World Championships in Belgrade, Yugoslavia.

In 1970, Tal Brody officially made Aliyah (in Hebrew, literally "going up" – an expression meaning "immigrated to Israel") and became an Israeli citizen. Brody gave up a promising career in the NBA to become an Israeli and explained the dramatic move in these words:

[I was drafted thirteenth in the NBA draft,] after being chosen as an All-American among the ten best players in the United States with guys like Rick Barry, Bill Bradley and Billy Cunningham.... I went to Baltimore at the time and after going through rookie camp, I went to the Maccabiah Games with the United States team. Through playing in the games, which...I got permission from the [Baltimore] Bullets to do, Maccabi Tel Aviv and the [Israeli] Minister of Sports presented me with a challenge. Baltimore was not giving no-cut contracts at the time; Jerry Sloan was their first draft pick and they had some good guards already. So I said I'll take a year out of my life and go to Israel, see what it's like to live in a foreign country. Because I have a Jewish background, I decided to take up that challenge. [And soon] I saw what the result was and I saw the vision of what we could do, of the impact [it had on Israel] whenever we beat another team in Europe. I felt it was bigger than myself and felt it had to be continued, because I saw what the results were.[61]

---

61. "50 Years Interview: Tal Brody, Maccabi Tel Aviv," www.euroleague.net.

The six-foot-one-and-a-half-inch star played the next ten years for Maccabi Tel Aviv, winning ten national championships and appearing in eighty-one European Cup games where he scored 1,378 points. Brody also played for the Israeli national team, scoring 1,219 points in seventy-eight games. The highlight of his basketball career was in 1977 when Maccabi Tel Aviv was matched against the Soviet champions, CSKA Moscow, in the European Cup semi-finals. The Soviet Union had broken off diplomatic relations with Israel during the 1967 Six-Day War and had politically and militarily backed Israel's Arab enemies. The USSR was also severely persecuting its three million Jewish citizens and had closed the "Iron Curtain" to Jewish emigration. CSKA Moscow refused to go to Tel Aviv and would not agree to host the Israeli club on Soviet soil. The Red Army Champions finally agreed to meet the Israelis on neutral territory in Virton, Belgium. Tal Brody remembered preparing for the history-making game:

> Before we played CSKA, when it was decided that we would play on a neutral floor, even though we would have preferred to play in Tel Aviv and Moscow, we saw a video of their game against Real Madrid. At that period of time it was very difficult to win in Madrid, as they had great teams with [terrific players like] Brabender, Szczerbiak and Corbalan. And we saw that CSKA won [even] in Madrid, and about six or seven of those guys from CSKA were on the Olympic team that beat the United States in the Olympics. So the hopes weren't that high as far as the public was concerned. Our first concern was not to be embarrassed. We never saw them individually before, so we didn't really know. I knew [the famous Russian team captain Sergei] Belov, because we played against each other at the world championships in 1970 in Yugoslavia and I knew some of their players and I knew they were good.

I didn't think we couldn't win, but [our general goal was just] not to be disgraced. And when we went to this town of Virton, Belgium, and we went into the small gymnasium that was there and as captain of the team I walked in with [our] flag alongside Belov, and I saw we were going to exchange flags for the first time. When I walked into the stadium and was greeted by so many Israel flags and [Hebrew] singing, it gave our team a real adrenaline shot. I saw that CSKA felt a little bit shattered by the fact that everyone was rooting for us and I think we played above and beyond...and we won the game by twelve points.... At the end of the game, as we were going off the floor with all the excitement after the victory and people dancing around, the announcer came to me with the microphone and the feeling was after beating the Russians that we are on the map, we are staying on the map, not just in sports, but in everything. It meant that here was the hope that we could accomplish things in every field like we did in basketball. It just came out of my heart at that instant.[62]

Maccabi Tel Aviv won the game 91–79 and Israelis felt as if they had defeated their people's greatest enemy, the Soviet Union. The historic victory lifted the soul of the tiny nation. Hundreds of thousands of Israelis, who had been watching the Maccabi games in the European League each Thursday night on television, rushed out of their homes to celebrate in the streets. Over 150,000 fans partied at Kikar Malchei Yisrael (now Rabin Square) in front of the Tel Aviv municipality, many jumping into the square's famed fountain. Interviewed at the end of the game, Tal Brody made remarks that touched the hearts and souls of every Israeli and are forever inscribed in the Jewish nation's history books. In his thick American accent, he said in Hebrew, "We are on the map and we are staying on the map – not only in sports, but in everything!"

---

62. Ibid.

Destiny could not be halted and Maccabi Tel Aviv went on to defeat Mobilgirgi Varese, Italy's champion, in the Euroleague final at Belgrade, 78–77, for the European Cup championship. Tal Brody, team captain, hoisted the European Cup on high, as millions of Israelis cheered their national heroes. Back at home, in Israel's National Park, over 200,000 Israelis celebrated Maccabi Tel Aviv's victory over twenty-two other European national basketball champions. The victory was more than a sports accomplishment. It showed Israelis and the world what a tiny team and nation could do with hard work, drive and determination. Tal Brody, the quintessential sportsman and gentleman, taught his new country valuable lessons. In 1979, he would become the first athlete to be awarded the coveted Israel Prize, Israel's highest civilian honor. In 1996 Tal was inducted into the International Jewish Sports Hall of Fame and in 2004 he lit one of the twelve torches at the national ceremony on Mount Herzl opening Israel's fifty-sixth Independence Day celebrations.

Since his retirement, Tal has not only pursued a successful career in insurance, he has given generously of his time and money to the children of Israel. He started the "Let's Play Ball" program, which benefited over 200,000 needy youth in development towns and economically challenged neighborhoods, and founded one of the largest basketball schools in the world in Herzliya. Tal has also become active in his country's politics and in 2009 was a candidate for a spot on the Likud Knesset list.

Tal Brody, one of Israel's most famous and beloved citizens, grew up thousands of miles away from the "Promised Land" in Trenton, New Jersey's state capital. As you drive into Trenton from nearby Philadelphia, you will cross the Delaware River Bridge, which has a neon light inscription across it stating, "Trenton Makes – The World Takes." The bridge, affectionately known as the "Trenton Makes Bridge," touted Trenton's manufacturing prowess in years gone by. There is no denying, however, that one of Trenton's greatest exports has been Tal Brody. He helped Israel win their first European League basketball championship and put Israel on the world map in sports. He has set a profound personal example for Israelis, young and old, as an athlete, as a gentleman, and most importantly, as a Zionist. Tal Brody has shown Jews from around the world that Israel can be a wonderful home and country, even for Jews from the affluent United States. He has been, and always will be, a winner…on and off the court.

YONATAN BEN-MEIR
AND THE HEROES AT HOME

> **Yonatan Ben-Meir (1987–)**
> - Officer in Haruv Battalion of Kfir Infantry Brigade
> - Hero of battle near Kissufim in 2009 Operation Cast Lead
> - Chosen as Outstanding Officer in Kfir Brigade
> *"No fear, no pain!"*

In December 2008, war erupted in Gaza, after the Hamas terrorist organization fired thousands of missiles and mortar shells into Israeli cities and towns. Hamas has openly declared that its goal is the destruction of Israel and the genocide of its Jewish people. The Israeli military operation, which lasted approximately one month, was given the name Cast Lead, and its purpose was to destroy terrorist infrastructure in Gaza. It was during those days that I had a unique opportunity to observe the heroic quality of my people from a personal angle.

I am a Jewish history teacher at the Alexander Muss High School in Israel and spend much of my life teaching others about Jewish heroes, but during the war in Gaza I had the privilege to witness true heroism among my friends. I am divorced with three grown children. My youngest son, Yair, is in the Israeli Armor Corps and his older brother, Meron, serves in an elite unit of the Givati Infantry Brigade. I have a dear friend named Ruth Ben-Meir, who made Aliyah to Israel many years ago from Waltham, Massachusetts. Ruth, like me, is divorced and has four children of her own. We live together in the seaside city of Netanya, and Ruth's children are now like family to me. Ruth has a full-time job in the accounting department of a large international pharmaceutical corporation, in addition to single-handedly raising her three sons and daughter. Her second son, Yonatan, was drafted into the Israel Defense Forces in 2006 and serves as an officer in the Haruv Battalion of the Kfir Infantry Brigade.

When Operation Cast Lead began, Yonatan was sent with his combat unit to the Kissufim Crossing along the Gaza border. On the morning of Thursday, January 8, 2009, Yonatan and his men followed their beloved company commander, Major Roi Rosner, into battle against Hamas terrorists in the area. The Haruv soldiers came under intense fire from the Hamas which also launched several anti-tank missiles at their unit. One of the missiles passed right by Yonatan and shrapnel from the explosion cut Roi's neck, killing the company commander. Yonatan kept his cool in the face of battle and prepared the counterattack. He shouted to his soldiers, "No fear, no pain!" and led the counterassault. As he charged the terrorists, his assault weapon malfunctioned. Yonatan took his fallen commander's rifle and helped lead the frontal charge that annihilated the Hamas terrorist force.

Roi, who was buried that evening in his hometown of Holon, would have been very proud of Yonaton and his Haruv soldiers. Roi Rosner was twenty-seven years old and had just gotten married ten months earlier to his sweetheart, Sharon. The couple had just bought an apartment in Holon, near Roi's family. Roi's brother, Yaniv, was in the middle of combat training at the Tzeelim base near Gaza, after having received an emergency call-up the previous Saturday night. Yaniv was preparing to go into Gaza with his combat unit when he was informed of his brother's heroic death. The Rosners are a microcosm of the commitment and sacrifice of this heroic people called Israel.

Meanwhile, back in Netanya, Ruth heard on the radio that an officer from the Haruv Battalion was killed in action near Kissufim Crossing. Sitting at her desk at work she broke down in tears with worry over her son and his comrades at arms. Shortly afterwards, Yonatan's girlfriend, Yael, called and informed Ruth that Yonatan had been in a tough battle but that he was unhurt. Sadly though, Yael continued, his beloved company commander, Roi, was dead. Ruth shed tears now for this fallen hero who had been an inspiration to her son and so many others.

Yonatan, like many of our young sons and daughters in uniform, is a true hero but in many ways so are Ruth, his mother; Yael, his girlfriend; and his siblings, Noa, Nadav and Itai. While our brave children in the Israel Defense Forces fight on for our survival and security, their mothers, fathers, girlfriends and brothers and sisters back at home spend sleepless nights worrying about and praying for their soldiers at the front. Not content to just pray for our soldiers, Ruth, and many others like her, sent packages to the soldiers at the front and even ordered food supplies from a grocer in Sderot to help support the embattled town's economy. In fact, during the 2006 Second War in Lebanon, while thousands of Hizbullah rockets rained down on northern Israeli cities, Ruth invited two strangers, a single mother and her young daughter from a bombed-out Haifa suburb, to share her home for over a month.

It is that kind of selfless heroism that needs to be passed down to our children as a legacy. It is not only the soldiers of Tzahal who deserve our kudos but also their brave family and friends back at home who continue on with life's challenges in the face of never-ending adversity. Back in America, many parents are worried about the financial crisis and what college their children will get into. Our worries in Israel can be quite different at times. During Operation Cast Lead, Ruth and Yael, Noa, Nadav and Itai were all worried about Yonatan and were praying that he would return home safely, after fighting to protect his country. He and all the Israeli soldiers, like their families – the heroes back at home – are what keep our nation and people secure.

❖   ❖   ❖

IRV AND MIRIAM KATZ
LETTERS FROM ISRAEL

Irving Katz (1928–1996)
Miriam Katz (1928–1999)
Beloved parents and heroes to the author
*"We in America must continue to help them
by doing all we can for Israel..."*

My late beloved father, Irving Katz, grew up in an economically poor home in North Philadelphia. Today that neighborhood, around 9th and Diamond Streets, is one of the toughest ghetto areas in the United States. When my father lived there it was no less poor but was rich in Jewish culture and love. My dad had to leave school to help support his family but became a highly educated man through his own studies and readings. He eventually became a textile engineer and put up pipes and shelving in the many suit factories that were based in Philly in the 1950s and '60s.

I was the second of three children born to my father and his loving wife, Miriam. We grew up in a lower middle-class neighborhood in Philly's Great Northeast and were educated from birth by my parents to be proud and committed Jews. My dad was president of our synagogue, which he literally helped build with his hands. At home he would make passionate speeches around the dinner table each night on Israel and Judaism. My dad demanded that we be involved in a Jewish youth group and attend Hebrew school. He made Judaism and Israel the most important priorities in our lives. Much due to his teaching and ideals, I decided to make Aliyah to Israel in 1978 and moved there the day after I finished my college finals at Temple University.

My dad was so proud of me for making Aliyah and even prouder when I won the Israeli National Boxing Championship, but he was most proud of me when I became a reconnaissance soldier in the Israel Defense Forces. In many ways I felt I was carrying out a mission he would have liked to have done himself. One of the most moving moments I can remember is when my dad came to Israel for three weeks with Sar-El Volunteers for Israel. He arrived in Israel and was taken to his base at Tzrifin, near Rishon LeZion. At the same time I was on combat duty in the Israeli army reserves in the Golan Heights and received permission to visit my dad.

I traveled to his base and asked if the Volunteers for Israel group from Philadelphia had arrived. An officer pointed me to a bus of American volunteers in Israeli army fatigues and I asked if Irv Katz was on the bus. Their escort shouted to the back of the bus, "Mr. Katz, there is a soldier here looking for you." My dad ran to the front of the bus and suddenly saw me in uniform. We embraced each other with tears in our eyes. The other volunteers asked why Irv was hugging a soldier and one of dad's friends recognized me and shouted to the rest of the bus, "That's his son – he's in the Israeli army!" The two of us were not only reunited in Israel but fate had brought us together at that moment in the uniform of Tzahal, the Israel Defense Forces.

Though my parents were rich in love and the things that matter, they remained financially disadvantaged for the rest of their lives. When I was married in 1980, my parents couldn't afford to come to my wedding, but my Dad's brothers passed around the hat and bought him a ticket. He showed up at my wedding at the last minute and it was a wonderful surprise. The textile business died in Philly by the 1970s and most of the suit factories moved to the south or to Asia. It became tougher and tougher for my dad to earn a livelihood and in 1983 he was laid off when the small textile company he worked for closed. My dad was very worried about how he'd support his wife and family and became very depressed.

It was precisely in those days of the summer of 1983 that I was preparing to go on a mission to the USA as an emissary on behalf of the State of Israel. I was very worried about my dad and didn't know what I could do to help him. As I pondered my dad's situation, I remembered that his hero was Israel's Prime Minister Menachem Begin. I wrote a letter in the summer of 1983 to Prime Minister Begin and told him all about my dad. I wrote him that the State of Israel is always honoring wealthy American Jews but perhaps it should also honor those Jews who give of their hearts and souls. I told Mr. Begin that my dad had raised me to make Aliyah and serve in the Israeli army. I then explained that he had recently been laid off from work and was depressed. I concluded by asking the prime minister if he could write a note of encouragement to my dad, who looked up to him. I didn't tell my family about my letter to Menachem Begin and after a couple of weeks forgot about it. In mid-September, my mom called me, all excited. She said my dad had just received a registered letter from the Israeli prime minister's office. She read it to me over the phone:

September 13, 1983

Dear Mr. Katz,

In these days of awe between Rosh Hashana and Yom Kippur I write to wish you and your wife a G'mar Chatima Tova.

I am aware of the devotion you have shown to our people, of the education you have provided your children, and of the influence you have had on your son who lives here in Eretz Israel, and has served in the Israel Defense Forces.

May you have *nachas* [pride and pleasure] from your children and grandchildren, and may you enjoy blessings of good health in the years ahead.

Sincerely,

Menachem Begin

The letter was balm to my father's injuries. It gave him needed support and encouragement in his time of distress. It was hand signed by the prime minister of Israel and my dad was so proud to have received it. Menachem Begin is arguably one of Israel's greatest prime ministers. He set the highest standards of honesty and dedication for his office, bombed the nuclear reactor in Iraq, helped bridge the gap between Ashkenazic and Sephardic Jews in Israel, initiated Project Renewal to address infrastructure and other needs, helped save Ethiopian Jewry and did so much more...but for me he will always be the hero who wrote to my dad in his time of despair and lifted his spirit. Menachem Begin, like my beloved father, will forever be a light and inspiration to me.

On December 10, 2008, my mother would have celebrated her eightieth birthday but sadly, she passed away nine years earlier on December 24, 1999, after a long illness. My mom, Miriam Katz, or Mimi as her friends called her, was a true *Eshet Chayil* – a Woman of Valor. In recent years it has become fashionable for celebrities to trash their moms in public, as Rosanne Barr did several years ago. Perhaps it is unfashionable for me to sing my mother's praise but she and my father gave me all the love and warmth they could and left me a legacy of love and commitment to the Jewish people, the Torah and Israel.

Both my parents were true leaders who set personal examples for their children. While my dad was president of our synagogue, my mom was president of the parent-teacher council in Philadelphia which administered all the Hebrew schools in our city. At home my parents were warm and loving but set standards for us to follow and gave us a wealth of Jewish ideals and values. Every night our family of five ate dinner together and in between the first and second courses, my dad would talk to us about Israel and Jewish identity. He made fiery, passionate speeches every night and taught us more over the dinner table than I would ever gain in years of college.

Economically we were on the lower end of the middle class but my mom made sure we were always well fed and dressed even if it meant at times taking food off her own plate to give to her kids. When my brother told my parents that the synagogue's youth group was boring, my parents told him: "You must be involved in a Jewish youth group! That is not open for discussion. But if you care and want to make a difference, you can become a leader and make the youth group vibrant and rewarding." Following their direction and sound advice both my brother and I went on to become regional presidents of Philadelphia Region USY (United Synagogue Youth). Today too many parents follow their children's lead and try to be their kids' friends. I believe we need more parents who act like parents and give their children love, values and priorities.

My mom developed diabetes during childbirth and sadly, other painful conditions followed. She had triple bypass surgery, lost her kidneys and had to receive dialysis several times a week. My dad, who was known to most on the outside as a strong tough guy, spent years taking tender loving care of my sick mom – cooking for her, bathing her and driving her to and from dialysis treatments. In 1996 my dad had a massive heart attack and died hours later at the age of sixty-eight. My sister moved to Philadelphia and continued taking loving care of my mom.

Three years later my mom, who could not walk and had lost her eyesight to diabetes, felt a lump on her breast. She waited until my sister was out one day and called an ambulance, going to see her doctor secretly. She discovered that she had double breast cancer and would need a double mastectomy. My mom understood that without the ability to walk or see, and with this new tragic twist of fate, she would no longer have any quality of life. She called my brother and sister and informed them of what had transpired and that she was going to stop her dialysis treatments so she could die a few days later with dignity and not have to leave tough decisions for her children. I think my mom was one of the bravest and most selfless people I've ever known. She died on December 24, 1999.

I live in Israel and returned to Philadelphia to bury my mom and sit shivah with my brother and sister in the home we had grown up in.

One morning my sister and I were going through some of my mom's drawers and found a letter written on airmail tissue paper, as was once stylish and mandated by the postal authorities. It was a handwritten letter from my mom, Mimi, to her boyfriend Irv (the man who would become her husband and my father). It was dated August 26, 1949, and was sent from Israel where my mom was visiting as a young twenty-one-year-old tourist just days after the cease-fire went into effect at the end of Israel's War of Independence. Older Israelis tell me that my mom was probably the *only* young female tourist in Israel in 1949. They tell me that half the Palmach was trying to date her and all the Israeli soldiers were mesmerized by her sexy legs adorned with an ankle bracelet! It's hard to believe it but my mom was once young too. I want to share with you some of my mom's words and thoughts from that letter to her future husband. It carries with it the love and passion of Israel that she and my dad passed on to me and my siblings.

August 26,1949

Dear Irv,

Just returned home after a nine-day tour of the Galil. I decided to take the day off today just for writing letters and I've been at it now for four hours!! (That's some accomplishment for me since I've always disliked writing letters but loved to receive them. I've found out since I'm here that if I want to receive mail, I'd have to write also!) How are you? Are you still at the same job? What's the latest news in Philadelphia??

...It's six weeks that I've been here in Israel and I'm just getting a little homesick – not for America, but for my family and friends, even so I'm not thinking of returning home. This country is so beautiful and the people are just marvelous. You don't find the superficiality of most Americans here. The Israelis lead a plain, simple life. All of them are kind, friendly and most hospitable. For example, if you approach anyone on the street and ask for directions to reach a certain place, they will answer your question, take you there and tell you all about the place. If one goes to a kibbutz, one need not know a soul to feel at home! The kibbutzniks will befriend him, give him food and a place to sleep and he is welcome to stay as long as he desires.

...The housing situation is a problem. A four-room flat costs $12,000!!! I'll have to go back to the USA and work and save money to buy an apartment here. I've decided on the site for my home also – on Har HaCarmel in Haifa. It's so beautiful and airy – the most beautiful city in Israel!

...As for the beauty of the country itself, I can't describe it in words. If I could only paint! It has everything – the mountains, the sea, the tropical trees, and beautiful flowers and, oh yes, the desert which some day will also be full of trees and flowers. I carry my camera with me at all times – it's my most valuable possession. You can find here any type of life you like. There's Tel Aviv for people who like noise and the hustle and bustle of New York City. And Haifa for a quiet, peaceful but yet not-so-small-townish type of life.

For those who like the country or farm you have all the kibbutzim. And all the people are Jews!! There's no one to turn around and call you a "Dirty Jew"! In other words – it's just wonderful!

P.S.: I didn't mention Jerusalem above as there's no city like it in the world. You find atheists and the religious – very religious – boys with "payos," long black socks and long pants and coats; you find the ancient and the modern together. What a place! I could go on and on, but I haven't any more strength left. I've also been up since 6 a.m. and besides I have a cramp in my right hand by now. Before I close I want to get one thing straight. There are naturally many things here that are not right and need correction (important things!), but in the next few years I'm sure they'll be taken care of. For a country so young, it has done a marvelous job. We in America must continue to help them by doing all we can for Israel and raising more money than in the past few years. I don't pretend to be an authority on Israel because I've only been here a few weeks. I'm just an observer but in a couple of years I hope to be an Israeli citizen. It seems the "Zionist Bug" has bitten me too! Next time I'll write you more of my observations....

...Hoping to hear from you soon! As ever, Mimi

Israel has changed greatly since 1949. An apartment on Mount Carmel will cost half a million dollars today, not the $12,000 that so shocked my mother during her visit in 1949. Kibbutzim are pretty much out of date and Haifa is no longer such a quiet town! We've improved a lot of things in Israel but we've also messed up some things along the way. There are still many things that need improvement in Israel, but what my mom said in 1949 is still true today: "For a country so young, it's done a marvelous job! We in America must continue to help them by doing all we can for Israel!"

My mom returned to Israel several times but never had the chance to make Aliyah. Life for her and my dad wasn't easy but they lived it with passion, love and Jewish commitment rarely seen today. I graduated from Temple University in 1978 and a day later made Aliyah to Israel where I have lived for the past thirty years. After serving in the Israeli army, I joined the Alexander Muss High School in Israel where I have been a Jewish educator for over twenty-eight years. My daughter Inbal and her husband are Modern Orthodox, have three children and work in Jewish education in Ramat Gan. My middle son Meron served in an elite commando unit in the Israel Defense Forces and his younger brother, Yair, is now in the Israeli Armor Corps.

I hope my parents are proud of me and I know they must be proud of their grandchildren. Much of what is good in my children and in my brother and sister and in me comes from my parents. They passed down a precious legacy to their children and grandchildren through their ideals, teachings and personal example. They showed us that Jewish-Zionist education and Jewish commitment and love of Israel must be among the most important priorities in our lives. It is my hope and prayer that Jewish parents today and our children, tomorrow's parents, will find the appropriate ways to pass on this legacy to our future generations. I am lucky to have had the influence and guidance of two wonderful parents and they will always have my admiration and love. Their memories will always be a blessing.

Irv Katz on volunteers for Israel

❖ ❖ ❖

Epilogue
MEETING MY HERO

Since 1980 I have been working as a teacher of Jewish history and a tour guide at the Alexander Muss High School in Israel (AMHSI). AMHSI is a two-month program in Jewish history for high school students from the United States and combines classroom study with visits to the actual sites of historic events in Israel. One of the most moving moments I experienced as a teacher at AMHSI occurred in 1988 on the Judean Desert mountain fortress of Masada. There in the year 73 CE, 960 Jewish freedom fighters took their own lives the night before they were to be assaulted by an entire Roman legion. Knowing they could not defeat their Roman enemies, they chose to die as free people rather than to be subjected to Roman torture and slavery.

After spending seven hours climbing the mighty fortress and reliving its history with my class, I stood with my students on the southern ramparts and we shouted our pledge: "*Shenit Metzada lo tipol* (Massada shall not fall again)!" Just as our last words echoed in the distance, an Israeli F-16 fighter jet flew over our heads. (The Judean Desert around Masada is a regular training site for the Israeli Air Force.) Suddenly the pilot, seeing our group on the fortress edge, dived down towards us, saluted us by waving his fighter jet wings and then soared back into the blue sky leaving a white smoky trail behind. Chills went down our spines as we watched this brave son of Israel reassure us that today there are those who stand ready to fulfill the pledge we made that day at Masada. The symbolism of that sight will never be lost on those who beheld it.

Then in September 2004, on a fieldtrip with my class to the Golan Heights, we shared a moment, perhaps even more special, at Hermonit, site of the most concentrated tank battle in world history. The battle of the Valley of Tears took place in the 1973 Yom Kippur War. There, during three epic days in October 1973, eight tanks of the 77th Tank Battalion led by Lieutenant Colonel Avigdor Kahalani held back an onslaught of hundreds of Syrian tanks and armored personnel carriers. Their heroic stand stopped the Syrians and turned the tide of the Yom Kippur War in 1973. Kahalani, who had been severely burned and wounded in a heroic tank battle in the 1967 Six-Day War, won the Medal of Valor (Israeli equivalent of the American Medal of Honor) for his courage and leadership in 1973. His commander called him at the end of the battle and said straightforwardly, in no uncertain terms, "Avigdor, you have saved the State of Israel."

Without a doubt, Avigdor Kahalani is one of the great heroes in Jewish history and his story has inspired many Israelis including myself. I share his story twice every session with my students. The first time is on the second week of our history course at Masada when at the end of my lesson I tell my students how Kahalani had been sworn into the Israeli Armor Corps on Masada and had made the pledge of "*Shenit Metzada lo tipol!*" I try to help my students understand that Masada's significance is not in its historical importance but in its symbolic meaning, the very symbolism that helped Kahalani and his men save our people in 1973. It's then that we stand on the mountain's edge and pledge, "*Shenit Metzada lo tipol!*"

The second time I tell Kahalani's story is on our last fieldtrip to the Golan Heights at the Hermonit battle site, as we learn about the 1973 Yom Kippur War. Masada fell in 73 CE and Kahalani's story takes place exactly nineteen hundred years later. Though 1973 is in modern times and every form of high-tech and nuclear weapon existed, it was this one man's leadership and heroism that saved Israel. I tell my students that for our Jewish people, *individuals* do make a difference and *they* are the individuals who will need to make that difference for today and tomorrow.

As I finished my lesson that day at Hermonit, a swarthy, proud-looking, smiling man approached me. It was Avigdor Kahalani. He had been speaking to a group of VIPs on the spot and noticed our group of American Jewish teenagers. The security guard who was traveling with my group, Gideon Meiri, knew Kahalani from the Israeli army and asked him if he would speak to our group. Graciously, this warm-hearted hero stood in front of our class and in perfect English explained to us how he had fought on this spot thirty-one years ago and how he had seen many of his friends die in battle. Kahalani told us how his own brother and brother-in-law were killed in combat during the Yom Kippur War. Then he proudly described how his own sons serve today in the same tank battalion as he did, carrying on the family tradition of fighting to protect the Jewish state and people.

Kahalani closed by saying: "We must do everything we can to protect and strengthen our Jewish homeland! You must be ambassadors of Israel and go back to the USA and tell everyone what you saw and learned. The motto of the Israeli Armor Corps is '*Ha'ish hu haplada* (human beings – they are the armor of our nation)!' You must be that armor!" Kahalani remained behind to take a picture with our class and I am sure that moment will remain captured in all of our hearts forever. As we prepared to board our bus, our driver, a broad-shouldered, middle-aged man with a ponytail and gruff beard, stepped forward towards Kahalani, saluted and said, "Commander – It's me, Amitai, I fought under your command in 1973!" Kahalani smiled and warmly embraced Amitai. Only in Israel can a class of American Jewish students run into our people's greatest living hero and find out that their bus driver is a hero too.

I was most impressed with Avigdor Kahalani as a human being and as a mensch (Yiddish word for "man" meaning a person of integrity and honor). He looked like he could be the neighbor next door and even reminded me of my dad. Though he was on a busy schedule with a VIP group he felt that the youth are our people's future and gave us of his time and heart. Most of all, it was an honor and a privilege meeting one of my heroes, Avigdor Kahalani, in person! It was important to see that heroes are real people; knowing that makes them even more special in my eyes.

In each and every one of us is the ability to be a hero. I hope this book will inspire the reader to reach for that potential. Jews, and free people everywhere, face existential threats and challenges today, and we all need to be the armor of our nations. Without that armor, our freedom will be lost. I have shared with you in this book the stories of some famous as well as unsung Jewish heroes in the hope that the readers will not only learn about the past, but more importantly, will find the resolve and courage to be the heroes of the future. "*Ha'ish hu haplada!*" Human beings are the armor of our nation! We must be that armor.

Avigdor Kahalani with Author's class

Bibliography

Abbey, Alan D. *Journey of Hope: The Story of Ilan Ramon, Israel's First Astronaut.* Jerusalem: Gefen Publishing House, 2003.

Aldouby, Zwy, and Jerrold Ballinger. *The Shattered Silence: The Eli Cohen Affair.* New York: Coward, McCann and Geoghegan, 1971.

Altschuler, David. *Hitler's War against the Jews.* New York: Behrmann House, 1978.

Arad, Yitzhak, Israel Gutman, *et al. Documents on the Holocaust: Selected Sources on the Destruction of the Jews of Germany and Austria, Poland, and the Soviet Union,* 8th ed. Lincoln, NE: University of Nebraska Press, 1999.

Banai, Yaakov. *Chayalim almonim: Sefer mivtse'ei Lehi* [Unknown soldiers: The operation book of Lehi]. Tel Aviv: Hug Yedidim, 1958.

Barkai, Meyer, ed. *The Fighting Ghettos.* Philadelphia: J.B. Lippincott, 1962.

Bar-Zohar, Michael, ed. *Lionhearts: Heroes of Israel.* New York: Warner Books, 1998.

—. *Spies in the Promised Land.* Boston: Houghton Mifflin, 1972.

Begin, Menachem. *The Revolt: Story of the Irgun.* New York: H. Schuman, 1951.

Bell, J. Bowyer. *Terror out of Zion: Irgun Zvai Leumi, Lehi, and the Palestine Underground, 1929–1949.* New York: St. Martin's Press, 1977. Reprint, *Terror out of Zion: The Fight for Israeli Independence.* Piscataway, NJ: Transaction Publishers, 1996.

Ben-Hanan, Eli. *Our Man in Damascus.* Tel Aviv: ADM Publishing House, 1968.

Berkman, Ted. *Cast a Giant Shadow.* Garden City, NY: Doubleday, 1962.

Berman, Yisrael. "Im H.N. Bialik b'Kishinev [With C.N. Bialik in Kishinev]." In *HaPogrom b'Kishinev b'Mil'ot Shishim Shana, 1903–1963*, edited by Chaim Shorer. Tel Aviv: HaIgud HaOlami shel Yehudei Bessarabia (World Federation of Bessarabian Jews), 1963.

Blady, Ken. *The Jewish Boxers' Hall of Fame*. New York: Shapolsky Publishers, 1988.

Blazer, Phil. *Pioneers of Israel: Modern-Day Heroes of the State of Israel*. Sherman Oaks, CA: Blazer Communications, 2004.

Bodner, Allen. *When Boxing Was a Jewish Sport*. Westport, CT: Praeger, 1997.

Century, Douglas. *Barney Ross: The Life of a Jewish Fighter*. New York: Schocken, 2006.

Dawidowicz, Lucy S. *The War against the Jews, 1933–1945*. New York: Holt, Rinehart and Winston, 1975.

Eisen, Yosef. *Miraculous Journey: A Complete History of the Jewish People from Creation to the Present*. Jerusalem: Targum Press, 2004.

Elkins, Michael. *Forged in Fury*. London: Corgi Books, 1982.

Elon, Amos. *Herzl*. New York: Holt, Rinehart and Winston, 1975.

Encyclopedia Judaica. Jerusalem: Keter Publishing House, 1972.

Engle, Anita. *The Nili Spies*. London: Hogarth Press, 1959.

Finkelstein, Louis. *Akiba: Scholar, Saint and Martyr*. New York: Covici Friede, 1936.

Frank, Gerold. *The Deed*. New York: Simon and Schuster, 1963.

Gera, Gershon. *Anshei HaShomer b'hayeihem u'bemotam* [Members of HaShomer in life and in death]. Tel Aviv, 1991.

Golan, Zev. *Free Jerusalem: Heroes, Heroines and Rogues Who Created the State of Israel*. Jerusalem: Devora Publishing Company, 2003.

Greenfield, Murray S., and Joseph M. Hochstein. *The Jews' Secret Fleet*. Jerusalem: Gefen Publishing House, 1987.

Gurion, Itzhak. *Triumph on the Gallows*. New York: Brit Trumpeldor of America, 1950.

Halpern, Yirmiyahu. *Avi, Michael Halpern* [My father, Michael Halpern]. Tel Aviv, 1964.

Hay, Peter. *Ordinary Heroes: Chana Szenes and the Dream of Zion.* New York: G.P. Putnam's Sons, 1986.

Hertzberg, Arthur. *The Zionist Idea: A Historical Analysis and Reader.* New York: Atheneum, 1969.

Herzl, Theodor. *The Jewish State.* Vienna, 1896. Reprint, Mineola, NY: Dover Publications, 1988.

—, and Reuben R. Hecht, Ohad Zemorah. *When the Shofar Sounds: Herzl – Image, Deeds and Selected Writings.* Haifa: Moledeth, 2006.

Herzog, Haim. *Heroes of Israel: Profiles of Jewish Courage.* Boston: Little, Brown, 1989.

—. *The War of Atonement.* London: Weidenfeld and Nicolson,1975.

Hoffman, Lawrence A. *Israel: A Spiritual Travel Guide; A Companion for the Modern Jewish Pilgrim.* Woodstock, VT: Jewish Lights Publishing, 2005.

Israel Ministry of Defense. *Yizkor: In Memoriam. Biographies and Photographs of the Fallen in the Ranks of the Israel Defense Forces Beginning with the Breakout of the Yom Kippur War until the Day of Signature of the Disengagement Agreement on the Syrian Front* [in Hebrew]. 2 vols. Tel Aviv: Ministry of Defense Publishing, 1981.

The JPS Hebrew-English Tanakh. Philadelphia: Jewish Publication Society, 1999.

Kahalani, Avigdor. *The Heights of Courage: A Tank Leader's War on the Golan.* Westport, CT: Greenwood Press, 1984.

—. *A Warrior's Way: Israel's Most Decorated Tank Commander Relives His Greatest Battles.* New York: SPI Books, 1994.

Katz, Shmuel. *The Aaronsohn Saga.* Jerusalem: Gefen Publishing House, 2007.

—. *Days of Fire: The Secret History of the Irgun Zvai Leumi.* New York: Doubleday, 1966.

Laqueur, Walter. *A History of Zionism.* New York: Holt, Rinehart and Winston, 1972.

Levin, Nora. *The Holocaust: The Destruction of European Jewry, 1939–1945*. New York: Crowell, 1968.

Levine, Peter. *Ellis Island to Ebbets Field: Sport and the American Jewish Experience*. New York: Oxford University Press, 1992.

Lubetkin, Zivia. *Biyemei kilayon vamered* [In the days of destruction and revolt]. Tel Aviv: HaKibbutz HaMeuchad, 1953.

Milstein, Uri, ed. *Rahel* [in Hebrew]. Tel Aviv: Zmora-Bitan, 1985.

Nedava, Yosef. *Sefer olei hagardom* [Book of those who mounted the gallows]. Tel Aviv: Sefarim Shelah, 1952.

Netanyahu, Iddo. *Yoni's Last Battle: The Rescue at Entebbe, 1976*. Jerusalem: Gefen Publishing House, 2002.

Netanyahu, Jonathan. *Self-Portrait of a Hero: The Letters of Jonathan Netanyahu*. New York: Ballantine Books, 1980. Available in reprint as *The Letters of Jonathan Netanyahu: The Commander of the Entebbe Rescue Force*. Jerusalem: Gefen Publishing House, 2001.

Nordau, Anna, and Max Nordau. *Max Nordau: A Biography*. New York, 1943.

Pressburger, Chava, trans. *The Diary of Petr Ginz, 1941–1942*. New York: Atlantic Monthly Press, 2004.

Raviv, Dan, and Yossi Melman. *Every Spy a Prince*. Boston: Houghton Mifflin, 1990.

Raz, Simcha. *A Tzaddik in Our Time: The Life of Rabbi Aryeh Levin*. Jerusalem: Feldheim, 1976.

Sachar, Howard Morley. *A History of Israel*. New York: Knopf, 1976.

Schechtman, Joseph B. *The Life and Times of Vladimir Jabotinsky*. Vol. 1, *Rebel and Statesman: The Early Years*. Vol. 2, *Fighter and Prophet: The Last Years*. Silver Spring, MD: Eshel Books, 1986. Originally published as *The Vladimir Jabotinsky Story*. New York: T. Yoseloff, 1961.

Schroeter, Leonard. *The Last Exodus*. Seattle: University of Washington Press, 1979.

Schur, Maxine Rose. *Hannah Szenes: A Song of Light*. Philadelphia: Jewish Publication Society, 1986.

Senesh, Hannah. *Hannah Senesh: Her Life and Diary.* New York: Schocken, 1966. Reprint, Hannah Senesh, Marge Piercy, *et al.*, *Hannah Senesh: Her Life and Diary, The First Complete Edition.* Woodstock, VT: Jewish Lights Publishing, 2004.

Sharansky, Natan. *Fear No Evil.* New York: Random House, 1988.

Singer, Alex. *Alex: Building a Life; The Story of an American Who Fell Defending Israel.* Jerusalem: Gefen Publishing House, 1996.

Slater, Elinor, and Robert Slater. *Great Jewish Men.* Middle Village, NY: Jonathan David Publishers, 1996.

Slater, Leonard. *The Pledge.* New York: Simon and Schuster, 1970.

Soshuk, Levi, and Azriel Louis Eisenberg, eds. *Momentous Century: Personal and Eyewitness Accounts of the Rise of the Jewish Homeland and State, 1875–1978.* New York: Cornwall Books, 1984.

St. John, Robert. *They Came from Everywhere: Twelve Who Helped Mold Modern Israel.* New York: Coward-McCann, 1962.

Stewart, Steven. *The Spymasters of Israel.* New York: Macmillan, 1980.

Suhl, Yuri. *They Fought Back: The Story of the Jewish Resistance in Nazi Europe.* New York: Crown, 1967.

Sykes, Christopher. *Orde Wingate.* London: Collins, 1959.

Syrkin, Marie. *Blessed Is the Match.* Philadelphia: Jewish Publication Society, 1947.

Wiesel, Elie. *The Jews of Silence: A Personal Report on Soviet Jewry.* New York: Holt, Rinehart and Winston, 1966.

Wyman, David. *The Abandonment of the Jews: America and the Holocaust, 1941–1945.* New York: Pantheon, 1984.

Zion, Noam, and Barbara Spectre. *A Different Light: The Hanukkah Book of Celebration.* Jerusalem: Devora Publishing, 2000.

Ziv, Hani, and Yoav Gelber, ed. *The Bow Bearers.* Tel Aviv: Ministry of Defense Publishing, 1998.

About the Author

Yossi Katz was born and raised in Philadelphia. He was active in United Synagogue Youth (USY) and served as regional president and as an international board member. In 1989, Yossi was the recipient of the International USY Alumni of the Year Award. Yossi has also spent over fifteen years at Camp Ramah in the Poconos as a camper, counselor and division head. Yossi Katz graduated with honors from Temple University in Philadelphia and the Hebrew University in Jerusalem with a degree in Jewish and Arab history. He has studied at the Hebrew University's Center for Jewish Education in the Diaspora and is a licensed teacher.

Yossi Katz made Aliyah to Israel in 1978. He served in Tzahal (Israel Defense Forces) for over twenty-five years as a combat soldier in a reconnaissance unit of the Israeli Armored Corps. He has also served as assistant commander of the Jerusalem Information Unit, where he lectured on Jewish and Arab history and the military history of the Israel Defense Forces. Yossi is the former Israeli national light-middleweight boxing champion and has represented Israel in international competition. He is also an experienced boxing instructor and has coached youth in Israeli prisons and community centers.

Yossi was sent to the United States as a Shaliach (Emissary) of the State of Israel and the World Zionist Organization from 1983 to 1986 and again from 1991 to 1994 to work with American Jewish youth in order to help strengthen their Jewish identity and connection with the

State of Israel. In that capacity he traveled extensively across the United States and Canada lecturing before hundreds of synagogue, community and university groups, as well as to youth movements and schools. Yossi has also served as the official scholar in residence for the Jewish communities of Boca Raton, Seattle, Philadelphia and Orlando, as well as for scores of synagogue educational programs and retreats.

Yossi Katz has been an educator with the Alexander Muss High School in Israel (AMHSI) since 1980. He has taught both high school and adult sessions, directed the "USY High" program and made important contributions to the school's curriculum. A father of three and grandfather of three, Yossi resides in Netanya.

ALEXANDER MUSS

HIGH SCHOOL IN ISRAEL

Founded in 1972 by Rabbi Morris and Lenore Kipper together with the Greater Miami Jewish Federation, the **Alexander Muss High School in Israel** (AMHSI) is today the premier Israel educational experience program for Diaspora youth.

AMHSI's mission is to promote, build and strengthen lifelong bonds between youth and Israel through study of the history and culture of the people of Israel. Recognizing that using Israel as a living classroom boosts interest in and attachment to the land and its fascinating history, AMHSI revolutionized the way "Israel" is taught. AMHSI imbues each and every student with a distinctly educational, cultural and social experience specifically intended to enhance his or her connection to Israel and Judaism.

We are extremely proud that Yossi Katz joined the AMHSI staff in 1980. Throughout the past three decades he has taught and inspired thousands of high school students and adults. In addition, Yossi has served as Scholar-in-Residence for the Jewish communities of Boca Raton, Seattle, Orlando and Philadelphia on behalf of AMHSI.

Alexander Muss High School in Israel
78 Randall Avenue
Rockville Centre, NY 11570
(212) 472-9300 ph
(212) 472-9301 fax
www.amhsi.org